D0732641

论　　语

ANALECTS OF CONFUCIUS

中文译注　蔡希勤
英文翻译　赖　波
　　　　　夏玉和

华语教学出版社
北　京

First Edition   1 9 9 4

Second Printing   1 9 9 6

ISBN 7—80052—407—8

Copyright 1994 by Sinolingua

Published by Sinolingua

24 Baiwanzhuang Road, Beijing 100037, China

Printed by Beijing Foreign Languages Printing House

Distributed by China International

Book Trading Corporation

35 Chegongzhuang Xilu, P. O. Box 399

Beijing 100044, China

Printed in the People's Republic of China

序

辛冠洁

中国传统文化，是世界文化的一个瑰丽的宝藏，《论语》则是这个宝藏桂冠上的一颗最眩目的明珠。早在距今两千四百多年前的春秋末年和战国初期，这颗明珠即已熠熠发光。

《论语》记载了孔子及其弟子的言行，是其弟子所辑的"接闻于夫子之语"的思想汇编，后来成为儒家的最高经典，也是中国历史上最具权威性的文献典籍。《论语》篇幅并不大，仅一万二千字，二十篇，但内容宏富充实，且又言简意赅，故能两千年来流传不息，影响广大深入。它所包含的思想，久久以来，潜移默化，已经渗透到中国人的血液之中。任何一个中国人，不论是汉族人，还是少数民族成员的意识，都自觉或不自觉地受着它的影响，甚至制约。

《论语》讲"为政以德"（《为政》），至少自汉以来，两千多年间，任何一个统治阶级对此都不能置之不理，而被统治的老百姓也往往以此要求其上司。由此而引出的"道之以政，齐之以刑，民免而无耻；道之以德，齐之以礼，有耻且格"（《为政》），弥漫着有关道德与政治的关系的思考，形成为儒家强调德化教育的根据，也成为儒家思想的一大特色，后来还成为儒家文化圈内东方文化型的特色。《论语》讲仁讲礼，"人而不仁，如礼何"（《八佾》），"克己复礼为仁"。讲仁便引出忠恕，推己及人；讲礼便引出名教，要有等级制度，正己正人。政治道德的相互影响，仁与礼的相互制约，自然形成了一定社会秩序的安定统一系统。这个系统，明显显示着东方文化的特征。也是《论语》生命力所在。

文化各有其民族特色，但却无疆域的界限，它必以自己的特色，为他种文化所吸收，同时也吸收他种文化。所以《论语》早在世纪之初，已经传播到越南、朝鲜、日本及受其影响的地区，所谓儒家文化圈，便是这种传播影响的产物，及至十七世纪已开始向欧洲传播。公元1687年巴黎已出现《论语》的拉丁文本。历史的车轮辗入近代之后，《论语》在东西方文化撞击中，依然神彩奕奕，尤其第二次世界大战之后，更在全世界范围内蓬勃扩展开来。在若干地区，《论语》的某些内容成了经济活动的道德规范，甚至成为发财致富的指导手段，有一个时期"《论语》加算盘"，在日本经济界曾经是通向发达的一种特有智慧。

在此过程中，各种文字的《论语》版本曾经出现过不少，但多为外国人士所为，中国人把中文本《论语》翻译成外文的则很少。一百多年前辜鸿铭先生把《论语》翻译成英文本，一时成为美谈，后来作这种尝试的不能说没有，但委实不多见。几年前，华语教学出版社蔡希勤先生倡议把《论语》重新翻译成英文本，蔡先生首先把古文翻译成白话文，并以译本示我，作为蔡希勤白话《论语》的第一个读者，我感到十分高兴，蔡先生的白话本作得十分准确、精辟，为英文翻译提供了良好基础。现在由于蔡先生的努力，经过英语高手、大家的辛勤劳动，中国版的文白、汉英对照《论语》即将付梓，这是中国对国际文化交流的一大贡献，也是使中国文化走向世界的一个助力，蔡先生命为之为序，不敢竟辞，故略抒胸臆如上云尔。

1994 年 2 月于不知足斋

（辛冠洁先生为中国社会科学院哲学所教授，中国孔子基金会常务副会长）

FOREWORD

Chinese traditional culture is a treasure among the cultures of the world, and *Analects of Confucius* is the brightest pearl in its depository. This brilliant book began to show its splendour as early as 2,400 years ago between the Spring and Autumn and the Warring States periods.

Compiled by his disciples, *Analects of Confucius* recorded the sayings and deeds of the great sage and his disciples. It later became the major classic of Confucianism as well as the most authoritative book in Chinese history. With only 12,000 characters, it is terse but comprehensive, rich yet profound; it has influenced Chinese society for over 2,000 years. Its ideas have taken such firm root among the Chinese people that all Chinese, —— both Han and minority nationalities —— have been more or less influenced by it.

Analects of Confucius says: "A state should be ruled on a moral basis. "(II)For over 2,000 years since the Han Dynasty, every ruler has had to pay at least some heed to this, and the people also expected their ruler to act accordingly. Developing his ideas further, Confucius said: "Regulated by the edicts and punishments, the people will know only how to stay away out of trouble, but will not have a sense of shame. Guided by virtues and the rites, they will not only have a sense of shame, but also know how to correct their mistakes of their own accord." (II) This philosophy concerning the relationship between politics and morality formed the basis for the Confucian school's emphasis on moral education. Characteristic of Confucianism, this idea later became a distinguishing feature of Oriental or East Asian culture realm under the influence of Confucianism.

Analects of Confucius also discusses benevolence and rites: "What can a man do about the rites if he is not benevolent?" (III) "One who restrains himself in order to observe the rites is benevolent." (XII) After benevolence, Confucius talked about loyalty and forbearance: "Do to others what you do to yourself, while do not do to others what you do not do to yourself." His teaching also includes guides on social relationships. According to Confucius, society should include a social estate system in which everyone should observe certain rites before he can perform his social duties. Consequently, the interaction of politics and morality, and the mutual influence of benevolence and rites, formed naturally a stable and unified social system which is a fundamental characteristic of Oriental culture. The vitality of *Analects of Confucius* can also be found here.

Every culture has its own national features which are not limited by national boundaries. As a result, early in the beginning of this century, *Analects of Confucius* was introduced to Vietnam, Korea and Japan, as well as regions under their influence, thereby forming the "cultural circle" of Confucianism. Its spread to Europe dated back as early as the 17th century when a Latin version appeared in Paris in 1687. Even during cultural clashes between East and West in modern times, *Analects of Confucius* has lost none of its vigour; since World War II especially, it has become even more widespread throughout the world. In some localities, certain parts of the book have been incorporated as ethical codes in business activities, or even as guidelines for becoming rich. At one time, "*Analects of Confucius* plus abacus" represented a special wisdom leading to prosperity for Japanese businessmen.

During past centuries, several versions of the book have appeared in various languages, mostly written by foreigners. Last century, Gu Hongming translated the book into English, a version which was favourably accepted. Few translations were published subsequently. Several years ago, Cai Xiqin of Sinolingua suggested re—translating the book into English. He first converted its classical Chinses into modern Chinese, and then showed me the results. I was very pleased to be the first reader of his modern Chinese translation which is both accurate and incisive. Now through the efforts of Mr. Cai and several other admirable English translators, a new version of *Analects of Confucius* containing modern Chinese and English translations will soon be published in China. This is a major contribution to the cultures of the world — proving once more the universal significance of Chinese culture.

Xin Guanjie
From the Studio of the Insatiable
February 1994

(Xin Guanjie is a professor of the Institute of Philosophy in the Chinese Academy of Social Sciences, and a standing vice chairman of China Confucius Foundation)

目 录

前 言

注：《论语》本无篇名，是后人选每篇第一章前两个字（个别选三个字）作为篇名。

山东曲阜孔庙大成殿内孔子塑像

（庞守义　摄）

孔子讲学图

（李士伋　绘）

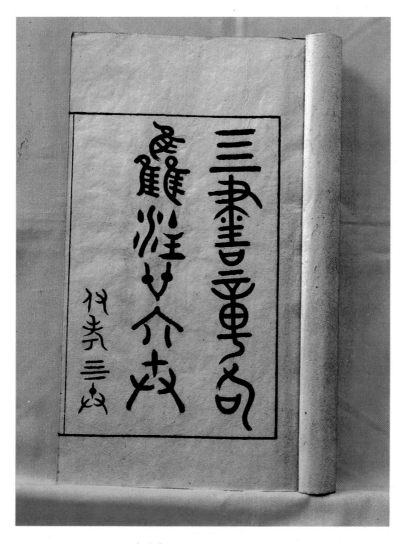

《四书章句》（北京大学图书馆藏）

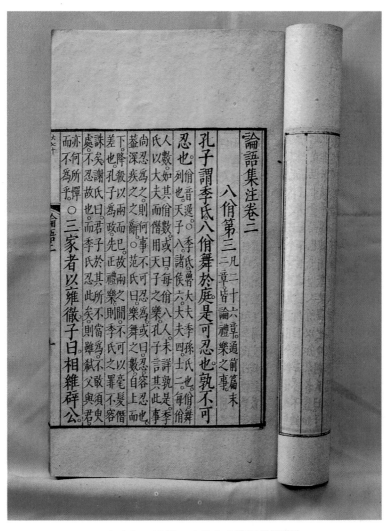

論語集注卷二

八佾第三 凡二十六章。通前篇末二章皆論禮樂之事。

孔子謂季氏八佾舞於庭是可忍也孰不可忍也。佾音逸。○季氏魯大夫季孫氏也。佾舞列也。天子八諸侯六大夫四士二。每佾人數如其佾數。或曰每佾八人。未詳孰是。季氏以大夫而僭用天子之樂孔子言其此事尚忍為之則何事不可忍為。或曰忍容忍也。蓋深疾之之辭。○范氏曰樂舞之數自上而下降殺以兩而已。故兩之間不可以毫髮僭差也。孔子為政先正禮樂則季氏之罪不容誅矣。謝氏曰君子於其所不當為不敢須臾處不忍故也。而季氏忍此矣則雖弑父與君亦何所憚而不為乎。○三家者以雍徹子曰相維辟公

《四书章句·论语》（北京大学图书馆藏）

前　言

孔子（前 551——前 479 年）名丘，字仲尼，山东曲阜（古称鲁国）人。是中国古代著名的思想家和伟大的教育家，是中国儒家学派的创始人。

《论语》是一部记载孔子及其若干弟子言行的书。这部书是孔子死后，由他的弟子和再传弟子辑录而成。内容广泛，比较系统的记述了孔子关于政治、哲学、文学艺术、教育和道德修养等方面的言论。是研究孔子思想的重要资料。

《论语》是一部语录体著作，内容丰富，语言简洁明快，含意深刻又通俗易懂。

《论语》成书于多人之手，而且这些作者的年代相去又不止三、五十年，这就不可避免的造成了书中各章多有重复、脱漏和错简。

《论语》问世后，注家蜂起，为了忠于"圣人之言"，大多是逐字翻译这部著作，由于原文的错漏和古今文化的变异，使一般读者对各注译本也是懵懵懂懂不得其要领。

为了帮助古文程度不高的青年读者能够读懂这部书，使这部儒家经典能在当今改革开放的经济大潮中为更多的人所掌握运用，我们在忠实于原文本意的基础上采用了意译，尽量使译文通俗易懂，内容连贯，易读易记，加深理解。需要说明的是我们虽然采取了不同于逐字翻译的传统译法，却参考了多种权威传统译本来校正这部意译本，以不使其"离经叛道"。

我们积极主张编译出版《论语》，是因为我们认为这部儒家经典对当前发展市场经济的新形势仍有着不可低估的现实意义。孔圣人在二千多年前的政治主张及其言行仍然值得我们深思。

PREFACE

Confucius (551-479 B.C.), born in Qufu, the State of Lu(today the south of Shandong Province), was a great thinker, educationist and the founder of Confucianism.

Lun Yu, or *Analects of Confucius*, records the words and deeds of Confucius as well as his disciples. The book was compiled by the disciples of Confucius and their disciples after their Master's death. It covers a wide scope of subjects, ranging from politics, philosophy, literature and art to education and moral cultivation. It is indispensable material for the study of the Master's thought.

In a conversational style, the book, rich in content but laconic and clear in language, is profound and understandable. Since it was compiled by scholars of different times, inevitabley, there are quite a few repetitions, omissions, and other lapses in some parts of the book. Although this book has been repeatedly interpreted since its compilation, for general readers it is still confusing and, in essence, by no means easy to grasp because, afraid of being unfaithful to the "Sayings of the Sage", almost all the interpreters and translators have fallen into literalism. They have failed to point out and correct the lapses, and to recognize the original meanings of some parts which have become obscure due to the modification of the cultural background with the passage of time.

To help young readers both at home and abroad who are not specialists in ancient Chinese language, a free approach is taken in translating this book into both modern Chinese and English, in the hope that the translations will be consistent and easy to read, recite and understand. Our basis throughout, however, has been to render faithfully the original meaning. It is necessary to mention that although our translation differs from traditional literalism, we correct a series of lapses with reference to many authoritative interpretations in traditional versions, which ensures that this freely translated version does not depart from the classic and go against the orthodoxy.

學而篇第一

1. 子曰:"學而時習之,不亦説乎? 有朋自遠方來,不亦樂乎? 人不知,而不愠,不亦君子乎?"

译文:

孔子说:"对学过的知识按时去实习它,不也是很好的事吗? 有朋友从远方来,不是很快乐的事吗? 不为别人不了解自己而抱怨,不是很有修养的君子风度吗?"

英文:

Confucius said, "Is it not a pleasure after all to practice in due time what one has learnt? Is it not a delight after all to have friends come from afar? Is it not a gentleman after all who will not take offence when others fail to appreciate him?"

2. 有子曰:"其爲人也孝弟,而好犯上者,鮮矣; 不好犯上,而好作亂者,未之有也。君子務本,本立而道生。孝弟也者,其爲仁之本與?"

译文:

有子说:"孝顺父母,敬爱兄长的人,却喜欢触犯上

级（司），这种人是不多的；从不触犯上级（司）
欢造反作乱，这种人从来没有过。君子致力于相
本树立了，治国做人的原则就会产生。孝敬父母
兄长，这就是仁爱的根本吧！"

注：

　　有子：姓有，名若，孔子的学生。

＊ **英文：**

　　You Zi (a disciple of Confucius') said, "It is rare for a man who is filial towards his parents and respectful to his elder brothers to go against his superiors; never has there been a person who does not like to go against his superiors and at the same time likes to start a rebellion. A gentleman devotes himself to basics. Once the basics are established, the principles of government and behaviour will grow there-from. The basics are to be filial toward one's parents and respectful to one's elder brothers!"

　　3. 子曰："巧言令色，鲜矣仁！"

译文：

　　孔子说："一贯花言巧语，伪装和善的人，不会有什么仁德。"

Confucius said, A man who speaks with honeyed words and pretends to be kind cannot be benevolent."

4. 曾子曰: "吾日三省吾身: 爲人謀而不忠乎? 與朋友交而不信乎? 傳不習乎?"

译文:

曾子说: "我每天都再三反省自己: 为别人办事是否尽心竭力了呢? 同朋友交往是否以诚相待了呢? 老师教的功课是否用心复习了呢?"

注:

曾子: 姓曾, 名参, 孔子的学生。

英文:

Zeng Zi (a disciple of Confucius') said, "Every day I examine myself once and again: Have I tried my utmost to help others? Have I been honest to my friends? Have I diligently reviewed the instructions from the Master?"

5. 子曰: "道千乘之國, 敬事而信, 節用而愛人, 使民以時。"

译文:

孔子说: "治理一个拥有兵车千乘的国家对政事的处

理要慎重，办事认真而讲信用，节省开支，爱护官吏，役使百姓也要不违农时。"

英文:

Confucius said, "A country of a thousand war-chariots should be governed in such a way that the ruler handles state affairs scrupulously and observes his promises strictly; that he keeps frugality and cherishes his inferiors; and that he employs the labour of the common people only in the right seasons."

6. 子曰："弟子，入則孝，出則悌，謹而信，汎愛衆而親仁。行有餘力，則以學文。"

译文:

孔子说："少年在家要孝顺父母，敬爱兄长，做事谨慎认真，说话诚实，博爱大众而亲近有仁德的人。如此之外还要学习文化知识。"

英文:

Confucius said, "At home, a young man should be dutiful towards his parents; going outside, he should be respectful towards his elders; he should be cautious in deeds and trustworthy in words; he should love everyone yet make close friends only with those of benevolence. If he has any more energy to spare, let him devote it to books."

7. 子夏曰: "賢賢易色; 事父母, 能竭其力; 事君, 能致其身; 與朋友交, 言而有信。雖曰未學, 吾必謂之學矣。"

译文:

子夏说: "对妻子, 重品德, 不重容貌; 事奉父母, 能尽心竭力; 为国家, 能鞠躬尽瘁; 和朋友交往, 诚实而守信。能够做到这样的人虽然没有入过学, 但我认为他已经学好了。"

注:

子夏: 姓卜, 名商, 字子夏, 孔子的学生。

英文:

Zi Xia (a disciple of Confucius') said, "If a man values the virtue of his wife more than her appearance, tries his best to serve his parents, sacrifices his life for his lord, and keeps his promises with his friends, I would then assert that he is well-educated, even though he may never have entered a school."

8. 子曰: "君子不重則不威, 學則不固。主忠信, 無友不如己者。過則勿憚改。"

译文:

孔子说: "君子不庄重就没有威仪, 不认真就学而无成。要重道德, 慎交友, 有过错, 随时改正。"

英文:

Confucius said, "A frivolous gentleman cannot command respect and his learnings cannot find a firm foundation. Therefore, he should pay great attention to loyalty and sincerity, and not make close friends with those whose morality is inferior to his. If he makes a mistake, he should not be afraid of correcting it."

9. 曾子曰: "慎終追遠, 民德歸厚矣。"

译文:

曾子说: "依礼对待父母的丧事, 虔诚地祭祀祖先, 这样做自然会导致民风淳厚了。

英文:

Zeng Zi said, "When funerals are conducted in accordance with the rites and sacrifices to the remote ancestors are given devoutly, the morality of the people will naturally reach its peak."

10. 子禽問於子貢曰："夫子至於是邦也，必聞其政，求之與？抑與之與？"子貢曰："夫子溫、良、恭、儉、讓以得之。夫子之求之也，其諸異乎人之求之與？"

译文：

子禽问子贡道："老师（指孔子）每到一个国家，就知道那个国家的政事，是他自己打听到的呢？还是人家主动告诉他的呢？"子贡说："他老人家以温和、善良、恭敬、俭朴、谦逊的态度而使人家乐于主动把这个国家的政事告诉他。他这种获得的方法，不同于别人吧？"

注：

子禽：姓陈，名亢，字子禽。子贡；姓端木，名赐，字子贡。孔子的学生。

英文：

Zi Qin asked Zi Gong (both disciples of Confucius'), "As soon as our Master arrives in a state, he always gets to know about its government. Does he seek the information or do people there tell him of their own accord?"

Zi Gong answered, "Our Master gets it by being cordial, kind, respectful, frugal and modest. The way our Master inquires is, perhaps, different from the ways others do."

11. 子曰："父在，觀其志；父沒，觀其行；三年無改於父之道，可謂孝矣。"

译文：

孔子说："在他父亲活着的时候看他的志向，父亲去世后看他的行为，如果他在父亲去世后三年之内能仍然坚持父亲的正确原则，就可以说他已经做到孝了。"

英文：

Confucius said, "Observe his aspirations when his father is alive, and observe his actions when his father passes away. He may well be called filial if he sticks to his father's way for three years after the latter's death.

12. 有子曰："禮之用，和爲貴。先王之道，斯爲美，小大由之。有所不行，知和而和，不以禮節之，亦不可行也。"

译文：

有子说："礼的应用，以遇事和顺为可贵。过去圣明君王治理国家，可贵之处就在这里，他们不管小事大事，都按这条原则处理。但也有不能实行的，那是因为只知道一味地求和顺，而不能用礼法节制约束它，也就行不通了。"

You Zi said, "In conducting the rites, seeking harmony is the most valuable principle. It was cherished by the ancient sage kings in handling state affairs. Great or trivial, they did everything according to this principle. If harmony is sought for its own sake without regulating it by the rites, however, the principle will not work."

13. 有子曰:"信近於義,言可復也。恭近於禮,遠恥辱也。因不失其親,亦可宗也。"

译文:

有子说:"信约符合道义,就可以实行。行为合于礼法,就可避免侮辱。依靠信得过的人,就靠得住。"

英文:

You Zi said, "Promises should be observed so long as they are in line with righteousness. Respect can keep one free from disgrace and insult so long as it is in line with the rites. And it also follows that one should rely on those with whom he is on intimate terms."

14. 子曰:"君子食無求飽,居無求安,敏於事而慎於言,就有道而正焉,可謂好學也已。"

译文:

孔子说:"君子吃饭不求饱足,居住不求舒适,办事敏捷,说话谨慎,向得道之人学习以改正自己的缺点,这样就可以说是好学了。"

英文:

Confucius said, "A gentleman seeks neither a full belly nor a comfortable home. Instead, he is quick in action yet cautious in speech. He learns from virtuous and accomplished men in order to correct his mistakes. Such can be called a man with eagerness to study."

15. 子貢曰:"貧而無諂,富而無驕,何如?"子曰:"可也,未若貧而樂,富而好禮者也。"

子貢曰:"《詩》云:'如切如磋,如琢如磨',其斯之謂與?"子曰:"賜也,始可與言《詩》已矣,告諸往而知來者。"

译文:

子贡说:"贫穷而不巴结人,富裕而不骄傲自大,这种人如何?"孔子说:"可以,但还不如虽贫穷而仍然快快乐乐,纵富贵却谦虚好礼的人。"

子贡说:"《诗经》上说:'治骨器玉器要精雕细刻后再磨光'就是这个意思吧?"孔子说:"赐呀,现在可以同你讨论《诗经》了,告诉你一件事,你就可以举一反三。"

Zi Gong asked, "What do you think of such a person who does not flatter when he is poor and does not boast when rich?"

Confucius said, "Good. But still better is a person who is poor but joyful, rich but polite."

Zi Gong said, "According to *The Book of Songs* 'Delicate jadework requires repeated cutting, carving and polishing'. Does this refer to the above?"

Confucius said, "Oh, Ci (given name of Zi Gong), now I can discuss *The Book of Songs* with you, since you will be able to tell what may happen in the future when you are told about the past."

16. 子曰："不患人之不己知，患不知人也。"

译文:

孔子说："不怕别人不了解自己，就怕自己不了解别人。"

英文:

Confucius said, "Don't worry about being misunderstood but about understanding others."

爲政篇第二

1. 子曰:"爲政以德, 譬如北辰居其所而衆星共之。"

译文:

孔子说:"国君如果用道德来治理国政, 自己就会像北极星受群星环绕一样受到百姓拥护。

英文:

Confucius said, "He who rules his state on a moral basis would be supported by the people, just as the Polar Star is encircled by all the other stars."

2. 子曰:"《詩》三百, 一言以蔽之, 曰:'思無邪'。"

译文:

孔子说:"《诗经》三百篇, 用一句话来概括它就是'思想纯正'。"

英文:

Confucius said, "The theme of the three hundred pieces in *The Book of Songs* can be summed up in one phrase, i.e. 'a pure and unadulterated mind'."

3. 子曰："道之以政，齊之以刑，民免而**無恥**；道之以德，齊之以禮，有恥且格。"

译文：

孔子说："靠行政命令和刑罚来制约人民，老百姓只知避免犯罪遭刑罚而不知道犯罪是耻辱的事情；如果用道德和礼教来引导人民，老百姓不仅知道犯罪是耻辱的事情，而且能自己改正错误。"

英文：

Confucius said, "Regulated by the edicts and punishments, the people will know only how to stay out of trouble but will not have a sense of shame. Guided by virtues and the rites, they will not only have a sense of shame but also know how to correct their mistakes of their own accord."

4. 子曰："吾十有五而志于學，三十而立，四十而不惑，五十而知天命，六十而耳順，七十而從心所欲，不踰矩。"

译文：

孔子说："我十五岁有志于做学问；三十岁立身处世

站稳了脚跟；四十岁掌握了各种知识遇事不迷惑；五十岁知道上天赋予自己的使命；六十岁对别人的话能辨别是非曲直；七十岁既使随心所欲也不会有越规的行为。"

英文：

Confucius said, "Since the age of 15, I have devoted myself to learning; since 30, I have been well established; since 40, I have understood many things and have no longer been confused; since 50, I have known my heaven–sent duty; since 60, I have been able to distinguish right and wrong in other people's words; and since 70, I have been able to do what I intend freely without breaking the rules."

5. 孟懿子問孝，子曰："無違。"

樊遲御，子告之曰："孟孫問孝於我，我對曰，無違。"樊遲曰："何謂也?"子曰："生，事之以禮；死，葬之以禮，祭之以禮。"

译文：

孟懿子向孔子请教什么是孝道，孔子说："不要违背礼节。"

一次，樊迟为孔子赶车，孔子便告诉他说："孟孙向我问孝道，我答复他说，不要违背礼节。"樊迟问："这是什么意思?"孔子说："父母活着时，按礼节侍奉他们，父母去世后，按礼节埋葬他们并照礼节祭祀他们。"

注:

孟懿子: 姓孟孙，名何忌，鲁国大夫。

樊迟: 姓樊，名须，字子迟。孔子的学生。

英文:

Meng Yizi (then minister of the Lu State) asked what being filial meant. Confucius answered, "Do not disobey the rites."

Once when Fan Chi (a disciple of Confucius') was driving a carriage for Confucius, Confucius said, "Meng Yizi asked me what being filial meant and I answered, 'Do not disobey the rites'." "What did you mean?" asked Fan. The Master replied, "When the parents are still alive, serve them according to the rites; and when they pass away, bury and then make sacrifices to them according to the rites."

6. 孟武伯问孝，子曰: "父母唯其疾之忧。"

译文:

孟武伯向孔子请教什么是孝道，孔子说: "特别为父母的疾病担忧。"

注:

孟武伯: 姓孟孙，孟懿子的儿子。

When Meng Wubo (son of Meng Yizı) asked about being filial, Confucius replied, "A son should show special concern for the health of his parents."

7. 子游問孝。子曰: "今之孝者，是謂能養。至於犬馬，皆能有養。不敬，何以别乎?"

译文:

子游向孔子请教孝道。孔子说: "现在所谓孝道，只是说能够供养父母就行了。就是狗马，也能做到这一点。如果对父母不心存孝敬之情，那和狗马有什么区别呢?"

注:

子游: 姓言，名偃，字子游。孔子的学生。

英文:

Zi You (a disciple of Confucius') asked about being filial. Confucius said, "Nowadays, one is called a filial son only because one is able to support one's parents. Actually, however, even dogs and horses are no less able to do this. If one does not treat one's parents with reverent respect, what is then the difference between him and animals?"

8. 子夏問孝。子曰:"色難。有事,弟子服其勞;有酒食,先生饌。曾是以爲孝乎?"

译文:

子夏向孔子请教什么是孝道。孔子说:"侍奉父母经常保持和颜悦色最难。有事情,儿子为父母效劳;有酒食,让父母吃喝。难道做到这些就算孝吗?"

英文:

Zi Xia asked about being filial. Confucius said, "It is most difficult for a son to serve his parents with a consistently joyful expression on his face. If he does nothing more than labouring for his parents whenever needed and sharing food and drink with them whenever he has some, how could he deserve to be called filial?"

9. 子曰:"吾與回言終日,不違,如愚。退而省其私,亦足以發,回也不愚。"

译文:

孔子说:"我整天和颜回讲学,他从来不提反对意见和疑问,好像很愚笨。可是我发现他私下研究时,也能发挥,可见他并不愚笨。"

颜回: 姓颜，名回，字子渊，亦称颜渊，孔子的学生。

英文:

Confucius said, "Yan Hui (a disciple of Confucius') never disagrees with me even when we talk for a whole day. Thus, it seems as if he were slow. But when he studies on his own, he is quite creative. Yan Hui is actually not slow at all."

10. 子曰: "视其所以，观其所由，察其所安。人焉廋哉? 人焉廋哉?"

译文:

孔子说: "了解一个人，要看他的所作所为，不仅了解他的过去，还要观察他的现在，这样的话，对那个人的了解还会不全面吗?"

英文:

Confucius said, "We can understand a man by observing what he does, how he arrived at his present position and how he feels about it. Then, is there anything about him we do not understand?"

11. 子曰: "温故而知新，可以为师矣。"

译文:

孔子说: "温习学过的知识时，能从中获得新知识的人，就可以做老师了。"

英文:

Confucius said, "If one is able to acquire new knowledge by reviewing old knowledge, he is qualified to be a tutor."

12. 子曰: "君子不器。"

译文:

孔子说: "君子应有广博的知识。"

英文:

Confucius said, "A gentleman should not be like a utensil. (He should have broad knowledge and not be confined to one use.)"

13. 子貢問君子。子曰: "先行其言而後從之。"

译文:

子贡问怎样才能做个君子。孔子说: "君子总是把想到的事先实行再说出来。"

英文:

Zi Gong asked about how to become a gentleman. Confucius answered, "A gentleman always puts his idea into action before he expresses it."

14. 子曰: "君子周而不比, 小人比而不周。"

译文:

孔子说: "君子讲团结而不互相勾结, 小人互相勾结而不讲团结。"

英文:

Confucius said, "Gentlemen unite instead of conspiring; petty men conspire instead of uniting."

15. 子曰: "學而不思則罔, 思而不學則殆。"

译文:

孔子说: "只读书不思考, 就不会分析。只空想不读书, 就不明事理。"

英文:

Confucius said, "It throws one into bewilderment to read without thinking whereas it places one in jeopardy to think without reading."

16. 子曰: "攻乎異端, 斯害也已。"

译文:

孔子说: "批判异端邪说, 祸害自消。"

英文:

Confucius said, "The plague of heterodox theories can be eliminated by fierce attack."

17. 子曰: "由! 誨女知之乎? 知之爲知之, 不知爲不知, 是知也。"

译文:

孔子说: "由! 我讲的你懂了吗? 懂就说懂, 不懂就说不懂, 才是聪明人。"

注:

由: 姓仲, 名由, 字子路, 又字季路, 孔子的学生。

英文:

Confucius said, "You (given name of Zi Lu, a disciple of Confucius')! Do you understand what I taught you? If you do, say you do; if not, say you do not. Only then are you an intelligent man."

18. 子張學干祿，子曰：“多聞闕疑，慎言其餘，則寡尤；多見闕殆，慎行其餘，則寡悔。言寡尤，行寡悔，祿在其中矣。”

译文：

子张向孔子请教求官的方法，孔子说：“多听少讲，不讲没把握的话，对有把握的话也要谨慎地讲，就可以少犯错误；多观察，不做没把握的事，对有把握的事情要细心去做，就可以少干错事。不说错话，不干错事，官职的俸禄就在这里面。”

注：

子张：姓颛孙，名师，字子张，孔子的学生。

英文：

Zi Zhang (a disciple of Confucius') consulted Confucius about the proper way of seeking officialdom. Confucius said, "Open your ears to all kinds of advice and opinions, set aside what is dubious and put forward those assured ones discreetly. You will thereby make fewer mistakes. Open your eyes to all kinds of things, set aside the doubtful ones and practice those assured ones carefully. You will thereby have fewer regrets. Officialdom is obtained by those who make fewer mistakes and have fewer regrets."

19. 哀公問曰：“何爲則民服？”孔子對曰：“舉直錯諸枉，則民服；舉枉錯諸直，則民不服。”

译文：

鲁哀公问孔子：“怎样做才能使百姓信服呢？”孔子回答说：“选用正直的人，压制邪恶的人，老百姓就会信服；如果选用邪恶的人，而把正直的人压下去，老百姓就不会信服。”

注：

哀公：姓姬，名蒋，鲁国国君。

英文：

Duke Ai of Lu asked Confucius, "How can I make my people obedient to me?" Confucius replied, "People will obey you if you promote righteous men and suppress evil men. And they will disobey you if you do the contrary."

20. 季康子問："使民敬、忠以勸，如之何？"子曰："臨之以莊，則敬；孝慈，則忠；舉善而教不能，則勸。"

译文：

季康子问："要让百姓对上恭敬，做事尽心竭力和互相勉励，应该怎么办？"孔子说："你行为端正，他们就会对你恭敬；你尊老爱幼，他们就会对你尽心竭力；你选用能者为师，他们就会互相勉励。"

注:

季康子：姓季孙，名肥，鲁国的大夫。"康"是谥号。

英文:

Ji Kangzi (Jisun Fei, then a minister of Lu) asked, "What can I do to make the people respect and be loyal to their superiors and try their best in service?" Confucius said, "Be upright in their presence, and they will hold you in respect; be filial and benevolent, and they will be loyal to you; use the righteous and instruct the unqualified, and they will try their best in service."

21. 或謂孔子曰："子奚不爲政?"子曰："《書》云：'孝乎惟孝，友于兄弟，施於有政，是亦爲政，奚其爲爲政?"

译文:

有人对孔子说："你为什么不做官参政呢？"孔子说："《尚书》上说：'孝顺父母，友爱兄弟'。我把这种风气影响到政治上去，也是参政了，不一定只有当官才算参政嘛！"

Someone asked Confucius, "Why don't you participate in government?" Confucius answered, "In *The Book
of Historical Documents*, we read, 'Be filial to your parents and love your brothers.' If I am able to influence
government by spreading this idea, then I am actually involved in government.What is meant by Participating in
government if you think what I am doing has nothing to
do with government?"

22. 子曰:"人而無信，不知其可也。大車無輗，小
車無軏，其何以行之哉？"

译文:

孔子说:"一个人不讲信用，怎么可以立身处世。这
就好比大车没有輗（古代牛车车辕前面横木上两端套牲
口用的木销子），小车没有軏（古代马车车辕前面横木
上两端套牲口用的木销子），它怎么能行走呢?"

英文:

Confucius said, "How can one be acceptable without being trustworthy in words? This is just like a cart
without a collar-bar or a carriage without a yoke-bar.
How can it move forward?"

23. 子張問："十世可知也?"子曰:"殷因於夏禮，所損益可知也；周因於殷禮，所損益可知也；其或繼周者，雖百世，可知也。"

译文：

子张问:"十代以后的礼仪制度可以知道吗?"孔子说:"殷朝继承夏朝的礼仪制度，所废除的，增加的，是可以知道的；周朝继承殷朝的礼仪制度，其中有废除和增加的内容也是可以知道的。那么，继承周朝的朝代甚至一百代以后的朝代，它的礼仪制度也是可以依此类推而知道的。"

英文：

Zi Zhang asked, "Is it possible for us to know the system of rites ten generations on?"

Confucius answered, "It is possible to know the system of rites that the Yin (Shang) Dynasty inherited from the Xia Dynasty and the revisions they made; it is possible to know the system of rites that the Zhou Dynasty inherited from the Yin Dynasty and the revisions they made. Therefore, it is also possible to know the system of rites of the ensuing dynasties, even those a hundred generations afterward."

24. 子曰:"非其鬼而祭之，諂也。見義不爲，無勇也。"

孔子说: "不是你应该祭祀的鬼神而去祭祀, 这是谄媚。见到合乎正义的事而不敢挺身去做, 是怯懦的表现。"

英文:

Confucius said, "It is only flattery if one offers sacrifices to the dead who are none of one's concern. It is cowardice not to dare to defend righteousness when it is endangered."

八佾篇第三

1. 孔子謂季氏，"八佾舞於庭，是可忍也，孰不可忍也？"

译文：

孔子谈到季氏时说："他竟用天子祭祀乐舞，这样违礼的事他都做得出来，还有什么事他做不出来呢？"

注：

季氏：季孙氏，即季孙意如，鲁国大夫。

八佾：古代奏乐舞蹈的行列，一行称一佾，每佾8人，八佾共64人。周礼规定，天子用八佾（64人），诸侯用六佾（48人），大夫用四佾（32人），士用二佾（16人）。季氏应用四佾而用八佾，故孔子说他违背周礼。

英文：

Confucius said of Jisun Shi (Jisun Yiru, then a minister of Lu), "He got eight rows of dancers to perform in his courtyard. If this violation of the rites could be tolerated, what else might he tolerate?"

Note: Eight rows, each of which consists of eight dancers, was the line-up of an ancient royal dance with musical accompaniment. It was arranged only when the

Monarch offered sacrifices to Heaven. According to the Zhou rites, the Monarch, or the Son of Heaven, could have eight rows of dancers, the dukes six rows, and the ministers four rows. Since Jisun Shi was a minister, he should have had four rows instead of eight rows. That was why Confucius accused him of going against the rites.

2. 三家者以《雍》徹。子曰: "'相維辟公，天子穆穆'，奚取於三家之堂?"

译文:

孟孙氏、叔孙氏、季孙氏三家祭祖时用天子之礼。孔子说: "天子之礼怎么能用在大夫的庙堂上呢?"

注:

三家: 指孟孙、叔孙、季孙，鲁国三家大夫。当时由这三家把持了鲁国政权。

英文:

The Three Noble Families of Lu (Mengsun Shi, Shusun Shi and Jisun Shi) offered sacrifices to their ancestors by performing the *Yong* ode. Confucius rebuked, "The ode sings: 'Accompanied by dukes only, the Son of Heaven shows great solemnity.' How is then this ode relevant to sacrifices in the halls of the Three

Families?"

3. 子曰："人而不仁，如禮何？人而不仁，如樂何？"

译文：

孔子说："如果一个人没有仁爱之心，还能讲礼仪吗？如果一个人没有仁爱之心，还能讲音乐吗？"

英文：

Confucius said, "What can a man do about the rites if he is not benevolent? What can he do about music if he is not benevolent?"

4. 林放問禮之本，子曰："大哉問！禮，與其奢也，寧儉；喪，與其易也，寧戚。"

译文：

林放问礼的本质是什么，孔子说："你提的问题太大了！就一般礼仪上说，与其铺张浪费，不如节俭朴素；就办丧事来说，与其看仪式上的隆重，不如看内心悲痛的程度。"

注：

林放：鲁国人。

英文：

Lin Fang (a man of Lu) asked about the basis of the rites. Confucius answered, "What a grand question that is! For the ordinary rites, frugality is better than extravagance. For mourning, the inner grief is more important than the formalities."

5. 子曰: "夷狄之有君, 不如諸夏之亡也。"

译文:

孔子说: "文化落后的国家虽有君主而没有礼仪, 还不如文明国家虽无国君而有礼仪。"

英文:

Confucius said, "A backward state with a ruler and no rites is inferior to a cultured state with rites, even if it has no ruler."

6. 季氏旅於泰山。子謂冉有曰: "女弗能救與?" 對曰: "不能。" 子曰: "嗚呼! 曾謂泰山不如林放乎?"

译文:

季氏要去祭祀泰山。孔子对冉有说: "你能劝阻他吗?" 冉有回答说: "不能。" 孔子说: "哎呀! 难道泰山之神还不如鲁国的林放懂礼, 竟会接受季氏越礼的祭祀吗?"

注:

林放：鲁国懂礼的人。按周礼，只有天子和诸侯才能祭祀泰山，季氏是大夫，所以他祭祀泰山是越礼行动。

冉有：孔子学生冉求，字子有，当时为季氏家臣。

英文：

Jisun Shi (Jisun Yiru) intended to offer sacrifices to the God of Mount Tai. Confucius asked Ran You (a disciple of Confucius' then serving Jisun Shi), "Can you persuade him out of doing that?" Ran You replied, "No, I can't." Confucius said, "Is it true that the God of Mount Tai knows less about the rites than Lin Fang, being so tolerant as to accept Jisun Shi's inappropriate offerings?"

Note: Lin Fang was an expert on rites in Lu. According to the rites of Zhou, only emperors could offer sacrifices to the God of Mount Tai. Jisun Shi was only a minister and therefore this sacrifice was inappropriate.

7. 子曰："君子無所爭。必也射乎！揖讓而升，下而飲。其爭也君子。"

译文：

孔子说："君子与世无争。如果有所争，那一定是射箭比赛吧！即使参加比赛，也是先谦让再上场，射完箭下场又相互敬酒，不失其君子风度。"

Confucius said, "There is no contention among gentlemen. The only exception is archery. When it begins, two parties will bow and make way for each other; when it ends, they will drink together. Even the way they contend is quite gentlemanly."

8. 子夏問曰: "'巧笑倩兮, 美目盼兮, 素以爲絢兮。'何謂也?"子曰: "繪事後素。"曰: "禮後乎?"子曰: "起予者商也! 始可與言《詩》已矣。"

译文:

子夏向孔子请教: "'动人的笑容, 美丽的眼睛, 像画出来的花儿一样', 这几句诗是什么意思?"孔子说: "先施匀净的白色作底, 然后才画出花儿来。"子夏说: "要这样, 是否能说只在仁义基础上才能产生礼仪呢?"孔子高兴地说: "你能这样发挥, 现在可以和你谈论《诗经》了。"

英文:

Zi Xia consulted Confucius, " 'An attractive smile and beautiful eyes are exactly like flowers painted on a plain background.' What does this verse mean?"

Confucius answered, "It is only after the white

background is prepared that any painting is possible."

Zi Xia said, "In that case can we say that the rites can only base themselves on benevolence?"

Confucius said joyfully, "Since you have thrown some new light on this verse, now I can begin to discuss *The Book of Songs* with you."

9. 子曰: "夏禮，吾能言之，杞不足徵也；殷禮，吾能言之，宋不足徵也。文獻不足故也。足，則吾能徵之矣。"

译文:

孔子说: "夏朝的礼，我能讲明白，但它后代杞国我讲不清；殷朝的礼，我也能讲清楚，它后代宋国我也讲不清。这是因为杞国和宋国文献不足的缘故，如果文献充足，我就可以讲明白。"

英文:

Confucius said, "I am able to discourse on the rites of the Xia Dynasty, but not on that of Qi (descendants of Xia), I am able to discourse on the rites of the Yin Dynasty, but not on that of Song (descendants of Yin).

This is because Qi and Song are not well enough documented. If they were, I would be able to talk about them.

10. 子曰: "禘自既灌而往者，吾不欲觀之矣。"

译文:

孔子说: "禘祭的仪式，从第一次献酒以后，我就不想看了。"

注:

禘: 古代一种隆重祭祀祖先的典礼。据《礼记》说，这种仪式只有天子才能举行。孔子认为鲁国国君实行禘祭是一种越礼行为，所以他不愿看。这就是他主张的"非礼勿视"了。

英文:

Confucius said, "I do not want to continue to watch the Di ceremony (a ceremony of offering sacrifices to ancestors) after the first offering of wine."

Note: The Di ceremony could only be performed by the son of Heaven, i.e. the Emperor of the Zhou Dynasty. In Confucius' time, however, it was often performed by the Dukes. Confucius could not tolerate the obvious violation of the rites.

11. 或問禘之説，子曰: "不知也; 知其説者之於天下也，其如示諸斯乎!"指其掌。

译文:

有人问孔子关于禘祭的理论，孔子说：“我不知道。知道这种理论的人治理天下可以说易如翻掌。”

英文：

Someone asked about the theory behind the Di ceremony. Confucius answered, "I don't know. Those who know it may rule the country as easily as turning one's palm."

12. 祭如在，祭神如神在。子曰："吾不與祭，如不祭。"

译文：

孔子认为祭祀祖先要虔诚，就像祖先在面前，祭神时就像看到了神。所以他说："如果让别人代理自己祭祀，那和不祭是一样的。"

英文：

Confucius thought one should offer sacifices to one's ancestors devoutly and sincerely as if they were still alive. He should offer sacrifices to gods devoutly and sincerely too as if they were present. Confucius said, "If I entrust others to go to offer sacrifices in my stead, that is no different from not offering any sacrifice at all."

13. 王孫賈問曰: "與其媚於奧, 寧媚於竈, 何謂也?" 子曰: "不然。獲罪於天, 無所禱也。"

译文:

王孙贾问孔子: "与其巴结奥神, 宁可巴结灶神, 是什么意思?" 孔子说: "不对, 如果得罪上天, 巴结谁都没用。"

注:

王孙贾: 卫国的大夫。

奥神、灶神: 古人认为室内西南角为尊位, 有神, 称奥神。其职位高于灶神。但灶神有"上天言事"之特权, 故当时有"与其媚于奥, 宁媚于灶"之俗说。

英文:

Wangsun Jia (then a minister of Wei) asked, "What is meant by 'It is better to curry favour of Zao (the kitchen god) rather than of Ao (a god believed to dwell in the southwest corner of a room)'?"

Confucius answered, "It is not true. For, if you offend Heaven, it is no use flattering anything else."

Note: The ancient people believed that the southwest corner of a room was a reverend place where the god of Ao, who was superior to that of Zao, dwelt. However, the latter has the privilege or prerogative to go to Heaven to report. Hence the saying, "One would flatter Zao rather than Ao".

14. 子曰: "周監於二代, 郁郁乎文哉! 吾從周。"

译文:

孔子说: "周朝的礼仪制度是借鉴夏、商两代的制度建立起来的, 十分丰富多彩所以我赞成周礼。"

英文:

Confucuis said, "By learning from the Xia and Yin dynasties the Zhou Dynasty established its own rites and institutions. What a rich culture! That is why I am in favour of the Zhou rites."

15. 子入太廟, 每事問。或曰: "孰謂鄹人之子知禮乎? 入太廟, 每事問。"子聞之, 曰: "是禮也。"

译文:

孔子进入周公庙, 对每件不明白的事情都向别人请教。有人背后说: "谁说鄹大夫的儿子懂得礼呢? 他到太庙, 每件事都问别人。"孔子听说后就说: "不懂就问这就是礼嘛。"

注:

鄹: 地名, 在山东曲阜县东南十里。孔子的父亲叔梁纥曾做过鄹大夫, 故称"鄹人"。

Confucius asked about everything he didn't understand whenever he entered the temple of the Duke of Zhou. Someone ridiculed him, saying, "How can you say that the son of the Zou fellow (i.e. Shu Lianghe, the father of Confucius, who had been a minister of Zou) knows the rites well? He had to ask about everything when he entered the temple." On hearing this, Confucius said, "It accords with the rites to do that."

16. 子曰: "射不主皮，爲力不同科，古之道也。"

译文:

孔子说: "演习礼乐时射箭，不一定要穿破箭靶子，因为各人的力量不一样，以中不中为输赢，这是古时候的规矩。"

英文:

Confucius said, "When performing archery, it is not necessary for the performer to shoot the arrow through the target, for different people have different strength, but to hit the target. This is an ancient rule."

17. 子貢欲去告朔之餼羊。子曰: "賜也! 爾愛其羊，我愛其禮。"

译文：

子贡想把每月初一祭祖庙时的活羊免去，孔子对他说："你看重的是羊，我看重的是礼，还是不免去为好。"

英文：

Zi Gong wanted to withdraw the live goat from the ancestral sacrifice held on the first day of every month. Confucius said, "Oh, Ci! What you cherish is the goat and what I hold dear to are the rites. The goat should not be spared."

18. 子曰："事君盡禮，人以爲諂也。"

译文：

孔子说："以臣下之礼侍奉君主，别人却以为是向君主献媚邀宠。"

英文：

Confucius said, "To serve a ruler in perfect accordance with the rites is sometimes regarded by others as currying his favour."

19. 定公問："君使臣，臣事君，如之何？"孔子對曰: "君使臣以禮, 臣事君以忠。"

译文:

鲁定公问: "君主怎样使用臣子, 臣子怎样服事君主?"孔子答道: "君主使用臣子应该按照礼节, 臣子事奉君主应该忠心耿耿。"

注:

定公: 姓姬, 名宋, 鲁国国君。

英文:

Duke Ding of Lu asked, "How should a ruler employ his ministers and his ministers serve him?" Confucius answered, "A ruler should employ his ministers according to the rites and the ministers should serve him loyally."

20. 子曰: "《關雎》樂而不淫, 哀而不傷。"

译文:

孔子说: "《关雎》这首诗, 欢快而不放荡, 悲哀而不痛苦。"

英文:

Confucius said, "The poem *Guanju* is full of joy but not licentiousness, of sadness but not grief."

21. 哀公問社於宰我。宰我對曰："夏后氏以松，殷人以柏，周人以栗，曰，使民戰栗。"子聞之，曰："成事不說，遂事不諫，既往不咎。"

译文:

鲁哀公问宰我，做土地神的神主应用什么木。宰我回答说："夏朝时用松木，商朝时用柏木，周朝用栗木，意思是使百姓战战栗栗。"孔子听了这话，告诫宰我说："已经做过的事不便再解释，已经完成的事不宜再规劝，已经过去的事不要再责备了。"

注:

哀公: 姓姬，名蒋，鲁国国君。

宰我: 名予，字子我，孔子的学生。

英文:

Duke Ai of Lu asked Zai Wo (a disciple of Confucius') what tree to use for a memorial tablet to the god of the earth. Zai Wo answered, "Pine was used in the Xia Dynasty, cypress in the Yin Dynasty, and chestnut in the Zhou Dynasty. The reason for the latter was to make common people tremble." * At this, Confucius admonished Zai Wo, "Do not explain what has been done, do not try to advise about what is finished, and do not reprimand what has happened."

Note: In Chinese, the same character "li" can mean either "chestnut tree" or "tremble".

22. 子曰:"管仲之器小哉!"或曰:"管仲儉乎?"曰:"管氏有三歸,官事不攝,焉得儉?""然則管仲知禮乎?"曰:"邦君樹塞門,管氏亦樹塞門。邦君爲兩君之好,有反坫,管氏亦有反坫。管氏而知禮,孰不知禮?"

译文:
孔子说:"管仲的器量太小。"有人问:"管仲节俭吗?"孔子说:"管仲有丰厚的收入,众多的家人,那里说得上节俭呢?"那人又问:"管仲是不是很懂礼节?"孔子又道:"管氏府第陈设和国君一样,如果说这样的人懂礼,那还有不懂礼的人吗?"

注:
管仲: 春秋时齐国人,名夷吾,做过齐桓公的宰相。

英文:
Confucius said, "Guan Zhong (the prime minister under Duke Huan of Qi) was rather narrow-minded." Somebody remarked, "Was Guan frugal?" Confucius answered, "Guan had a large income and a multitude of attendants. How could he be called 'frugal'?" "Did he know the rites well?" Confucius answered, "There was no difference between the arrangement of Guan's residence

and that of the ruler's. If such a person understood the rites, did anyone not understand them?"

23. 子語魯大師樂，曰："樂其可知也：始作，翕如也；從之，純如也，皦如也，繹如也，以成。"

译文:

孔子把演奏音乐的道理告诉鲁国的乐师，说："开始的时候，发音合奏；继尔奏出和谐明快的曲调，在馀音袅袅中结束。"

英文:

Confucius talked with the Grand Musician of Lu, saying, "Is it possible to understand music in such a way: music begins with an ensemble, develops into pure and clear melodies, and comes to an end with continuous tones?"

24. 儀封人請見，曰："君子之至於斯也，吾未嘗不得見也。"從者見之。出曰："二三子何患於喪乎？天下之無道也久矣，天將以夫子爲木鐸。"

译文:

卫国仪地的边防长官请求会见孔子，并说："凡到这里的有道德学问的人我都见过。"于是，孔子的学生带他去见孔子。会见后他出来对孔子的学生说: "你们不要急着做官，天下黑暗的日子已经太久，你们的老师将给人民带来光明。"

英文:

An officer in the border area of the State of Wei requested to have an interview with Confucius, saying, "I have never failed to see any gentleman who has been here." Then the disciples presented him to Confucius. After that, the officer told Confucius' disciples, "Do not be anxious to become officials. The world has been dark too long, and it is the Decree of Heaven that your Master will surely bring light to the people."

25. 子謂《韶》: "盡美矣，又盡善也。"謂《武》: "盡美矣，未盡善也。"

译文:

孔子说《韶》乐: "形式好，内容也好。"说《武》乐: "形式好，内容欠佳。"

注:

韶乐: 传为舜时乐曲名。

武乐: 传为周武王乐曲名。

舜天子之位由尧禅让而来，武王之位由伐纣而来，故孔子有此评论。

英文:

Confucius said of the Music of *Shao* (a piece of music in the Shun period), "The form and content are both good." He said of the Music of *Wu* (a piece of music in commemorating King Wu of Zhou), "The form is good but not the content."

Note: Shun inherited the office peacefully from Yao while King Wu of the Zhou State came to power by fighting against king Zhou of the Yin Dynasty. The former possessed higher virtue than the latter.

26. 子曰："居上不寬，爲禮不敬，臨喪不哀，吾何以觀之哉？"

译文:

孔子说："居上位而不能宽宏大量，行礼时不恭敬严肃，参加丧礼时不悲哀，这种样子我不忍看。"

英文:

Confucius said, "I cannot put up with a person who, in high position, is narrow-minded, who is irreverent in performing the rites and not sad in mourning."

里仁篇第四

1. 子曰: "里仁爲美。擇不處仁，焉得知?"

译文:

孔子说: "选择住处要选在风俗淳美的地方，否则怎么能算明智呢?"

英文:

Confucius said, "One should choose to dwell in such a place where there are men of benevolence. Otherwise, how can one be said to be wise?"

2. 子曰: "不仁者不可以久處約，不可以長處樂。仁者安仁，知者利仁。"

译文:

孔子说: "道德修养差的人不能安贫乐富。道德修养高的人安于实行仁，聪明人知道利用仁。"

英文:

Confucius said, "Ill-cultivated men can neither be content in poverty nor happy in wealth. The well-cultivated man is content in benevolence, and the wise man knows how to use benevolence."

3. 子曰: "唯仁者能好人, 能恶人。"

译文:

孔子说: "只有仁人才能够做到爱憎分明。"

英文:

Confucius said, "Only a benevolent man is able to tell whom to love and whom to hate."

4. 子曰: "苟志於仁矣, 無惡也。"

译文:

孔子说: "实行仁德, 没有坏处。"

英文:

Confucius said, "One who sets his heart on benevolence will be free from evil."

5. 子曰: "富與貴, 是人之所欲也; 不以其道得之, 不處也。貧與賤, 是人之所惡也; 不以其道得之, 不去也。君子去仁, 惡乎成名? 君子無終食之間違仁, 造次必於是, 顛沛必於是。"

译文:

孔子说: "金钱和地位,这是人人都想得到的,但君子不会用不正当的方法得到它。贫穷和下贱,这是人人都厌恶的,但君子不会用不正当的方法摆脱它。君子离开了仁德还怎么称得上君子呢? 君子在任何情况下都不会忘记实行仁德。"

英文:

Confucius said, "Everyone desires money and high position, but a gentleman would not accept them unless he got them in a right way. Everyone hates poverty and low status, but a gentleman would not get rid of them in an unjust way. How can one be called a gentleman if one betrays benevolence? Under no circumstances should a gentleman forget to practice benevolence."

6. 子曰: "我未見好仁者,惡不仁者。好仁者,無以尚之;惡不仁者,其爲仁矣,不使不仁者加乎其身。有能一日用其力於仁矣乎? 我未見力不足者。蓋有之矣,我未之見也。"

译文:

孔子说: "我没见过爱好仁德的人,也没见过憎恶不仁的人。爱好仁德的人,当然好;憎恶不仁的人,只不过是怕不仁的人影响自己而已。其实谁有力量在一天内实行仁德呢？这样的人大概是有的，只是我没有见过。"

英文:

Confucius said, "I have neither seen a man who really loves benevolence, nor a man who really hates unbenevolence. A man who really loves benevolence is the highest in virtue, and a man who really hates unbenevolence may only be considered benevolent in the sense that he would not allow unbenevolent people to contaminate him. Is there anyone who is willing to devote all his energy to benevolence for a whole day? Though I could find no one who does not possess the energy, yet I have never seen such a man who has devoted himself to it. Or perhaps there is such a person, but I have not yet come across him."

7. 子曰："人之過也，各於其黨。觀過，斯知仁矣。"

译文:

孔子说："人所犯的错误性质，往往和他们的社会地位有关。所以考察一个人的错误，就知道他的社会地位。"

Confucius said, "The mistakes one makes has to do with one's social position. By looking at someone's mistakes we can see what type of person he is."

8. 子曰: "朝闻道, 夕死可矣。"

译文:

孔子说: "早晨学得真理, 当天晚上死掉也不后悔。"

注:

意即"生命不止, 学习不停"。

英文:

Confucius said, "If one learns the truth in the morning, one would never regret dying the same evening."

9. 子曰: "士志於道, 而恥惡衣惡食者, 未足與議也。"

译文:

孔子说: "既有志于追求真理, 但又以贫困为耻辱的人, 不值得与他讨论真理。"

英文:

Confucius said, "It is not worthwhile to have discussions with a scholar who is willing to search for the truth, but is ashamed of poor food and dress."

10. 子曰:"君子之於天下也，無適也，無莫也，義之與比。"

译文:

孔子说:"天下的事情，并没有规定一定怎样干，君子只是根据实际情况决定怎样干。"

英文:

Confucius said, "In dealing with the world, there are no definite rules as to how things should be done. A gentleman simply does things according to the actual situation."

11. 子曰:"君子懷德，小人懷土；君子懷刑，小人懷惠。"

译文:

孔子说:"君子怀念道德，小人怀念乡土；君子关心法纪，小人关心私利。"

英文:

Confucius said, "While the gentleman cherishes virtue, the petty man cherishes his native place; while the gentleman cherishes the law, the petty man cherishes his self interests."

12. 子曰: "放於利而行，多怨。"

译文:

孔子说: "办事从个人利益出发，必会招来怨恨。"

英文:

Confucius said, "One will incur ill will if one does things to one's own interest."

13. 子曰: "能以禮讓爲國乎，何有？不能以禮讓爲國，如禮何?"

译文:

孔子说: "用礼让来治理国家，会有什么困难呢？如果不用礼让来治理国家，又怎样实行礼呢?"

英文:

Confucius said, "If a state is governed by showing deference, what difficulty will there be in performing the rites? If a state is not governed by showing deference, how can the rites be performed?"

14. 子曰:"不患無位,患所以立。不患莫己知,求爲可知也。"

译文:

孔子说:"不愁没有职位,只愁没有任职的本领。不怕别人不知道自己,只求自己创造出成绩来。"

英文:

Confucius said, "Don't worry about having no official position, but do worry about your ability to fulfill a post. Don't worry when others don't appreciate you, but you should strive to make achievements."

15. 子曰:"參乎!吾道一以貫之。"曾子曰:"唯。"子出,門人問曰:"何謂也?"曾子曰:"夫子之道,忠恕而已矣。"

译文:

孔子说:"参呀!我的学说贯穿一个基本观念。"曾子说:"是。"孔子出门以后,别的同学问曾子:"这是什么意思?"曾子说:"他老人家的学说,只是忠恕罢了。"

注:

忠恕:朱熹注:"尽己之谓忠,推己之谓恕。而已矣者,竭尽而无余之辞也。"

Confucius said, "Shen! There is one consistent idea penetrating into my doctrine!" Zeng Zi answered, "Yes." After Confucius went out, the other disciples asked Zeng, "What did he refer to?" Zeng answered, "He simply referred to Zhong Shu * ."

Note: "Zhong Shu" is one of the most important concepts of Confucianism. "Zhong" literally means loyal and "Shu" means forgiving. According to Confucian explanation, it implies that "do to others what you do to yourself while do not do to others what you do not do to yourself."

16. 子曰：“君子喻於義，小人喻於利。”

译文:

孔子说：“君子明白义，小人懂得利。”

英文:

Confucius said, "The gentleman sees righteousness; The petty man sees profit."

17. 子曰：“見賢思齊焉，見不賢而内自省也。”

孔子说:"遇见才德好的人,就应该向他看齐,遇到无德才的人,就应反省自己有没有和他同样的毛病。"

英文:

Confucius said, "When you meet a man of virtue, learn from him. When you meet a man without virtue, examine yourself to see if you have the same defects as he has."

18. 子曰:"事父母幾諫。見志不從,又敬不違,勞而不怨。"

译文:

孔子说:"对父母的缺点要委婉地劝说,父母不听,仍要恭顺,虽心忧而不可怀恨。"

英文:

Confucius said, "In serving one's parents, one should dissuade them from doing wrong in the gentlest way. When the advice is ignored, one should remain reverent and obedient. One should not complain even when one is laden with anxiety."

19. 子曰:"父母在,不遠遊,遊必有方。"

译文:

孔子说:"父母在堂,不出远门,如必须外出,一定要让父母知道去处。"

英文:

Confucius said, "When one's parents are alive, one should not go far away. If one has to, one should tell them where one is going."

20. 子曰:"三年無改於父之道,可謂孝矣。"

译文:

孔子说:"如果在父亲去世后三年之内仍然坚持父亲留下的正确原则,就可以说他已经做到孝了。"

注:

这段话和第一篇第十一节重复。

英文:

Confucius said, "A man can be called filial if he sticks to his father's ways for three years after the latter's death."

Note: This is a repetition from I—11.

21. 子曰:"父母之年,不可不知也。一則以喜,一则以惧。"

译文:

孔子说: "父母的生日不能不时时记在心里。一方面为他们长寿而高兴, 一方面为他们又老一岁而忧虑。"

英文:

Confucius said, "One must always keep in mind one's parents' birthdays. On the one hand, one is glad to offer birthday congratulations; on the other, one is worried to see they grow one year older."

22. 子曰: "古者言之不出, 耻躬之不逮也。"

译文:

孔子说: "古人不轻易说大话, 因为怕自己说得出而做不到。"

英文:

Confucius said, "In ancient times, people didn't say things lightly, as they would be ashamed not to be able to match up to their words."

23. 子曰: "以约失之者鲜矣。"

译文:

孔子说: "能约束节制自己行为的人很少犯错误。"

英文:

Confucius said, "Seldom does a man who regulates his behaviour according to the rites make mistakes."

24. 子曰: "君子欲訥於言而敏於行。"

译文:

孔子说: "君子应该说话谨慎, 做事勤劳敏捷。"

英文:

Confucius said, "A gentleman should be careful in speech and quick to act."

25. 子曰: "德不孤, 必有鄰。"

译文:

孔子说: "有道德的人不会孤立的, 一定会有志同道合者相从。"

英文:

Confucius said, "A man of virtue can never be isolated. He is sure to have like—minded companions."

26. 子游曰:"事君數,斯辱矣;朋友數,斯疏矣。"

译文:

子游说:"对君主屡屡进谏,就会被猜忌;对朋友劝告太多,就会被疏远。"

英文:

Zi You said, "One will suffer humiliation if one repeatedly remonstrates with one's ruler, and one will suffer isolation if one repeatedly advises one's friends."

公冶長篇第五

1. 子謂公冶長:"可妻也。雖在縲絏之中,非其罪也。"以其子妻之。

译文:

孔子谈起公冶长时说:"可以把女儿嫁给他。虽然他曾被关进监狱,但那不是他的罪过。"于是便把自己的女儿嫁给他。

注:

公冶长:姓公冶,名长,字子长。孔子的学生和女婿。

英文:

When talking about Gongye Zhang (a disciple of Confucius'), Confucius said, "He is a suitable choice for a husband. He once went to prison, but he was innocent." Then he married his daughter to Gongye.

2. 子謂南容:"邦有道,不廢;邦無道,免於刑戮。"以其兄之子妻之。

译文:

孔子谈到南容时说:"国家政治清明,他有官做;国家政治黑暗，他也不致被刑罚。"于是便把自己的侄女嫁给他。

注:

　南容: 姓南宫，名适，字子容，孔子的学生。

英文:

　　Confucius said of Nanrong (a disciple of Confucius') that when the state and government were in order, he held an official position and was not cast aside, and that when the state and government were benighted, he was free from penalty. Then he married his niece to Nanrong.

　　3. 子謂子賤,"君子哉若人! 魯無君子者，斯焉取斯?"

译文:

　　孔子谈论子贱时说:"这人是真君子呀! 若说鲁国无君子，他是从哪里学到这种好品德呢?"

注:

　子贱: 姓宓，名不齐，字子贱，孔子的学生。

英文:

　　When talking about Zi Jian (a disciple of Confucius'), Confucius said, "What a gentleman he is! If there were no gentlemen in Lu, where could he have acquired such virtue?"

4. 子貢問曰: "賜也何如?" 子曰: "女, 器也。" 曰: "何器也?" 曰: "瑚璉也。"

译文:

子贡问孔子: "你看我这个人怎么样?" 孔子说: "很有才能, 但还不是全才。"

英文:

Zi Gong asked, "What do you think of me?" Confucius answered, "You are like a vessel." "What kind of vessel then?" "A precious one used in grand sacrifices."

Note: It implies that Zi Gong had a special talent in one aspect, yet he was far from a perfect gentleman.

5. 或曰: "雍也仁而不佞。" 子曰: "焉用佞? 禦人以口給, 屢憎於人。不知其仁, 焉用佞?"

译文:

有人说: "冉雍有仁德而不善辩。" 孔子说: "何必要善辩呢? 整天强嘴利舌地同人辩驳, 被人讨厌。冉雍未必仁, 但为什么一定要善辩呢?"

　　冉雍: 姓冉，名雍，字仲弓，孔子的学生。

英文:

　　Some one said, "Ran Yong (a disciple of Confucius') is benevolent but is a poor orator." Confucius said, "Why bother with clever speech? If one is always using clever arguments, he will be hated by others. I don't know if Ran Yong is benevolent, but why must he be a good orator?"

　　6. 子使漆彫開仕，對曰:"吾斯之未能信。"子説。

译文:

　　孔子叫漆雕开去做官，漆雕开回答说:"我对做官没有信心。"孔子听了很高兴。

注:

　　漆雕开: 姓漆雕，名开，字子若，孔子的学生。

英文:

　　Confucius told Qidiao Kai (a disciple of Confucius') to take office. Qidiao said, "I cannot trust myself to do so." On hearing this, Confucius was very pleased.

　　7. 子曰:"道不行，乘桴浮于海，從我者，其由與?"

子路聞之喜。子曰:"由也好勇過我,無所取材。"

译文:

孔子说:"如果我的主张不能实行,就坐小船到海外去,那时跟随我的大概只有仲由吧!"子路听了这话很高兴。孔子又说:"仲由只是勇气过人,却别无长处。"

英文:

Confucius said, "If my doctrines are not accepted, and I have to go abroad on a raft, the only one who will follow me would probably be Zhong You." On hearing this, Zi Lu was overjoyed. Then Confucius continued, "But Zhong You has nothing except extraordinary courage."

8. 孟武伯問:"子路仁乎?"子曰:"不知也。"又問。子曰:"由也,千乘之國,可使治其賦也,不知其仁也。""求也何如?"子曰:"求也,千室之邑,百乘之家,可使爲之宰也,不知其仁也。""赤也何如?"子曰:"赤也,束帶立於朝,可使與賓客言也,不知其仁也。"

译文:

孟武伯再三问子路有没有仁德。孔子说:"我只知道仲由可以在一个有千乘兵车的国家里主管军政工作,但不知道他是否有仁德。"孟武伯又问:"冉求这个人怎么样?"孔子回答说: "冉求可以胜任在一个千户人家的县里当县长, 或者在大夫封地当总管。至于有无仁德, 我不知道。"孟武伯问到公西赤, 孔子说: "公西赤最适合接待外宾的工作, 我也不知道他是否有仁德。"

注:

冉求: 姓冉, 名求, 字子有, 孔子的学生。

公西赤: 孔子的学生。字子华, 通称公西华。

孔子对自己的学生, 了解很全面。这里说"不知道", 只是委婉语气。并非真不知道。如对冉求, 他称其"千室之邑, 百乘之家, 可使为之宰也。"但又斥责他帮助季氏"聚敛而附益之。"孔子肯定每个学生的某方面的特长和才能, 同时又认为他们还有不足, 还不是完人。所以说不知道他们是否有仁德。

英文:

Meng Wubo asked repeatedly whether Zi Lu was benevolent. Confucius said, "Zhong You can be given the responsibility of managing military affairs in a state of one thousand chariots, but whether he is benevolent or not, I don't know." Meng Wubo asked, "What about Ran Qiu (another disciple of Confucius')?" Confucius answered, "Ran Qiu can be appointed magistrate of a town with one thousand households, or steward in a noble manor with a hundred chariots, but whether he is benevolent, I don't know." Meng Wubo asked again, "What about Gongxi Chi (another disciple of

Confucius')?" Confucius answered, "Gongxi Chi is a suitable choice for the job of receiving foreign guests, but whether he is benevolent or not, I don't know."

Note: Confucius knew all his disciples very well. When he said "I don't know," it only served the purpose of politeness. Take Ran Qiu for example. Confucius said that Ran could be appointed steward of a noble manor with a hundred chariots, but on the other hand he criticised Ran for his helping the Ji Family gather more and more profit. Confucius showed his appreciation for the special talents of his disciples while believing that they had their own weaknesses, far from perfect. Therefore, he said he did not know whether they were benevolent or not.

9. 子謂子貢曰："女與回也孰愈?"對曰："賜也何敢望回? 回也聞一以知十，賜也聞一以知二。"子曰："弗如也; 吾與女弗如也。"

译文:

孔子问子贡："你和颜回谁更强一些?"子贡回答说: "我怎么敢和颜回相比呢，他学到一个道理可以推知十个道理，而我学到一个道理却只能推知两个道理。"孔子听后说："是这样的，我同意你的说法。"

英文:

Confucius asked Zi Gong, "Who is wiser, you or Hui?" Zi Gong answered, "How dare I compare myself with Yan Hui? When he is told one thing, he understands ten. When I am told one thing, I understand only two." Confucius said, "I agree that you are no match for him."

10. 宰予畫寢。子曰："朽木不可雕也，糞土之墙不可杇也。於予與何誅?"子曰："始吾於人也，聽其言而信其行；今吾於人也，聽其言而觀其行。於予與改是。"

译文:

孔子的学生宰予白天睡觉。孔子很生气地说："已腐朽了的木头不能精雕细刻，粪土一样的墙壁不能粉刷。对宰予，我也不责备他。"又说："以前，我对人是听他的话就相信了他；现在我是听了他的话还要观察他行为才肯相信。这是从宰予的表现使我改变了对人的态度。"

注:

宰予：孔子的学生。又名宰我，字子我。

英文:

Zai Yu always slept in the daytime. Confucius said resentfully, "One cannot expect to carve on a piece of rotten wood, nor can one expect to whitewash a filthy wall. As for Zai Yu, what is the use of scolding him?"

Confucius added, "I used to trust what people said, now I want to see what they do before I trust them. It is from Zai Yu that I have learnt to change my attitude in dealing with people."

11. 子曰: "吾未見剛者。" 或對曰: "申棖。" 子曰: "棖也慾，焉得剛？"

译文:

孔子说: "我没有看见过刚毅的人。" 有人说 "申棖就是这样的人。" 孔子说: "申棖欲望太多，怎么能刚毅。"

注:

申棖: 姓申，名棖，字周，孔子的学生。

英文:

Confucius said, "I have never met anyone who is truly unyielding." Someone said, "Shen Cheng (a disciple of Confucius') is such a person." Confucius said, "He is full of desires. How can he be unyielding?"

12. 子貢曰: "我不欲人之加諸我也，吾亦欲無加諸人。" 子曰: "賜也，非爾所及也。"

译文:

子贡说: "我不想让别人欺侮我，我也不想欺侮别人。"孔子说:"你现在还做不到这一点。"

英文:

Zi Gong said, "I do not want others to impose things on me, and nor do I want to impose things on others." Confucius commented, "Ci, you have yet been far from practising this."

13. 子貢曰:"夫子之文章,可得而聞也;夫子之言性與天道,不可得而聞也。"

译文:

子贡说:"我们只听老师讲过文献方面的学问,却没听过关于人性和天道的知识。"

英文:

Zi Gong said, "We can get to know the ancient literature the Master taught us, but we have never heard of his views on human nature and the way of Heaven."

14. 子路有聞,未之能行,唯恐有聞。

译文:

子路学到知识一定要实行之后才肯接受新的知识。

Zi Lu would not try to acquire any more knowledge before he had practised what he had learnt.

15. 子貢問曰: "孔文子何以謂之'文'也?"子曰: "敏而好學，不恥下問，是以謂之'文'也。"

译文:

子贡问道: "孔文子为什么谥他为'文'呢?"孔子说: "他聪明好学，谦虚好问，所以加给'文'字作谥号。"

注:

孔文子: 孔圉，卫国大夫。"文"是谥号。

英文:

Zi Gong asked, "Why was Kong Wenzi (a previous minister of Wei) called 'Wen' (a title that means "cultured")?" Confucius answered, "Because he was quick and eager to learn, modest and never ashamed of asking questions. That is why he was honored as 'Wen'."

16. 子謂子產: "有君子之道四焉: 其行己也恭，其事上也敬，其養民也惠，其使民也義。"

译文:

孔子评论子产说: "他具有君子的四种美德: 行为端

庄，对君主负责，对百姓不忘教育和爱护。"

注:

子产: 姓公孙, 名侨, 字子产, 郑国贤相, 是一位杰出的政治家。

英文:

When talking of Zi Chan (a previous minister of Zheng), Confucius said, "He had four virtues that a gentleman should have: He was respectable in manners and respectful to his ruler; he educated the common people and used their labour reasonably."

17. 子曰: "晏平仲善與人交, 久而敬之。"

译文:

孔子说: "晏平仲善于与人交朋友, 交往越久, 别人越尊敬他。"

注:

晏平仲: 姓晏名婴, 字仲, "平" 是谥号。齐国大夫。

英文:

Confucius said, "Yan Pingzhong (a minister of Qi) was good at making friends. The longer the friendship, the more his friends respected him."

18. 子曰: "臧文仲居蔡, 山節藻梲, 何如其知也?"

译文:

孔子说: "臧文仲的聪明不过是给卜卦用的乌龟盖一间豪华的住室, 其实这是违礼的。"

注:

臧文仲: 姓臧孙, 名辰, 鲁国的大夫。

英文:

Confucius said, "The wisdom of Zang Wenzhong (a minister of Lu) in building a luxurious dwelling—place for a tortoise was actually in contravention of the rites."

19. 子張問曰: "令尹子文三仕爲令尹, 無喜色; 三已之, 無慍色。舊令尹之政, 必以告新令尹。何如?"子曰: "忠矣。"曰: "仁矣乎?"曰: "未知, 焉得仁?" "崔子弑齊君, 陳文子有馬十乘, 棄而違之, 至於他邦, 則曰: '猶吾大夫崔子也。'違之。之一邦, 則又曰: '猶吾大夫崔子也。'違之。何如?"子曰: "清矣。"曰: "仁矣乎?"曰: "未知, 焉得仁?"

译文:

子张问孔子: "楚国的令尹子文三次担任令尹, 不露高兴的颜色; 三次被免职, 亦不露怨恨的样子。而且每次被免职时都把一切政令告诉接任的人。这个人怎么样?"孔子说:"算得上对国家忠心耿耿了。"子张问:"这算不算仁呢?"孔子说:"不知道,这能算仁吗?"

子张又问:"齐国的大夫崔杼杀了齐庄公,陈文子因此弃官不做,离开了齐国。他先后到了两个国家又都离开了,因为他看出那两个国家的执政者和崔杼是一类人。你觉得这个人怎么样?"孔子说:"这人很清高。"子张问:"算得仁吗?"孔子说:"不知道,这能算仁吗?"

注:

令尹子文:令尹,楚国官名,相当宰相之职。子文:姓斗,名谷於菟,字子文,楚国贤相。

崔子:姓崔名杼,齐国的大夫。

陈文子:姓陈名须无,齐国的大夫。

英文:

Zi Zhang asked, "Zi Wen, the prime minister of Chu, neither looked happy when he was appointd to office three times, nor did he look unhappy when he was removed from office three times. Moreover, before leaving, he always told his successor what he had done in his term of office. What do you think of him?" Confucius answered, "We can say that he was loyal to his state." Zi Zhang asked, "Can we say that he was benevolent?" Confucius answered, "I don't know, but how can this be called benevolence?"

Zi Zhang asked again, "When Cui Zi, a minister of

Qi, assassinated Duke Zhuang of Qi, Chen Wenzi, another minister of Qi, gave up his position and left his state. He went to two other states, then left again, for he found the rulers of these two states were just like Cui Zi. What do you think of him?" Confucius answered, "He was very pure." Zi Zhang asked, "Can we say he was benevolent?" Confucius answered, "I don't know, but how can this be called benevolence?"

20. 季文子三思而後行。子聞之，曰：“再，斯可矣。”

译文：

季文子办事谨慎总要考虑再三才实行。孔子听后说：“也太谨小慎微了，遇事考虑两次就可以了。”

注：

季文子：姓季孙，名行父，“文”是谥号，鲁国的大夫。

英文：

Ji Wenzi (Jisun Xingwen, a minister of Lu) always thought again and again before taking action. When Confucius was told of this, he commented, "He was overcautious. Thinking twice is enough."

21. 子曰：“甯武子，邦有道，則知；邦無道，則愚。其知可及也，其愚不可及也。"

译文：

孔子说："宁武子在国家政治清明的时候，便聪明；在国家政治黑暗的时候，便装糊涂。他的聪明，别人可以做到；他的'糊涂'，别人就做不到。"

注：

宁武子：姓宁，名俞，"武"是谥号。卫国大夫。

英文：

Confucius said, "Ning Wuzi (a minister of Wei) was intelligent when the state and government were enlightened. He pretended to be stupid when the state and government were benighted. Others could match him in intelligence, but no one could equal him in stupidity."

22. 子在陳，曰："歸與！歸與！吾黨之小子狂簡，斐然成章，不知所以裁之。"

译文：

孔子出游陈国仍然挂念留在家里的学生，一再对随行学生说："回去吧！回去吧！那些学生都是志向远大，文彩又都斐然可观，只是不知道节制自己。"

When he was in the State of Chen, Confucius missed his disciples at home. He said again and again to those who accompanied him, "Let's go home! Let's go home! My students at home all have great ambitions and have the qualities of literary men, but they do not know how to regulate themselves."

23. 子曰: "伯夷、叔齐不念舊惡，怨是用希。"

译文:

孔子说: "伯夷、叔齐两兄弟不记过去的仇恨，别人对他们的怨恨也少。"

注:

伯夷、叔齐: 商朝末年孤竹君的两个儿子，父亲死后，兄弟两个互相让位而同时逃到周文王那里。周武王起兵伐商纣，他们曾扣马而谏。周朝统一天下后，他们不食周粟，隐居首阳山，终于饿死。

英文:

Confucius said, "The brothers Bo Yi and Shu Qi did not bear grudges in mind and that was why they incurred little ill will."

Note: The brothers Bo Yi and Shu Qi were sons of the king of the Guzhu State in the late Shang Dynasty.

After their father's death, neither of them succeeded to the throne. Instead, they both fled to King Wen of the State of Zhou. When King Wu of Zhou waged a war against the tyrannical King Zhou of the State of Shang, they stopped the army and remonstrated with King Wu against the war. After the unification of the Zhou, they took it a shame to live on the food under the rule of Zhou, so they secluded themselves from the world and finally starved to death in Mount Shouyang.

24. 子曰: "孰謂微生高直? 或乞醯焉, 乞諸其鄰而與之。"

译文:

孔子说: "谁说微生高直爽? 别人向他借点醋, 他不肯说自己没有, 却向邻居借来转给那人。"

注:

微生高: 姓微生, 名高, 鲁国人, 以性格直爽著称。

英文:

Confucius said, "Who said Weisheng Gao (a man of Lu) was a straightforward man? Once, when someone asked him for some vinegar, instead of saying that he had not got any, he borrowed some from his neighbour and gave it to him."

25. 子曰:"巧言、令色、足恭,左丘明恥之,丘亦恥之。匿怨而友其人,左丘明恥之,丘亦恥之。"

译文:

孔子说:"花言巧语,**伪装和善**,过分卑恭,对内心怨恨的人表面上却装出友好的样子,左丘明认为这种处世态度是可耻的,我也认为是可耻**的**。

注:

左丘明:春秋时杰出史学家。鲁国人,曾任鲁太史,相传为《左传》、《国语》作者。

英文:

Confucius said, "Flattery, false amiability and obsequiousness, these Zuo Qiuming (a historian of Lu) found shameful. So do I. To be friendly towards some one while concealing one's hostility, this Zuo Qiuming found shameful. So do I."

26. 顏淵、季路侍。子曰:"盍各言爾志?"子路曰:"願車馬衣裘與朋友共,敝之而無憾。"顏淵曰:"願無伐善,無施勞。"子路曰:"願聞子之志。"子曰:"老者安之,朋友信之,少者懷之。"

译文:

　　有一次颜渊、季路在老师身边听讲。孔子说:"说说你们自己的志向好吗?"子路说:"我愿意把车马衣服同朋友共同使用,用坏了也决不抱怨。"颜渊说:"我只想做到不夸耀自己的长处,不表白自己的功劳。"子路对孔子说:"很想听听您的志向。"孔子说:"我愿老年人得到安逸,朋友们相互信任,少年人得到关怀。"

英文:

　　Once Yan Yuan and Ji Lu were standing in attendance, Confucius asked, "Would you tell me your aspirations?" Zi Lu answered, "I would like to share my carriage and clothes with my friends and would never complain even if they wear them out." Yan Yuan answered, "I would only like never to boast of my own merits or show off what I have done." Zi Lu asked Confucius, "I would like to hear your aspirations." Confucius said, "I wish for the old to live in peace and comfort, friends to trust each other and the young to be taken good care of."

　　27. 子曰:"已矣乎! 吾未見能見其過而內自訟者也。"

译文:

　　孔子说:"算了吧! 我没看到过能够自我批评的人。"

Confucius said, "That's enough! I have not yet seen a man who is able to criticise his own errors."

28. 子曰: "十室之邑，必有忠信如丘者焉，不如丘之好學也。"

译文:

孔子说: "凡有人家居住的地方，都有像我这样忠诚和信实的人，只是不如我爱好学习罢了。"

英文:

Confucius said, "Wherever people live, there are honest and trustworthy people like me; but they are not so eager to learn as I am."

雍也篇第六

1. 子曰: "雍也可使南面。"

译文:

孔子说: "冉雍是可以做大官的。"

注:

雍: 姓冉，名雍，字仲弓，孔子的学生。

英文:

Confucius said, "Ran Yong could be made an important official."

2. 仲弓問子桑伯子，子曰: "可也簡。"仲弓曰: "居敬而行簡，以臨其民，不亦可乎? 居簡而行簡，無乃大簡乎?"子曰: "雍之言然。"

译文:

冉雍问子桑伯子这个人怎么样，孔子说: "还可以，他办事很简约。"冉雍说: "既严肃认真又办事简约不是治理百姓的好方法吗? 如果一味图简约，那不是有点不负责吗?"孔子说: "你的话很有道理。"

注：

　　子桑伯子：人名，事迹不详。

英文：

　　Ran Yong asked about Zisang Bozi. Confucius said, "He is quite good, and does things in a simple manner." Ran Yong said, "Aren't simplicity, along with strictness and conscientiousness, a good means of ruling the common people? And isn't it a bit irresponsible to be merely simple?" Confucius replied, "There is some point in what you said."

　　3. 哀公問："弟子孰爲好學?"孔子對曰："有顏回者好學，不遷怒，不貳過。不幸短命死矣。今也則亡，未聞好學者也。"

译文：

　　鲁哀公问孔子："你的学生中谁最爱学习?"孔子回答说："有一个叫颜回的最爱学习，对人和气，且知过能改。不幸短命死了。现在没有像他那样爱学习的人了。"

英文：

　　Duke Ai of Lu asked, "Among all your students, who was the most eager to learn?" Confucius answered, "Yan Hui was. He was always friendly toward others and he never made the same mistake twice. Unfortunately he died young. No longer do I hear of anyone who is as eager to learn as he was."

4. 子華使於齊，冉子爲其母請粟，子曰："與之釜。" 請益，曰："與之庾。"冉子與之粟五秉。子曰："赤之適齊也，乘肥馬，衣輕裘。吾聞之也：君子周急不繼富。"

译文:

公西华被派到齐国去作使者，冉有为他的母亲向孔子请求补贴些谷子，孔子说："给她六斗四升。"冉有请求多给一些，孔子说："再给她二斗四升。"冉有提出给她八十石。孔子说："公西华到齐国去，乘坐着肥壮的马驾的车子，穿着又轻又暖的皮袍。我听说过：君子救济穷人急难而不是给富人增加更多的财富。"

英文:

Ran You asked Confucius for grain for the mother of Gongxi Hua who had gone away on a mission to the State of Qi. Confucius said, "Give her 64 litres." Ran asked for more. Confucius said, "Give her 24 litres more." Ran You, however, actually gave ber 80 hectolitres. Confucius said, "Gongxi Hua went off to Qi in a carriage drawn by well-fed horses, dressed in a light, warm fur coat. I heard that 'A gentleman gives help to the needy, not to the rich.'"

5. 原思爲之宰，與之粟九百，辭。子曰："毋！以與
爾鄰里鄉黨乎！"

译文:

原思在孔子家当总管，孔子给他九百斗谷子，原思
推辞不受。孔子说："不要推辞，你可以把多馀的谷子给
家乡的穷人嘛！"

注:

原思: 姓原，名宪，字子思，孔子的学生。孔子在鲁国任司
寇时，他在孔子家当总管。

英文:

When Yuan Si (a disciple of Confucius') became
Confucius' steward, Confucius gave him 90 hectolitres of
grain. Yuan declined. Confucius said, "Do accept it. You
can distribute excess to the other people in your
neighbourhood."

6. 子謂仲弓，曰："犁牛之子骍且角，雖欲勿用，山
川其舍諸？"

译文:

孔子谈论冉雍时说："冉雍虽然出身贫贱，但凭他的

才能是可以做官的。"

注:
孔子的话是比喻，字面意思是：依礼祭祀不能用耕牛，但耕牛生的小牛，毛色红润而且双角端正，虽不能用它祭祀，但山川之神是不会舍弃它的。

英文:

When talking about Ran Yong, Confucius said, "Although his origins are poor, his ability is sufficient to become an official."

Note: Literally, this passage means: "A calf, born of ploughing oxen, though with red hair and well-formed horns, shouldn't be used as a sacrifice to the gods. However, would the gods of the mountains and rivers refuse to accept such a well-built calf? The calf described in this passage is a metaphor for Ran Yong.

7. 子曰："回也，其心三月不违仁，其餘则日月至焉而已矣。"

译文:

孔子说："只有颜回能够长期坚持仁德，至于其餘的学生只不过有时想一下罢了。"

英文:

Confucius said, "Only Yan Hui was able to devote himself to benevolence constantly; the other disciples only thought of it occasionally."

8. 季康子問: "仲由可使從政也與?" 子曰: "由也果, 於從政乎何有?" 曰: "賜也可使從政也與?" 曰: "賜也達, 於從政乎何有?" 曰: "求也可使從政也與?" 曰: "求也藝, 於從政乎何有?"

译文:

季康子问孔子: "仲由可以做官么?" 孔子说: "仲由遇事果断, 做官有什么困难呢?" 季康子又问: "端木赐可以做官么?" 孔子说: "端木赐通达人情事理, 做官有什么困难呢?" 季康子又问: "冉求可以做官么?" 孔子说: "冉求多才多艺, 做官有什么困难呢?"

注:

季康子: 姓季孙, 名肥, "康"是谥号, 鲁国大夫, 哀公时任宰相。

英文:

Jikang Zi asked, "Can Zhong You be an official?" Confucius answered, "Zhong is resolute, what difficulties could there be?"

Jikang Zi asked again, "Can Zi Gong be an

official?" Confucius answered, "Zi Gong is a sensible man. What difficulties could there be?"

Jikang Zi finally asked, "Can **Ran** Qiu be an official?" Confucius answered, "Ran is versatile, what difficulties could there be?"

9. 季氏使閔子騫爲費宰。閔子騫曰:"善爲我辭焉! 如有復我者,則吾必在汶上矣。"

译文:

季氏派人请闵子骞做费邑县长。闵子骞对来人说: "请回去替我美言几句辞掉吧! 如果再来人召我,那我 一定逃到汶水那边去了。"

注:

季氏: 季孙氏,鲁国大夫。

闵子骞: 姓闵,名损,字子骞,孔子的学生。

汶: 汶水,在山东省,当时是鲁、齐两国的界河。因季氏不 忠于鲁国国君,故闵子骞不奉召任职。暗示再召即逃往齐国。

英文:

Jisun Shi wanted to make Min Ziqian head of Fei county. Min told the messenger, "Please decline the offer for me tactfully. If anyone comes back for me, I shall flee to the other side of River Wen."

Note: River Wen is situated in today's Shandong

Province. It was then a bordering line between the State of Lu and that of Qi. Because Jisun Shi was disloyal to the Duke of Lu, Min Ziqian refused the appointment, implying that he would flee to the State of Qi if summoned again.

10. 伯牛有疾，子問之，自牖執其手，曰："亡之，命矣夫！斯人也而有斯疾也！斯人也而有斯疾也！"

译文：

伯牛生病，孔子去探望他，拉着他的手劝慰一番说："生死有命呀！"又叹道："没想到这样的人竟得了这样的病！"

注：

伯牛：姓冉，名耕，字伯牛，孔子的学生。

英文：

Bo Niu (a disciple of Confucius') was ill, and Confucius went to wisit him. He held his hands to console him, saying, "Life and death are both preordained." Then, he sighed once and again, "I have never expected that such a man could have such a disease!"

11. 子曰："賢哉，回也！一箪食，一瓢飲，在陋巷，人不堪其憂，回也不改其樂。賢哉，回也！"

译文：

孔子说："颜回的修养多好呀，粗茶淡饭很满足，住在简陋的巷子里，别人都受不了那种困苦，而他却依然快快乐乐，并不因此改变自己的志向。这样好的修养只有颜回才能做到。"

英文：

Confucius exclaimed, "What a man of virtues Yan Hui was! Living in a mean alley on homely fare was a hardship others would find intolerable, but Hui was still no less cheerful and would never change his aspirations. Only Yan Hui was able to cultivate such a virtue!"

12. 冉求曰："非不說子之道，力不足也。"子曰："力不足者，中道而廢，今女畫。"

译文：

冉求对老师说："不是我不喜欢您的学说，是我的接受能力不够。"孔子说："如果真是能力不够，好比一个人走路走到半道再也走不动了，而你还没有起步就说走不动了。"

英文：

Ran Qiu said, "It is not that I dislike your doctrines,

but that I do not have enough energy." Confucius said, "If it were a case of not having enough energy, one would give up half way through, but you have not yet taken a step."

13. 子謂子夏曰: "女爲君子儒，無爲小人儒。"

译文:

孔子对子夏说: "你要做一个道德高尚的学者，不要做道德低下的儒生。"

英文:

Confucius said to Zi Xia, "You should be a virtuous scholar, not a petty scholar."

14. 子游爲武城宰。子曰: "女得人焉耳乎?"曰: "有澹臺滅明者，行不由徑，非公事，未嘗至於偃之室也。"

译文:

子游做鲁国武城县长的时候，孔子问他: "你发现什么人才了吗?"子游说: "有一个叫澹台灭明的人，从不走邪道，每次有求于我，必为公事。"

注:

女: 同"汝"，你。

澹台灭明: 姓澹台，名灭明，字子羽，鲁国武城人，为人公正，后为孔子学生。

When Zi You was the governor of Wu County in Lu, Confucius asked him, "Have you found any talented people there?" Zi You answered, "There is one called Dantai Mieming (later he became a disciple of Confucius") who never takes shortcuts and never calls on me except on public business."

15. 子曰："孟之反不伐，奔而殿，将入門，策其馬，曰：'非敢後也，馬不進也。'"

译文:

孔子说："孟之反这个人从不夸耀自己，有一次和齐国打仗败退下来，他走在最后，掩护全军，将入城门时，人们都赞扬他敢于殿后的勇气，他却用鞭子打着马说：'不是我敢于殿后，是这匹马跑不快。'"

注:

孟之反：鲁国大夫。

奔：逃奔，败走。公元前484年，鲁国和齐国打仗，鲁军大败，全军溃逃，孟之反留在最后掩护。

英文:

Confucius said, "Meng Zhifan (a minister of Lu)

never boasts of himself. Once his army was routed, he stayed at the back to cover the retreating army. On entering the city—gate, he was praised for his courage. He, however, whipped his horse, saying, "It was not courage that made me stay at the back, it was my horse that refused to go any faster."

16. 子曰："不有祝鮀之佞，而有宋朝之美，難乎免於今之世矣。"

译文:

孔子说："如果没有祝鮀的口才，而又有宋朝的美貌，在当今社会里怕是祸害难免了。"

注:

祝鮀：字子鱼，卫国大夫，以能言善辩著称。

宋朝：宋国公子，名明，容貌美丽。曾两次因貌美而引起乱子。故孔子有此说。

英文:

Confucius said, "It would be difficult for one to avoid trouble, if one only had the good looks of Song Chao (a prince of Song) without having the eloquence of Zhu Tuo (a minister of Wei)."

17. 子曰："誰能出不由戶？何莫由斯道也?"

译文:

孔子说: "谁能够不经屋门而走出去呢? 为什么就没有人经过我这条仁义之路呢?"

英文:

Confucius said, "Who can go out of a room except through its door? So why is no one following my way of benevolence?"

18. 子曰: "質勝文則野，文勝質則史。文質彬彬，然後君子。"

译文:

孔子说: "一个人朴实多于文彩，就未免显得粗俗，如果文彩多于朴实，就未免显得虚浮，文彩和朴实配合适当，这才是君子风度。"

英文:

Confucius said, "One would seem uncouth with more simplicity than refinement, and seem superficial with more refinement than simplicity. Only when these two qualities are well-balanced can one become a real gentleman."

19. 子曰: "人之生也直, 罔之生也幸而免。"

译文:

孔子说: "人的生存在于正直, 不正直的人也能生存, 那是由于侥幸。"

英文:

Confucius said, "Man's existence lies in his integrity. A man without integrity can exist merely through his luck."

20. 子曰: "知之者不如好之者, 好之者不如樂之者。"

译文:

孔子说: "懂得学业的人不如喜爱学业的人, 喜爱学业的人不如以从事学业为快乐的人。"

英文:

Confucius said, "To be fond of knowledge is better than merely to acquire it; to take delight in it is still better than merely to be fond of it."

21. 子曰: "中人以上, 可以語上也; 中人以下, 不可以語上也。"

译文:

孔子说: "对具有中等接受水平以上的人, 可以传授高深知识; 对中等水平以下的人, 不可以传授高深知识。"

英文:

Confucius said, "Advanced knowledge can be transmitted to those who are above the average, but never to those who are below the average."

22. 樊遲問知, 子曰: "務民之義, 敬鬼神而遠之, 可謂知矣。"問仁, 曰: "仁者先難而後獲, 可謂仁矣。"

译文:

樊迟问怎样才算聪明, 孔子说: "善于劝导人民重义, 对鬼神敬而远之, 可以算是聪明了。樊迟又问怎样才算有仁德, 孔子说: "对艰难的工作抢先去做, 在论功行赏的时候退居人后, 这样的人便算有仁德了。"

注:

樊迟: 姓樊, 名须, 字子迟, 孔子的学生。

英文:

Fan Chi asked what wisdom was. Confucius said, "If one gives sound advice to the common people so that they will cherish what is right and just, and respects the spirits of the dead and the gods while keeping them at a distance, then he can be called wise." Fan asked what benevolence was, Confucius said, "If one is the first to take a difficult job and the last to think about reward, then one can be called benevolent."

23. 子曰: "知者樂水, 仁者樂山。知者動, 仁者静。知者樂, 仁者壽。"

译文:

孔子说: "聪明人喜欢水, 有仁德的人喜爱山。聪明人好动, 有仁德的人好静。聪明人生活快乐, 有仁德的人能享高寿。"

英文:

Confucius said, "The wise take delight in water, the benevolent in mountains. The wise are active while the benevolent are still. The wise enjoy life while the benevolent achieve longevity."

24. 子曰: "齊一變, 至於魯; 魯一變, 至於道。"

译文:

孔子说: "齐国如果实行政治改革, 可以达到鲁国现

在的水平；如果鲁国能实行政治改革，便进而合于大道
了。"

英文：

Confucius said, "If reform is carried out in Qi, it will
catch up with Lu; and if Lu reforms, it will be on the way
to benevolence."

25. 子曰："觚不觚，觚哉！觚哉！"

译文：

孔子叹道："现在的觚不像觚的样子，这能算是觚
吗！"。

注：

觚：古代盛酒的器皿，亦为礼器。上圆下方，有四条棱角。
孔子时代的觚，已改成圆形无棱。孔子以此为喻，表示对当时社
会改革的不满。

英文：

Confucius sighed again and again, "The shape of the
present *gu* (an ancient wine and sacrificial vessel) is no
longer what it used to be, how can it still be called *gu*?"

Note: This implies that Confucius was unhappy
about those who were casting away traditions.

26. 宰我問曰: "仁者, 雖告之曰, '井有仁焉', 其從之也?" 子曰: "何爲其然也? 君子可逝也, 不可陷也; 可欺也, 不可罔也。"

译文:

宰我问道: "有仁德的人, 就是告诉他: '有人掉进井里', 他会跟着跳下去吗?" 孔子说: "你怎么能这样提问题呢? 君子可以把井里的人救出来, 却不应该也跳进去, 因为君子可能被欺骗, 却不可以受愚弄。"

英文:

Zai Wo asked, "If you tell a man of benevolence that a man has fallen into the well, will he jump in after him?" Confucius answered, "How can you raise such a question? A gentleman will rescue the man in the well, but he wouldn't jump in himself. He may be cheated but will never be fooled into taking unintelligent actions."

27. 子曰: "君子博學於文, 約之以禮, 亦可以弗畔矣夫!"

译文:

孔子说: "君子广泛地学习文化典籍, 并用礼来约束自己, 就可避免离经叛道了。"

英文:

Confucius said, "A gentleman will not go astray so long as he studies extensively and regulates himself with the rites."

28. 子見南子，子路不説。夫子矢之曰："予所否者，天厭之！天厭之！"

译文:

孔子去见南子，子路很不高兴。孔子发誓说："我如果做了不正当的事，天理不容！天理不容！"

注:

南子：卫灵公夫人，当时把持朝政，且名声不好。所以子路反对老师去和她见面。

英文:

Confucius visited the famous lady Nan Zi (Queen Consort of Wei), and Zi Lu was unhappy about it. Confucius swore, "If I have done anything inappropriate, may Heaven curse me! May Heaven curse me!"

29. 子曰："中庸之爲德也，其至矣乎！民鲜久矣。"

译文:

孔子说："中庸作为最高道德，人们已经很久不提它了。"

Confucius said, "The Mean is the supremest virtue! However, it has been rare among the people for a long time now."

30. 子貢曰:"如有博施於民而能濟衆,何如? 可謂仁乎?"子曰:"何事於仁! 必也聖乎! 堯舜其猶病諸! 夫仁者,己欲立而立人,己欲達而達人。能近取譬,可謂仁之方也已。"

译文:

子贡问孔子:"如果有人能广泛地给人民带来好处,使大家生活富裕,怎么样? 这个人可算得仁人吗?"孔子说:"何止是仁人! 简真是圣人了! 只怕连尧、舜也做不到这样呢! 仁人就是自己想树立的也帮别人树立,自己想达到的也帮别人达到。凡事能推己及人,这就是仁人的处世态度。"

注:

尧、舜: 中国传说中两位上古的君主,孔子心中圣君的榜样。

英文:

Zi Gong asked, "What do you think of one who can

bring bountiful benefits and a better life to all the people? Is he benevolent?"

Confucius answered, "Far more than benevolent, he would be a sage for whom Yao and Shun (two ancient sages) would be no match. A benevolent man is one who helps others establish what he himself wishes to establish, helps others achieve something he wishes to achieve. To be capable of treating others as one would be treated oneself is the best way to be benevolent."

述而篇第七

1. 子曰："述而不作，信而好古，竊比於我老彭。"

译文：

孔子说："阐述古籍而不随意创作，相信而爱好古代文化，我私下自比于老子和彭祖。"

注：

老彭：老子和彭祖。老子，春秋末杰出思想家，道家创始人。彭祖，传说中的人物。

英文：

Confucius said, "I transmit out do not innovate randomly. I am so faithful to and so fond of ancient culture that privately, I compare myself to Lao Zi and Peng Zu."

Note: Lao Zi, the great thinker at the end of the Spring and Autumn Period and the founder of Taoist School; Peng Zu, a legendary figure.

2. 子曰："默而識之，學而不厭，誨人不倦，何有於我哉？"

译文:

孔子说:"把所见所闻默记在心,学习努力而不满足,教导别人不知疲倦,这些事情我做到了吗?"

英文:

Confucius asked, "To keep silently in mind what one has seen and heard, to study hard and never feel contented, to teach others tirelessly—have I done all of these things?

3. 子曰:"德之不修,學之不講,聞義不能徙,不善不能改,是吾憂也。"

译文:

孔子说:"不培养品德,不讲习学问,合乎义礼的事不能亲身去做,有缺点不能及时改正,这些都是我忧虑的事。"

英文:

Confucius said, "Not to cultivate virtue, not to review what one learned, not to practice personally what is righteous, and not to correct one's mistakes in time—these are all my worries."

4. 子之燕居，申申如也，夭夭如也。

译文:

孔子在家闲住的时候，衣着整齐，心情舒畅。

英文:

During his leisure time at home, Confucius was neatly dressed, relaxed and cheerful.

5. 子曰:"甚矣，吾衰也! 久矣，吾不復夢見周公!"

译文:

孔子说:"我老了，已经很长时间没有梦见周公了。"

注:

周公: 姓姬，名旦，周文王之子，武王之弟，鲁国始祖。传西周礼乐制度是他制定的，是孔子心目中最崇拜的圣人之一。

英文:

Confucius said, "I must be old and feeble, for it is a long time since I last dreamt of the Duke of Zhou."

Note: A son of King Wen of Zhou and younger brother of King Wu of Zhou, Duke Zhou was the founding father of the State of Lu. He was said to have formulated the ritual system of Western Zhou. He was one of Confucius' most worshipped sages.

6. 子曰："志於道，據於德，依於仁，**遊於藝**。"

译文:

孔子说:"志向在道，根据在德，依靠在仁，游习于六艺之中。"

注:

艺: 指六艺 (礼、乐、射、御、书、数)，这是孔子教育学生的六门功课。

英文:

Confucius said, "Stick to the way to your goal, base yourself on virtue, lean upon benevolence, and take your recreation in the six arts (i.e. music, the rites, archery, carriage driving, classic books and arithmetic)."

7. 子曰："自行束脩以上，吾未嘗無誨焉。"

译文:

孔子说:"凡成童 (十五岁) 来学习，我没有不教诲的。"

注:

束脩: 束发修饰。古代男孩子十五岁左右则束发为髻，表示成童，开始受教育。还有一种解释是一束干肉，学生向老师交的拜师礼物。

Confucius said, "I never refuse to teach those fifteen-year old children who are reaching adolescence."

Note: In the original text above, Shuxiu means the decoration of hair by binding a piece of silk or cloth. In ancient time when boys came of age at fifteen, they would have their hair worn in a bun or coil, indicating the beginning of his adolescence and education. There is another interpretation for Shuxiu: a private tutor's remuneration or emolument, usually a bundle of dried meat prepared in honour of the tutor.

8. 子曰:"不憤不啓，不悱不發。舉一隅不以三隅反，則不復也。"

译文:

孔子说:"我教学生的方法是: 不到他们苦思冥想也不能明白的时候，不去开导他们; 不到他们心里想说又总说不明白的时候，不去启发他们; 我教给他们某种知识，如果他们不能举一反三，我就不再教他们了。"

英文:

Confucius said, "I will not instruct my students until they have really tried hard but failed to understand. If I give them one instance and they cannot draw inferences from it, I will not teach them any more."

9. 子食於有喪者之側，未嘗飽也。

译文:

孔子和死了亲属的人一块吃饭，不曾吃饱过。

英文:

Confucius never ate enough food at a meal when he found himself seated next to someone who had been bereaved.

10. 子於是日哭，則不歌。

译文:

孔子为吊丧哭泣过，终日不再唱歌。

英文:

Confucius did not sing for the rest of the day as he usually would do after he had wept at a funeral.

11. 子謂顏淵曰："用之則行，舍之則藏，惟我與爾有是夫!"子路曰："子行三軍，則誰與?"子曰："暴虎馮河，死而無悔者，吾不與也。必也臨事而懼，好謀而成者也。"

译文:

孔子对颜渊说:"用我,就干,不用我,就不露面,能做到这样的只有我和你吧!"子路问道:"您若指挥军队打仗,愿意找谁共事?"孔子说:"赤手空拳敢打老虎,徒步敢过大河,死了都不知道后悔的人,虽勇敢无比,我也是不会和他共事的。同我共事的人应该遇事谨慎小心,善于思考问题能完成任务的人。"

英文:

Confucius said to Yan Yuan, "Only you and I are able to get down to work when needed and to stay in the background when not required." Zi Lu asked, "If you were an army commander, whom would you like to be together with?"Confucius said, "I would not want anyone who is brave enough to fight a tiger with his bare hands, or walk across a river, and would not regret for dying in the process. Even though he could be very courageous, I don't need him as my colleague. I would want someone who carries things out cautiously and is capable of completing his tasks by strategy."

12. 子曰:"富而可求也,雖執鞭之士,吾亦爲之。如不可求,從吾所好。"

译文:

孔子说: "财富如果来路正当, 就是替人执鞭的下等差役我也可以干。如果财富不能合理求得, 还是做我自己爱好的事情。"

英文:

Confucius said, "I would pursue wealth so long as it could be obtained legitimately, even by being a common cart driver. If wealth could not be obtained legitimately, I would rather follow my own preferences."

13. 子之所慎: 齋, 戰, 疾。

译文:

孔子谈到斋戒, 战争, 疾病三件事时最为谨慎。

英文:

Confucius was most cautious about fasting, warfare and diseases.

14. 子在齊聞《韶》, 三月不知肉味, 曰: "不圖爲樂之至於斯也。"

孔子在齐国听到《韶》的乐曲，很长时间吃肉都不知道味道。于是感叹说："想不到欣赏音乐竟到了这种境界。"

注:

《韶》: 舜时乐曲名。

英文:

In the State of Qi, Confucius heard the *Shao* music, and for a long time afterwards, he could not tell the taste of the meat he ate. He sighed and said, "I never thought I could be so lost in music!"

15. 冉有曰："夫子爲衞君乎?"子貢曰："諾，吾將問之。"入，曰："伯夷、叔齊何人也?"曰："古之賢人也。"曰："怨乎?"曰："求仁而得仁，又何怨?"出曰："夫子不爲也。"

译文:

冉有问子贡："老师会帮助卫君吗?"子贡说："等我去问问他。"子贡进去问孔子："伯夷、叔齐是怎样的人?"孔子说："古代的贤人。"子贡又问："后来他们互相怨恨吗?"孔子说："他们所为只是想得到仁德，他们都得到了，还怨恨什么呢?"子贡出来对冉有说："老师不会帮助卫君的。"

注:

　　卫君: 卫灵公的孙子蒯辄。卫灵公的儿子蒯聩因得罪卫灵公夫人南子而出逃晋国。卫灵公死后，孙子蒯辄即位，蒯聩借晋国之力回国与儿子争夺君位，他们的行为和伯夷、叔齐兄弟互让君位的行为正好相反，所以子贡只问孔子对伯夷、叔齐的态度就知道他不会帮助卫君的。

　　伯夷、叔齐: 商朝末年孤竹君两个儿子，孤竹君死后，兄弟两个为让君位不约而同出逃。周灭商后，又隐居首阳山，因不食周粟而饿死。所以子贡问他们是否有怨恨。

英文:

　　Ran You asked Zi Gong ," Will the Master help the ruler of Wei (i.e. Kuai Zhe, who was then struggling with his father for the throne)?" Zi Gong answered, "I shall go and ask him about it." He went in and asked, "What sort of people were Bo Yi and Shu Qi?" (Both of them insisted on giving up the throne to the other.) Confucius answered, "They were both men of virture in ancient times." Zi Gong asked, " Did they resent each other after giving up the throne?" Confucius answered, " They sought benevolence and they got it. What would they resent?" On coming out, Zi Gong said, "The Master will not help the ruler of Wei."

　　16. 子曰:"飯疏食飲水，曲肱而枕之，樂亦在其中矣。不義而富且貴，於我如浮雲。"

译文:

孔子说: "吃粗粮，喝冷水，随地而卧，其中也有乐趣。用不正当的手段得来的富贵，对我来说就像浮云一样。"

英文:

Confucius said, "There is happiness in eating coarse food, drinking cold water and sleeping on the floor. Ill—gotten wealth and rank are just like fleeting clouds to me."

17. 子曰: "加我數年，五十以學《易》，可以無大過矣。"

译文:

孔子说: "如果让我多活几年，到五十岁的时候再学习《易经》，就不会再有大的过错了。"

注:

《易》: 书名，又称《易经》，古代用以占卜的书。

英文:

Confucius said, "Give me a few more years so that at the age of fifty I shall study again *The Book of*

Changes and I shall never make any more major mistakes."

18. 子所雅言，《詩》、《書》、執禮，皆雅言也。

译文：

孔子诵读《诗》、《书》和赞礼时都用国语。

注：

雅言：当时以周朝京都地区的语言为标准的官话，时称雅言。孔子平时说鲁国方言，只在诵读《诗》、《书》和赞礼时用官话。

英文：

When teaching the *Odes* and the *Book of Documents* and performing the rites, Confucius always spoke in the standard language of the Zhou Dynasty (instead of the Lu dialect he spoke in daily life).

19. 葉公問孔子於子路，子路不對。子曰："女奚不曰，其爲人也，發憤忘食，樂以忘憂，不知老之將至云爾。"

译文：

叶公向子路问孔子的为人，子路不知如何回答。孔子对子路说："你为什么不这样说：他的为人，用功便忘记吃饭，快乐便忘记忧愁，不晓得衰老会要到来，如此而已。"

注:

叶公: 姓沈，名诸梁，字子高，楚国大夫。

英文:

The Duke of Ye asked Zi Lu about Confucius, Zi Lu failed to give a reply. Confucius said to him afterwards, "Why did you not say something like this. He is the sort of person who can be so diligent that he forgets his meals, so happy that he forgets his worries and is even unaware of approaching old age."

20. 子曰: "我非生而知之者，好古，敏以求之者也。"

译文:

孔子说: "我不是生来就有知识的人，而是由于爱好古代文化，靠了勤奋和敏捷求得知识的。"

英文:

Confucius said, "I was not born with knowledge, but, being fond of ancient culture, I was eager to seek it through diligence."

21. 子不語怪，力，亂，神。

译文:

孔子从不谈论怪异，勇力，叛乱和鬼神。

英文:

Confucius never talked of monsters, forces, disorder or spiritual beings.

22. 子曰:"三人行，必有我師焉。擇其善者而從之，其不善者而改之。"

译文:

孔子说:"有几个人一块走路，其中便一定有值得我学习的人。我选取那些优点而学习，看出那些缺点而改正。

英文:

Confucius said, "When walking in the company of other men, there must be one I can learn something from. I shall pick out his merits to follow and his shortcomings for reference to overcome my own."

23. 子曰:"天生德於予，桓魋其如予何!"

孔子说: "我的品德是上天赋于的, **桓魋**能把我怎么样! "

注:

桓魋: 宋国主管军事行政的官 (司马)。孔子周游列国时经过宋国, 和学生在一棵大树下演习礼仪。桓魋想杀孔子, 砍倒大树, 孔子于是只得离开那里, 弟子们怕桓魋追赶, 催孔子快跑, 孔子说了上面这句话。

英文:

Confucius said, "Heaven bestowed me with supreme virtue. What can Huan Kui (a general of Song, who intended to kill Confucius) do to me?"

24. 子曰: "二三子以我爲隱乎? 吾無隱乎爾。吾無行而不與二三子者, 是丘也。"

译文:

孔子说: "你们这些学生以为我会隐瞒什么不教给你们吗? 我不会对你们有所隐瞒的。我没有什么不可以告诉你们的, 这就是我孔丘的为人。"

英文:

Confucius said to his disciples, "My disciples, do you think that I have kept secrets from you? There is nothing I hide from you, and there is nothing that I will not tell you. This is what I am like."

25. 子以四教: 文, 行, 忠, 信。

译文:

孔子从四个方面教育学生: 文化知识, 社会实践, 对人忠诚, 信于朋友。

英文:

Confucius taught his disciples four disciplines: classics, social conduct, loyalty to superiors and faithfulness to friends.

26. 子曰: "聖人, 吾不得而見之矣; 得見君子者, 斯可矣。"子曰: "善人, 吾不得而見之矣; 得見有恒者, 斯可矣。亡而爲有, 虚而爲盈, 約而爲泰, 難乎有恒矣。"

译文:

孔子说: "圣人, 我不能看见了; 能看见君子, 也就可以了。"又说: "善人, 我不能看见了; 能看见有操守的人, 也就可以了。本来没有却假装有, 本来空虚却假装充实, 本来穷困却假装富有, 这样的人, 只怕连操守也没有了。"

Confucius said, "I cannot expect to see a sage, but it is enough for me to see a gentleman." He added, "I cannot expect to see a benevolent man, but it is enough for me to see a man who persists in principle. I'm afraid that even those who persist in principle cannot say that they have never pretended to have when they have not, pretended fullness when there is emptiness and pretended to be rich when poor."

27. 子釣而不綱，弋不射宿。

译文：

孔子钓鱼不用网，射鸟不射归巢歇宿的鸟。

英文：

Confucius fished with a hook but not with a net and he never shot birds in the nest.

28. 子曰："蓋有不知而作之者，我無是也。多聞，擇其善者而從之；多見而識之；知之次也。"

译文：

孔子说："我没有不懂装懂的毛病。我主张多听各种意见，选择其中好的来学习；多看各种事情，记在心里。这样得来的知识虽不是生而知之，但是靠得住的。"

英文:

Confucius said, "I am not one of those who pretend to understand what they do not. I suggest that one should listen to different views and choose the sound one to follow, see different things and keep them in mind. Knowledge obtained in this way is reliable, though not as good as innate knowledge."

29. 互鄉難與言，童子見，門人惑。子曰："與其進也，不與其退也，唯何甚! 人潔己以進，與其潔也，不保其往也。"

译文:

互乡是个野蛮的地方，但一个少年却受到孔子的接见，为此弟子们迷惑不解。孔子说："我赞成他们的进步，不赞成他们的落后，凡事不可太过分，人家既然改正缺点来学习，就应该受称赞，不要抓住人家过去的污点不放。"

英文:

A boy from Huxiang, an uncivilized place, came to Confucius and was received. The disciples were puzzled.

Confucius said, "I am for their progress and against their retrogression. We shall not be too demanding. Now that they have overcome their shortcomings and come for study, they should be encouraged. We shall not keep our eyes on their past."

30. 子曰: "仁遠乎哉? 我欲仁, 斯仁至矣。"

译文:

孔子说: "仁德离我们很遥远吗? 只要想达到, 就可以达到。"

英文:

Confucius said, "Is benevolence really far away from us? You only have to really want it and it will come."

31: 陳司敗問: "昭公知禮乎?"孔子曰: "知禮。"孔子退, 揖巫馬期而進之, 曰: "吾聞君子不黨, 君子亦黨乎? 君取於吳, 爲同姓, 謂之吳孟子。君而知禮, 孰不知禮?"巫馬期以告。子曰: "丘也幸, 苟有過, 人必知之。"

译文:

陈司败问孔子: "鲁昭公懂礼吗?"孔子答: "懂礼。"孔子走了以后, 陈司败请巫马期走近自己, 说: "我听说君子无所偏袒，难道孔子竟偏袒昭公吗？鲁昭公从吴国娶了一位夫人，鲁和吴是同姓，依礼同姓是不能通婚的，所以叫吴孟子而不称吴姬。鲁君若是懂礼，还有谁不懂礼呢？"巫马期把这话告诉孔子。孔子说："我很幸运，如果有错误，别人**就会**指出来。"

注：

　　陈司败：人名，一说官名。即陈国司寇，主管司法的官。

　　巫马期：姓巫马，**名施**，字之期，孔子的学生。

　　吴孟子：鲁昭公夫人。吴国人，姬姓，按当时国君夫人称号惯例应称吴姬。但吴国和鲁国国君同为姬姓，依周礼"同姓不婚"，故称吴孟子。陈司败也因此说鲁昭公不懂礼，说孔子的回答是有意偏袒。孔子虽然知道这一情况，但"臣不言君亲之恶"，最后只好归过于自己。

英文：

　　Chen Sibai asked, "Did Duke Zhao of Lu know the rites?" Confucius answered, "Yes." After Confucius went away, Chen greeted and approached Wuma Qi (a disciple of Confucius'), saying, "It is said that a gentleman is never partial. Why then should your Master be partial? The Duke took a lady from the Wu State as his wife in spite of the fact that she had the same clan name as himself, and renamed her Wu Mengzi. If the Duke knew the rites, who doesn't!" When Wuma Qi told Confucius about this, Confucius said, "What a fortunate man I am! If ever

I make a mistake, others always point it out."

Note: According to a matter of convention, Wu Mengzi, as the first lady of Lu, should be called Wu Ji. However, to call her Wu Mengzi was an attempt to cover the fact that she had the same clan name as the Duke, for it was clearly stipulated in the Zhou rites that "Thou shalt not marry if thou hast the same surname." Hence, Chen's remark. Knowing the truth too well, Confucius would rather bear the blame, for 'Ministers shall not speak ill of the royal family'.

32. 子與人歌而善，必使反之，而後和之。

译文:

孔子和别人一道唱歌，如果发现别人唱得好，就一定要求人家再唱一遍，然后再跟着唱。

英文:

When Confucius sang with others and found a good singer among them, he would always ask him to sing again and then join in again afterwards.

33. 子曰：“文，莫吾猶人也。躬行君子，則吾未之有得。”

译文:

孔子说:"书本上的知识,我已经差不多。但要做一个身体力行的君子,我还没有做到。"

英文:

Confucius said, "I have acquired quite enough knowledge from books, but I have not yet become a gentleman who earnestly practises in life what he has learned."

34. 子曰:"若聖與仁,則吾豈敢! 抑爲之不厭,誨人不倦,則可謂云爾已矣。"公西華曰:"正唯弟子不能學也。"

译文:

孔子说:"如果说我是圣人和仁人,实不敢当! 我不过是不懈的学习和工作,教诲别人从不知疲倦,不过如此而已。"公西华说:"这正是我们做不到的。"

英文:

Confucius said, "How can I deserve to be called a sage or a benevolent man? I simply study and work tirelessly and teach others patiently, and that is all." Gongxi Hua said, "This is just we disciples are unable to do."

35. 子疾病，子路請禱。子曰："有諸?"子路對曰："有之。《誄》曰:'禱爾于上下神祇。'"子曰:"丘之禱久矣。"

译文:

孔子病重，子路请求向鬼神祈祷。孔子问:"有这回事吗?"子路回答说:"有的,《誄》文说:'为你向天神地祇祷告。'"孔子说:"我早已祷告过了。"

英文:

When Confucius was seriously ill, Zi Lu asked to pray for him. Confucius asked, "Is there such a thing?" Zi Lu answered, "Yes. The prayer was: 'Pray for you to the gods above and below.'" Confucius said, "In that case, I have been offering my prayers for quite a long time."

36. 子曰:"奢則不孫，儉則固。與其不孫也，寧固。"

译文:

孔子说:"奢侈豪华就显得骄傲,俭省朴素就显得简陋。与其骄傲,宁可简陋。"

英文:

Confucius said, "Just as lavishness leads easily to arrogance, so frugality leads easily to shabbiness. However, the latter is better than the former."

37. 子曰:"君子坦荡荡,小人长戚戚。"

译文:

孔子说:"君子心胸坦荡,小人忧心忡忡。"

英文:

Confucius said, "A gentleman is always broad-minded while a petty man is always full of anxiety."

38. 子温而厉,威而不猛,恭而安。

译文:

孔子温和而又严厉,有威仪而不凶暴,庄重而安祥。

英文:

Confucius was cordial but strict, awe-inspiring but not harsh, grave but composed.

泰伯篇第八

1. 子曰："泰伯，其可謂至德也已矣。三以天下讓，民無得而稱焉。"

译文:

孔子说："泰伯，可以说是品德最高尚的人了，他屡次把君位让给弟弟季历，老百姓简直找不出合适的词来称颂他。"

注:

泰伯: 周朝祖先古公亶父的长子，又名太伯。古公亶父有三个儿子: 泰伯、仲雍、季历。他想把君位传三子季历，而不传长子泰伯。泰伯为顺从父亲的意愿，和二弟仲雍出走。泰伯的行为既孝父，又礼让，所以孔子称之为"至德"。

英文:

Confucius said, "Tai Bo could be called a man of the highest virtue. For several times he gave up his right to the throne in favour of Ji Li, his brother. The common people could not find a proper word to praise him for it."

Note: Tai Bo was the oldest son of Duke Dan Fu, the forefather of Zhou empire. The Duke had three sons: Tai Bo, Zhong Yong and Ji Li. He intended to pass the throne to Ji Li, the third son instead of Tai Bo, the oldest. To comply with the father's will, Tai Bo left with Zhong Yong. Tai's action shows filial piety as well as deference. Hence, Confucius' acclaim, "the highest virtue".

2. 子曰: "恭而無禮則勞, 慎而無禮則葸, 勇而無禮則亂, 直而無禮則絞。君子篤於親, 則民興於仁; 故舊不遺, 則民不偷。"

译文:

孔子说: "只会一味恭敬而不知礼未免劳倦。只知谨小慎微而不知礼, 就流于懦弱。只凭勇敢无畏而不知礼, 就会盲动闯祸。心直口快而不知礼, 就会因言语尖刻而伤人。上行下效, 在上位的人能以深厚感情对待亲族, 老百姓就会重视仁德的培养; 在上位的人不遗弃朋友, 老百姓就不会对人冷漠无情。"

英文:

Confucius said, "Courtesy without following the rites leads to tiredness; caution without following the rites leads to cowardice; courage without following the rites leads to rudeness; frankness without following the rites leads to harshness. Subordinates imitate their superiors: when a superior man devotes himself to his own kin, the people will cherish the cultivation of benevolence. When he does not forget his friends, people will not be indifferent to one another."

3. 曾子有疾, 召門弟子曰: "啓予足, 啓予手!《詩》云: '戰戰兢兢, 如臨深淵, 如履薄冰'。而今而後, 吾知免夫! 小子!"

译文:

曾子有病, 把他的学生召集到床前, 说: "看看我的脚, 看看我的手!《诗经》上说: '小心谨慎, 好像经常面临着深渊, 行走在薄冰之上。' 从今以后, 我知道自己可以免于祸害了! 你们可要注意呀!"

注:

曾子: 姓曾, 名参, 字子舆, 孔子的学生。

小子: 对弟子的称呼。

英文:

When Zeng Zi was ill, he summoned his disciples to the bed, saying, "Look at my feet. Look at my hands. *The Book of Songs* says, 'Be cautious and fearful as if you were often on the brink of the abyss or walking on thin ice.' From now on, I know how to be free from disasters. You must take care!"

4. 曾子有疾，孟敬子問之。曾子言曰："鳥之將死，其鳴也哀；人之將死，其言也善。君子所貴乎道者三：動容貌，斯遠暴慢矣；正顏色，斯近信矣；出辭氣，斯遠鄙倍矣。籩豆之事，則有司存。"

译文:

曾子有病，孟敬子去看望他。曾子对他说："鸟快死的时候，它的叫声是悲哀的；人快死的时候，他说的话是善意的。在上位的人接物待人要注意三个方面：容貌严肃，可以避免别人的懈怠和放肆；脸色庄重，说出的话使人容易相信；说话的时候，多考虑言辞和声调，就可以**避免鄙陋粗野**的错误。至于祭祀等礼仪方面的细节，自有主管人员负责。"

注:

孟敬子：姓仲孙，名捷，鲁国大夫。

籩豆之事：籩和豆是祭祀和典礼时用来盛祭品的器具。籩豆之事指祭祀等礼仪方面的具体事情。

英文:

When Zeng Zi was ill, Meng Jingzi (a minister of Lu) came to visit him. Zeng Zi said, "When a bird is dying, its cry is sad; when a man is dying, his words are kind. A gentleman should pay due attention to the following three points: He should look strict so as to prevent others from being slacks and wanton; he should look serious so as to make others believe him; and he should take care to speak the proper words in the proper tone of voice so as to avoid coarseness. As for the details of sacrifice and other rites, he should leave them to the care of those in charge."

5. 曾子曰: "以能問於不能, 以多問於寡; 有若無, 實若虛; 犯而不校。昔者吾友嘗從事於斯矣。"

译文:

曾子说: "勇于向能力比自己差的人请教; 向知识不如自己丰富的人请教; 满腹学问要像没有学问的人一样虚心好学; 才华过人要像很空虚的人一样; 纵被人欺侮也不计较。从前我的一位朋友做到了这样。"

英文:

Zeng Zi said, "I had a friend who did the following: Though capable, he asked the less capable for advice; though he knew a great deal, he consulted those who knew less; though he was a man of great learning, he studied as diligently as those who had little knowledge; though he had rich knowledge, he looked as if he were empty and never minded those who offended him."

6. 曾子曰: "可以託六尺之孤,可以寄百里之命, 臨大節而不可奪也。君子人與？君子人也。”

译文：

　　曾子说：“可以把年幼的君主和国家的命运都托付给他，而在安危存亡的紧要关头不动摇屈服。这种人是君子吗？是君子。”

注：

　　六尺之孤：指未成年而继位的君主。中国古代六尺约合今天一百三十多厘米。

英文：

　　Zeng Zi said, "If a man could be entrusted with a young ruler and the destiny of a state, and in a moment of crisis, he remains unyielding, is he a gentleman? He is indeed a gentleman."

　　7. 曾子曰：“士不可以不弘毅，任重而道遠。仁以爲己任，不亦重乎？死而後已，不亦遠乎？”

译文：

　　曾子说：“读书人要刚强而有毅力，因为他们肩负重任而前程远大。以实现仁德于天下，这担子还不重吗？为此目的，至死方休，这还不遥远吗？”

英文：

Zeng Zi said, "A scholar must be resolute and stead-fast, for his burden is heavy and his road is long. To practise the virtue of benevolence in the world is his burden. Is that not heavy? Only with death does his journey come to an end. Is that not long?"

8. 子曰: "興於詩，立於禮，成於樂。"

译文:

孔子说: "诗使我兴奋，礼是我立世之本，乐可以陶冶我的性情。"

英文:

Confucius said, "Find inspiration in *The Book of Songs*, take the rites as your basis and cultivate your mind by music."

9. 子曰: "民可使由之，不可使知之。"

译文:

孔子说: "对于老百姓，可以使他们照着规定的道路走，不必让他们知道那是为什么。"

英文:

Confucius said, "The common people can be made

to follow a path but not to understand it."

10. 子曰: "好勇疾貧，亂也。人而不仁，疾之已甚，亂也。"

译文:

孔子说: "喜好动武而又不安贫的人，常会作乱。对于不懂仁德的人，如不能因势利导也是一种祸害。"

英文:

Confucius said, "Those who are brave and cannot tolerate living in poverty are likely to riot. Those who know nothing about benevolence, if not carefully guided will also make trouble."

11. 子曰: "如有周公之才之美，使驕且吝，其餘不足觀也已。"

译文:

孔子说: "即使才华比得上周公的人，只要骄傲和吝啬，别的方面也不值得看了。"

注:

周公: 姓姬，名旦，周文王的儿子，武王之弟，成王之叔，据传是西周礼乐制度的制订者，孔子心目中的圣人。

Confucius said, "If a man is as gifted as the Duke of Zhou yet is arrogant and stingy, then his other qualities are not worthy of note."

12. 子曰: "三年學, 不至於穀, 不易得也。"

译文:

孔子说: "读书三年而不存做官的念头, 这种人已不容易找到了。"

英文:

Confucius said, "It is really hard to find one who can study for three years without making plans to become an official."

13. 子曰: "篤信好學, 守死善道。危邦不入, 亂邦不居。天下有道則見, 無道則隱。邦有道, 貧且賤焉, 恥也; 邦無道, 富且貴焉, 恥也。"

译文:

孔子说: "一个人应该有坚定的信仰和好学的精神, 誓死保卫治国做人的正确原则。不进入政局不稳的国家, 不居住在存在祸乱的国家。政治清明就出来做官, 政治黑暗就隐居不仕。国家政治清明而自己贫贱, 这是耻辱；国家政治黑暗而自己富贵，也是耻辱。"

英文:

Confucius said, "One should stick to one's faith, be eager to learn and ready to die for the just principle. He should not enter a state full of instability or live in a state full of rebellions. When government is enlightened, he would come out to take office; when government is benighted, he would live in obscurity and not take office. It is shameful to be poor and humble when the government is enlightened; it is also a shame to be rich and noble when the government is benighted."

14. 子曰："不在其位，不谋其政。"

译文:

孔子说："不居于那个职位，就不为它的政务谋划。"

英文:

Confucius said, "Do not interfere in others' business if you are not in their positions."

15. 子曰："師摯之始，《關雎》之亂，洋洋乎盈耳哉。"

译文:

孔子说: "太师挚奏乐从始到终, 优美动听。"

注:

师挚: 鲁国乐师, 名挚。

英文:

Confucius said, "From beginning to end, the performance of Zhi, the Grand Musician of Lu was wonderful and appealing to the ears."

16. 子曰: "狂而不直, 侗而不愿, 悾悾而不信, 吾不知之矣。"

译文:

孔子说: "狂妄而不正直, 幼稚而不老实, 无能而不讲信用, 我不知道这种人为什么会这样。"

英文:

Confucius said, "Men who are wildly arrogant and not upright, men who are ignorant and not honest, and men who are short of ability and not trustworty are quite beyond my understanding."

17. 子曰: "學如不及, 猶恐失之。"

孔子说: "学习怕赶不上, 学后怕忘了。"

英文:

Confucius said, "When learning something new, one should worry about being unable to reach it. When one has learnt something, one should worry about forgetting it."

18. 子曰: "巍巍乎, 舜禹之有天下也, 而不與焉。"

译文:

孔子说: "舜和禹不愧是高尚的圣君, 贵为天子, 富有四海, 整年为百姓辛劳而一点不谋私利。"

注:

舜、禹: 远古君主, 传说他们的君位都是通过禅让得来的, 这是孔子极为赞赏的。

英文:

Confucius said, "What lofty lords Shun and Yu were! All that was under Heaven was theirs, yet they sought no personal gain from it."

19. 子曰: "大哉, 堯之爲君也! 巍巍乎, 唯天爲大, 唯堯則之。蕩蕩乎, 民無能名焉。巍巍乎, 其有成功也，焕乎其有文章。"

译文:

孔子说: "尧是一位了不起的君主。天意是无限的，只有尧能够效法天。他的恩惠使老百姓不知如何称颂才好，他的功绩太大了，他的礼仪制度太美好了。"

注:

尧: 远古君主。

英文:

Confucius said, "What a great lord Yao was! Nothing is greater than Heaven, yet Yao was the only one who took it as a model. How boundless his kindness was! The common people did not know how to praise it! How great his achievements were and how brilliant his system of rites was!"

20. 舜有臣五人而天下治。武王曰: "予有亂臣十人。"孔子曰: "才難，不其然乎? 唐虞之際，於斯爲盛，有婦人焉，九人而已。三分天下有其二，以服事殷。周之德，其可謂至德也已矣。"

译文:

舜有五位治世贤臣，天下便太平无事。周武王也说过，"我有十位能治理天下的臣子。"孔子因此说道: "人才难得呀！唐尧、虞舜之后以武王时人才最盛，然而武王所说十位人才中还有一位妇女，实际上只有九人。周文王得天下，三分之二，却仍然向商纣称臣，周文王的道德可谓达到了最高境界。"

注：

妇人：传说指太姒，文王后妃，武王之母，能以德化天下。孔子不敢把她列为武王臣子之列，故说"九人而已"。

英文：

Shun had five good ministers and the empire was very well governed. King Wu of Zhou once said, "I have ten capable ministers." Confucius therefore commented, "Talented people are hard to find. Since the Yao and Shun Period, the time of King Wu of Zhou has become the period that possessed the most of talented people. But one of his ministers was a woman, so actually he only had nine. King Wen of Zhou (father of King Wu) had two thirds of the empire, yet he continued to pay homage to the Yin Dynasty. He really had the highest virtue."

Note: 'A woman' refers allegedly to Tai Si, one of King Wen's imperial concubines and mother of King Wu. She ruled the state with benevolence.

21. 子曰："禹，吾無間然矣！菲飲食而致孝乎鬼神，惡衣服而致美乎黻冕，卑宮室而盡力乎溝洫。禹，吾無間然矣。”

译文：

孔子说："对于禹，我挑不出他有什么毛病了。他自己吃得很坏，却把祭品办得很丰盛；平时穿的很坏，却把祭服做得很华美；住的也很坏，却把力量完全用于兴修水利上。对禹的一切都无可挑剔了。"

注：

禹：夏朝开国君主，在治理洪水方面立有功勋，一直受到后世称颂。

英文：

Confucius said, "I can not find any fault with Yu. He ate poorly but made abundant sacrifices. His everyday clothes were very poor but he dressed magnificently on sacrificial occasions. He lived in a humble house but put great effort into completing irrigation work. With Yu, I can find no fault at all!"

Note: Yu was the founding father of the Xia Dynasty. His achievement in establishing irrigation systems to tame floods has been extolled by later generations.

子罕篇第九

1. 子罕言利與命與仁。

译文：

孔子平时很少主动谈到功利，命运和仁德。

英文：

Seldom did Confucius talk about profit, fate and benevolence.

2. 達巷黨人曰："大哉，孔子！博學而無所成名。"子聞之，謂門弟子曰："吾何執？執御乎？執射乎？吾執御矣。"

译文：

达巷党的一个人说："孔子是伟大的，有广博的学问，可惜没有足以树立名声的专长。"孔子听了这话对学生们说："我干什么好呢？赶车？做射手？我赶马车好了。"

注：

达巷党：地名，古代五百家为一党。

A man from Daxiangdang said, "Confucius is great, and his learning wide and profound, but what a pity he has nothing to make a name for himself." When Confucius heard this, he said to his disciples, "What shall I take up? Cart–driving? Or perhaps archery? Perhaps I'd better take up driving."

Note: Daxiangdang is a place name. In ancient times, a "dang" was 500 households.

3. 子曰: "麻冕, 禮也; 今也純, 儉, 吾從衆。拜下, 禮也; 今拜乎上, 泰也。雖違衆, 吾從下。"

译文:

孔子说: "礼帽用麻料制作, 这是合于传统礼节的; 现在大家都改用丝料制作, 因为这样省俭, 所以我赞成大家的做法。臣见君, 按传统礼节, 先在堂下磕头, 升堂之后再磕头; 现在大家都免除了在堂下磕头, 直接升堂磕头, 这是目无尊上, 所以我仍然赞成原来的做法。"

英文:

Confucius said, "According to traditional rites, ceremonial hats were made out of hemp. Now people make them out of silk, I approve of the common practice since this is more economical. According to traditional rites, when a minister wanted to see the ruler, he would start to kowtow first at the bottom of the steps then again at the top. Now nobody kowtows at the bottom of the steps, but just kowtows after ascending steps. This is disrespectful, so I still advocate the former practice."

4. 子絕四: 毋意, 毋必, 毋固, 毋我。

译文:

孔子身上绝没有凭空揣测, 绝对肯定, 拘泥固执, 自以为是这四种毛病。

英文:

Confucius never made wild conjectures and never talked in terms of absolutes. He was neither obstinate nor egoistic. These he took to be four faults.

5. 子畏於匡, 曰: "文王既没, 文不在兹乎? 天之將喪斯文也, 後死者不得與於斯文也; 天之未喪斯文也, 匡人其如予何?"

译文:

孔子被匡地群众所拘禁, 他说: "周文王死了以后, 是我继承了古代文化, 如果天意要消灭文化, 我也就不会知道这种文化了; 如果天意要保存文化, 那匡人又能对我怎么样呢?"

注:

　　子畏于匡: 孔子离开卫国到陈国去, 经过匡地时, 匡地群众曾遭受鲁国阳货的掠夺和残杀, 孔子的相貌和阳货相似, 当地人误将孔子拘禁了五天。畏: 拘禁。匡: 地名。

　　文王: 周文王, 姓姬, 名昌, 武王之父。

英文:

　　When he was detained in Kuang, Confucius said, "I am the one who inherited the ancient culture after King Wen's death. If Heaven had intended to destroy this culture, I would not have mastered it; if Heaven intends to preserve it, what can the men in Kuang do to me?"

　　Note: When Confucius was passing the place of Kuang on his way from Wei to Chen, he was taken for Yang Huo, who had plundered and killed the Kuang people. For the similar looks, Confucius was held up for five days.

　　6. 太宰問於子貢曰: "夫子聖者與? 何其多能也?"子貢曰: "固天縱之將聖, 又多能也。"子聞之, 曰: "太宰知我乎! 吾少也賤, 故多能鄙事。君子多乎哉? 不多也。"

译文:

　　太宰问子贡: "孔老先生是圣人吗? 为什么如此多才

多艺呢?"子贡回答说:"这是天意让他成为圣人,又让他多才多艺。"孔子听到这些话后说:"太宰知道我呀!我小时候家里穷,为了谋生,所以学会很多鄙贱的技艺。真正的君子需要这些技艺吗?不需要的。"

注:

太宰:官名。这里的太宰不知其详。

英文:

A high official asked Zi Gong, "Is your Master a sage? If so, why is he skilled in so many ways?" Zi Gong answered, "It is Heaven that intended him to become a sage and capable of many skills." On hearing this, Confucius said, "That official understands me! I am from a poor family and I learned many humble crafts only to make a living. Does a real gentleman need to be skilled in many trades? No, he need not."

7. 牢曰:"子云:'吾不試,故藝。'"

译文:

牢说:"孔子说:'因为我不曾做官,所以学到多种技艺。'"

注:

牢:其人不详,有说是孔子的学生。

Lao (perhaps a disciple of Confucius') said, "The Master said, 'I have never been an official so I have learned many trades.'"

8. 子曰："吾有知乎哉？無知也。有鄙夫問於我，空空如也。我叩其兩端而竭焉。"

译文：

孔子说："我算有知识吗？其实没有。有个农夫向我提问，我却回答不出来。对他提出的问题我前后反复思考，也无法回答他。"

英文：

Confucius said, "Am I a learned man? No. Once a farmer asked me a question, and I failed to answer it. I thought about it again and again, but still could not give him an answer."

9. 子曰："鳳鳥不至，河不出圖，吾已矣夫！"

译文：

孔子说："天下无清明之望了，我也没什么盼头了！"

注：

凤鸟：即凤凰，传说中一种神鸟，祥瑞的象征。凤凰出现，便预示天下清明。

河图: 传说圣人受命, 黄河中就有龙马背负八卦图出现, 预示圣王将出世。孔子在这里是感叹天下无清明之望了。

英文:

Confucius said, "There is no hope of enlightenment in the world, and I have no future!"

Note: According to legend, during sagely and enlightened reign periods, phoenix were often seen and a magic chart appeared on the Yellow River, carried on the back of a dragon horse.

10. 子見齊衰者、冕衣裳者與瞽者, 見之, 雖少, 必作; 過之, 必趨。"

译文:

孔子和穿丧服的人、穿戴整齐的贵族以及瞎子这三种人相见时, 既使是年轻人, 也要站起来; 从他们面前走过时, 一定紧走几步, 以表示敬意。

英文:

When he met people in mourning dress or ceremonial dress or blind people, even if they were young, Confucius would stand up. When walking past them, he would quicken his step.

11. 顔淵喟然歎曰："仰之彌高，鑽之彌堅。瞻之在前，忽焉在後。夫子循循然善誘人，博我以文，約我以禮，欲罷不能。既竭吾才，如有所立卓爾。雖欲從之，末由也已。"

译文:

颜渊感汉地说："老师的学问道德，高深莫测。但他善于诱导我步步深入，用各种文献丰富我的知识，用礼节约束我的行为，使我想停止学习都不可能了。我虽然用尽了才力，却仍然不能攀上顶峰。"

英文:

Yan Yuan said with a deep sigh, "The more I look up at the Master's doctrine, the higher it soars; the more I delve into it, the deeper it becomes. It was just in front but suddenly it is behind. In spite of this, the Master is good at leading me forward step by step. He has broadened my mind with ancient culture and regulated me with the rites. I could not give up learning even if I wanted to. Although I am exhausted, it is still beyond me. However much I long to pursue it, I cannot achieve it."

12. 子疾病，子路使門人爲臣。病間，曰："久矣哉，由之行詐也！無臣而爲有臣。吾誰欺？欺天乎？且

予與其死於臣之手也，無寧死於二三子之手乎？且予縱
不得大葬，予死於道路乎？"

译文:

　　孔子病势沉重的时候，子路叫孔子的学生充当家臣
准备料理丧事。后来孔子病情好转知道了这件事，就
说："仲由这样做是欺骗人的呀！我没有家臣却装作有家
臣。这欺骗谁呢？难道是欺骗上天吗？而且我与其由家
臣料理丧事，还不如由你们这些学生来料理更好一些。
我虽然不能按大夫的隆重葬礼来安葬，难道我会死在路
上没人管吗？"

注:

　　臣: 家臣。当时大夫家才有家臣。孔子虽然当过大夫，但当
时已退位，没有家臣。子路让孔子的学生充当家臣，是准备仍以
大夫之礼安葬孔子的。所以孔子不同意这样做。

英文:

　　When Confucius was seriously ill, Zi Lu told the
other disciples to act as retainers to prepare the funeral.
After recovery, Confucius got to know about this. He
said, "Zhong You, this is deception! In pretending that I
have retainers while I have none, whom are we deceiving?
Are we deceiving Heaven? I would rather my funeral be
arranged by you, my students, than by retainers. Even if
I do not have an elaborate funeral, could I be left

unattended by the roadside?"

Note: At that time, retainers could only be found at the ministers' houses. Although he had been a minister, Confucius had already retired then with no retainers. Zi Lu asked the master's other disciples to act as retainers in order to arrange the Master's funeral according to the rites of the ministers. Hence Confucius disagreed.

13. 子貢曰:"有美玉於斯,韞匵而藏諸? 求善賈而沽諸?"子曰:"沽之哉! 沽之哉! 我待賈者也!"

译文:

子贡说:"我这里有一块美玉,是把它放在匣子里藏起来呢? 还是找一个识货的商人卖掉呢?"孔子道:"卖掉! 卖掉! 我就是在等识货者。"

注:

孔子和子贡的对话是借美玉比喻一个有才能的人是怀才作隐士呢? 还是出来作事。孔子赞成后者,但更强调要遇贤明的君主(识货者) 才可出来作官。

英文:

Zi Gong said, "Suppose you had a piece of beautiful jade, would you put it away in a box or sell it to a connoisseur?" Confucius said, "I would sell it! I would sell it! I am just waiting for a connoisseur."

Note: In this conversation, a piece of beautiful jade is a metaphor for a talented person: should he stay out of sight or come out to take office? Confucius was in favour of the latter, but he stressed that the talented came out only when the state was ruled by a wise and able monarch, just as a lovely jade could be sold for a good price only to a connoiseur.

14. 子欲居九夷。或曰: "陋, 如之何?"子曰: "君子居之, 何陋之有?"

译文:

孔子想到九夷去住。有人对他说: "那地方非常偏僻, 怎么好住?"孔子说: "有君子住在那里, 还能说偏僻吗?"

注:

九夷: 地名。

英文:

Confucius wanted to live in Jiuyi (a barbarian place). Somebody said to him, "That place is rather uncivilized, how can you live there?" Confucius answered, "If a gentleman lives there, can we still call it an uncivilized place?"

15. 子曰:"吾自衛反魯,然後樂正,《雅》、《頌》各得其所。"

译文:

孔子说:"我从卫国回到鲁国以后,对有关乐章按内容整理归并到《雅》、《颂》两类。"

注:

《雅》、《颂》: 中国最早的诗歌总集《诗经》中的两类诗。经孔子整理分类删减后传世。

英文:

Confucius said, "After my return from Wei to Lu I categorised all music as either *Ya* or *Song* according to their contents."

Note: *Ya* and *Song* were two types of poems in *The Book of Songs*, the earliest collection of poems in China. After Confucius' revision, editing and classification, they were handed down to later generations.

16. 子曰:"出則事公卿,入則事父兄,喪事不敢不勉,不爲酒困,何有於我哉?"

译文:

孔子说:"在外服事公卿,在家服事父兄,办丧事尽礼,饮酒不贪,这些事我都能做到吗?"

英文:

Confucius said, "Serve high officials at court; serve the elders at home. Arrange funerals according to the rites and do not be too fond of drink. Are these things really within my ability?"

17. 子在川上曰: "逝者如斯夫! 不舍晝夜。"

译文:

孔子站在河边感叹道: "过去的时光就像这河水一样, 日夜不停地流去。"

英文:

Standing by the side of a river, Confucius sighed, "Time is going on like this river, flowing away endlessly day and night."

18. 子曰: "吾未見好德如好色者也。"

译文:

孔子说: "我没见过有像喜爱美色那样喜爱道德的人。"

Confucius said, "I have never met any one who is as fond of virtue as he is of beauty."

19. 子曰："譬如爲山，未成一簣，止，吾止也。譬如平地，雖覆一簣，進，吾往也。"

译文：

孔子说："好比用土堆山，只差一筐土就堆成了，如果停下来，就会半途而废。又好比用土填坑，虽然刚倒一筐土，只要坚持下去，就会把坑填成平地。"

注：

孔子这段话是用堆山和平地作比喻，勉励学生自强不息，坚持不懈，不要半途停下来。

英文：

Confucius said, "In making a mound, the job is not finished until the last basketful of earth is in place; in filling in a hole, even if you've only poured in one basketful of earth, the job can surely be finished so long as you persist."

Note: In this passage, Confucius uses a metaphor to encourage his disciples to strive to improve themselves constantly and not to give up half way.

20. 子曰: "語之而不惰者，其回也與!"

译文:

孔子说: "能够听我说话始终不懈怠的，大概只有颜回吧!"

英文:

Confucius said, "There can only have been Yan Hui who could listen attentively to anything I said."

21. 子謂顏淵，曰: "惜乎! 吾見其進也，未見其止也!"

译文:

孔子谈到颜渊，说: "他死得太可惜了! 我看到他不断进步，从没见他停止过努力。"

英文:

Confucius said of Yan Yuan, "What a pity he is gone! I always saw him making progress and never did I see him stop making an effort."

22. 子曰: "苗而不秀者有矣夫! 秀而不實者有矣夫!"

译文:

孔子说:"有的庄稼苗虽壮却没有开花,有的虽开花却没有结实。"

注:

孔子这段话是比喻一个人没有成才和没有为国家作出贡献。

英文:

Confucius said, "Some seedlings spring up but never blossom, others blossom but never bear fruit."

23. 子曰:"後生可畏,焉知來者之不如今也? 四十、五十而無聞焉,斯亦不足畏也已。"

译文:

孔子说:"年轻人是大有作为的,谁能断定他们将来不如我们这一代呢? 如果一个人到了四、五十岁还没有什么名望,也就不会有什么作为了。"

英文:

Confucius said, "Young people have great potential for achievements. Who can say that they will not be our equals in the future? If someone hasn't distinguished himself by the age of forty or fifty, he will not amount to much."

24. 子曰:"法語之言,能無從乎? 改之爲貴。巽與之言,能無説乎? 繹之爲貴。説而不繹,從而不改,吾末如之何也已矣。"

译文:

孔子说:"对正确的意见,能不听吗? 但听了之后能改正错误才可贵。听了顺耳的话,能不高兴吗? 但要对这些话能够分析鉴别才可贵。对于不加分析地只愿听顺耳的话,表面接受批评意见,实际不改的人,我也没有办法教他的。"

英文:

Confucius said, "Is it possible not to listen to correct opinions? But they are only of value if you correct your mistakes after listening. Is it possible not to be pleased when you hear amenable words? But they are only of value if you can analyse them correctly."

25. 子曰:"主忠信,毋友不如己者,過則勿憚改。"

译文:

孔子说:"要重道德,慎交友,有过错,随时改正。"

注:

这段话译文见第一篇第八章。

Confucius said, "One should pay great attention to loyalty and sincerity, and not make close friends with those whose morality is inferior to one's own. If one makes a mistake, one should not be afraid of correcting it."

26. 子曰: "三军可夺帅也, 匹夫不可夺志也。"

译文:

孔子说: "军队可以丧失主帅, 一个人不可丧失志气。"

英文:

Confucius said, "An army may be deprived of its commanding officer, yet a man cannot be deprived of his will."

27. 子曰: "衣敝缊袍, 与衣狐貉者立, 而不耻者, 其由也与? '不忮不求, 何用不臧?'" 子路终身诵之。子曰: "是道也, 何足以臧?"

译文:

孔子说: "穿破旧衣服和穿着狐貉皮袍的人站在一起而不自惭的, 恐怕只有仲由能做到吧!《诗经》上说:

'不嫉妒，不贪求，为什么不好呢？'"子路听了，总念这两句诗。孔子又说："仅仅做到这样，就够了吗？"

英文:

Confucius said, "I am afraid there is only Zhong You who, in a worn-out gown, is able to stand unashamedly together with those in fox and racoon dog fur. As it says in *The Book of Songs*, 'Neither jealous nor greedy, is this not good?'"After hearing the line, Zi Lu kept on chanting it. Confucius said, "Is it good enough just to do this?"

28. 子曰："歲寒，然後知松柏之後彫也。"

译文:

孔子说："到了严寒的季节，才知道松柏树是最后落叶的。"

英文:

Confucius said, "Only when the weather turns cold can we see that the leaves of pines and cypresses are the last to wither and fall."

29. 子曰："知者不惑，仁者不憂，勇者不懼。"

孔子说: "聪明人不受欺骗, 品德高尚的人没有忧虑, 勇敢的人无所畏惧。"

英文:

Confucius said, "A wise man is never cheated, a virtuous man is never worried and a courageous man is never afraid."

30. 子曰: "可與共學, 未可與適道; 可與適道, 未可與立; 可與立, 未可與權。"

译文:

孔子说: "可以在一起学习的人, 未必能取得同样的成绩; 同样取得成绩的人, 未必都能坚持下去; 可以在一起坚持下去的人, 未必都能通权达变。"

英文:

Confucius said, "People who are good at studying together are not necessarily able to achieve the same; people who are able to achieve the same are not necessarily able to make persistent efforts; people who are good at making persistent efforts are not necessarily able to adapt to circumstances."

31. "唐棣之華，偏其反而，豈不爾思？室是遠而。"
子曰："未之思也，夫何遠之有？"

译文：

古代有一首诗说："唐棣树开花，摇摆翩翩。我不是
不想你，只因路途遥远。"孔子说："还是不想念，如果真
的想念，怎么会觉得遥远？"

注：

唐棣：一种植物名，又称棠棣。

英文：

An ancient poem reads：

"The flowers of 'Tang di' tree (differently explained
as poplar or cherry),

How they dance about!

It is not that I do not miss you，

But your home is so far away.

Confucius commented，"He did not really miss her；
if he truly missed her，how could he think it far away？"

鄉黨篇第十

1. 孔子於鄉黨，恂恂如也，似不能言者。其在宗廟朝廷，便便言，唯謹爾。

译文:

孔子在家乡，显得很温和恭顺，好像不善言辞。他在宗庙中、朝廷上却很健谈，只是很谨慎。

注:

乡党: 古代五百家为党，二十五党为乡。乡党，指家乡。

英文:

In his hometown, Confucius was very gentle and respectful, and behaved as if he could hardly express himself. However, at the ancestral temple or at court, he talked brilliantly but carefully.

2. 朝，與下大夫言，侃侃如也；與上大夫言，誾誾如也。君在，踧踖如也，與與如也。

译文:

孔子上朝的时候，同下大夫说话，显得温和而快乐；同上大夫说话，显得正直而恭敬。国君在场的时候，他显得局促不安，走路又轻又慢。

注：

大夫：官名，诸侯下面的一级。大夫又分上大夫和下大夫，孔子的地位相当于下大夫。

英文：

At court, when speaking with junior ministers, Confucius was affable and pleasant; when speaking with senior ministers, he was upright and respectful. In the presence of the ruler, he was uneasy and his steps become gentle and slow.

3. 君召使擯，色勃如也，足躩如也。揖所與立，左右手，衣前後，襜如也。趨進，翼如也。賓退，必復命曰："賓不顧矣。"

译文：

国君让孔子去接待外宾，他脸色矜持庄重，脚步也轻快起来。在迎送和接待宾客时，显得彬彬有礼，连衣服也显得飘逸而整齐。宾客走了以后，他一定向国君回报说："客人已经走远了。"

英文：

When he was summoned by the ruler to receive foreign guests, Confucius looked reserved and solemn and his steps became swift. When receiving and seeing off guests, Confucius was good-mannered, with his robe neat and elegant. When the guests left, he would invariably report to the ruler, "The guests are out of sight."

4. 入公門，鞠躬如也，如不容。立不中門，行不履閾。過位，色勃如也，足躩如也，其言似不足者。攝齊升堂，鞠躬如也，屏氣似不息者。出，降一等，逞顏色，怡怡如也。没階，趨進，翼如也。復其位，踧踖如也。

译文:

孔子一走进朝廷大门，就小心谨慎起来，好像没有容身之地。不敢站在门中间，进门不敢踩门坎。经过国君座位时，脸色庄重，脚步加快，说话也不敢高声。上堂时，他轻轻提起下摆，恭恭敬敬，似乎连气也不敢出。下堂后才轻轻松了一口气，现出和顺的样子。下了台阶，脚步加快，像鸟儿舒展翅膀，轻松了许多。回到自己的位置上后，又现出恭敬小心的样子。

英文:

On entering the door to the court, Confucius looked cautious, as if there was not enough room for him. He would neither dare to stand in the doorway nor would he step on the threshold. Walking past the throne, his look was serious, his steps were swift and his voice was soft. When ascending the steps, he lifted the hem of his robe respectfully, as if he were unable to breathe. After descending the steps, he felt relieved and relaxed. At the bottom of the steps, he quickened his steps, his arms extending like a bird's wings. When returning to his own position, he was as cautious and respectful as before.

5. 執圭，鞠躬如也，如不勝。上如揖，下如授。勃如戰色，足蹜蹜，如有循。享禮，有容色。私覿，愉愉如也。

译文：

孔子出使到外国，参加典礼时，非常小心谨慎，手中的圭好像有千斤重。向上举时像作揖，放下来时又好像要传给别人。面色庄重得好像在战栗。迈着碎步在一条直线上行走。在赠送礼物的仪式上，表现得和颜悦色。他以私人身分会见外国国君时，就没有这样紧张。

注：

圭：一种玉器，上圆下方，举行典礼时君臣都拿着。孔子出使外国，所持是代表君主的圭。

英文：

At a ceremony on his official mission to another

state, Confucius held a jade tablet very cautiously as if it were too heavy to carry. He raised it as though he were bowing, and he lowered it as though he were handing it to someone else. His expression was as solemn as if he were in fear and trembling. His steps were as restrained as if he were walking on a single thread. When presenting a gift, he looked calm and pleasant. When having a private interview with guests, he looked much more relaxed.

Note: A jade tablet (gui), with a round top and a square bottom, was usually held by monarchs or ministers at ceremonies. On his mission to other states, Confucius would carry a jade tablet, which symbolized his Lord's authority.

6. 君子不以紺緅飾，紅紫不以爲褻服。當暑，袗絺綌，必表而出之。緇衣，羔裘；素衣，麑裘；黃衣，狐裘。褻裘長，短右袂。必有寢衣，長一身有半。狐貉之厚以居。去喪無所不佩。非帷裳，必殺之。羔裘玄冠不以弔。吉月，必朝服而朝。

译文:

君子服饰是很讲究的，一般不用天青色和铁灰色的布作镶边，不用浅红和紫色的布做便服。夏天一般用麻布做单衣，里边一定要穿衬衣。穿皮袍时要注意和外边的罩衣颜色相配，黑色的羔羊皮袍配黑色的罩衣；白色的小鹿皮袍配白色罩衣；黄色的狐貉皮袍配黄色罩衣。平时在家里穿的皮袍样式可以实用随便一些。睡觉时一定盖被子，被长一身半。用狐貉的厚皮毛做坐垫。服丧期满才可佩带各种装饰品，不是礼服要裁边。不穿黑色衣服吊丧。每月初一日，上朝去朝拜君主时一定要穿礼服。

英文:

A gentleman is rather particular about what he wears. Usually he does not use dark red or grey for borders nor light red or violet for casual clothes. In the summer, he wears an unlined robe made of hemp over other clothes. He makes sure that the robe and the fur are well-matched. Under a black gown, he wears a black lambskin; under a white gown, a white fawnskin, under a yellow gown, a yellow fox fur. His day dress can be more casual and convenient. He must have a quilt which is half as long again as he is tall. He uses the thick fox or racoon dog fur for a cushion. He will not wear any ornaments until the period of mourning is over. Except for official occasions, his gowns are shorter than ceremonial dress. On visits of condolence, he is never in black. On the first day of the month, he always goes to court in full court dress.

7. 齊，必有明衣，布。齊必變食，居必遷坐。

译文:

斋戒沐浴时一定换上布做的浴衣，还必须戒酒肉，另室居住，不与妻妾同房。

英文:

In the period of fasting, one should wear a cotton bathrobe. One should also abstain from wine and meat and should live apart from one's wife.

8. 食不厭精，膾不厭細。食饐而餲，魚餒而肉敗，不食。色惡，不食。臭惡，不食。失飪，不食。不時，不食。割不正，不食。不得其醬，不食。肉雖多，不使勝食氣。唯酒無量不及亂。沽酒市脯，不食。不撤姜食，不多食。

译文:

粮食加工越细越好，鱼肉切得越细越好。不吃已经腐臭了的食物。不吃变色变味的食物。不吃生食和零食。不是正规宰杀的肉不吃。没有调料的肉不吃。在宴席上吃肉的量不能超过主食。酒可多饮，但不能醉。不吃从市上买来的酒和熟肉。吃完饭，再少吃一点姜去口中异味。

Rice (staple food) can never be refined too much; nor can meat be minced too much. Do not eat food that has gone off, or changed in colour or smell. Do not eat raw food or snacks. Do not eat meat that has not been killed in an orthodox fashion, nor meat with no seasonings. At a banquet, do not have more meat than rice; have plenty of wine but do not get drunk. Do not drink wine or eat cooked meat sold on the street. When you have finished eating, have a little ginger to clean the mouth.

9. 祭於公，不宿肉。祭肉不出三日。出三日，不食之矣。

译文：
参加国君祭祀典礼后，领来的祭肉不能过夜再吃。用来祭祀的肉不能超过三天。超过三天的肉，就不再吃了。

注：
不宿肉：肉不过夜。古代大夫、士有陪国君祭祀之礼，祭祀后可以领回一份祭肉，但国君祭祀要祭两天，所以分到的祭肉如果过夜再吃，就超过三天了。孔子认为超过三天的肉就不新鲜了，所以不吃。

After taking part in a sacrifice with the ruler, Confucius received a present of meat but did not keep it overnight before eating it. He would no longer eat sacrificial meat when it was kept more than three days.

Note: In ancient time, the ministers accompanied the monarch at the sacrificial ceremony, after which they would be granted a piece of sacrificial meat. As the sacrifice usually last two days, it would be more than three days if they ate the meat overnight. Confucius thought the meat kept beyond three days would no longer be fresh.

10. 食不語，寢不言。

译文:

吃饭的时候不交谈，睡觉的时候不说话。

英文:

He did not talk either at table or in bed.

11. 雖疏食菜羹，必祭，必齊如也。

译文:

虽然是粗茶淡饭，也要每餐必祭祀一番，而且态度要像斋戒那样恭恭敬敬。

英文:

Even if it was simple fare, he would offer a sacrifice for each meal, and looked as solemn as during the period of fast.

12. 席不正，不坐。

译文:

坐席摆放位置不合礼制，不坐。

英文:

If the mat was not properly set according to the rites, he did not sit on it.

13. 鄉人飲酒，杖者出，斯出矣。

译文:

同乡人一起饮酒，要等年长者退席之后才可出去。

英文:

When drinking with the people from his village, he

did not leave the table until the elderly had done so.

14. 鄉人儺，朝服而立於阼階。

译文:

本乡人举行迎神驱鬼仪式时，作为主人要穿着朝服站在东边台阶上。

英文:

When people from his village were expelling the evil spirits, as host, he would stand at the eastern steps in court dress.

15. 問人於他邦，再拜而送之。

译文:

托人给住在外国的朋友问候，要对受托人拜两次送别。

英文:

When sending a messenger to give his regards to a friend in another state, he would bow deeply twice before seeing him off.

16. 康子饋藥，拜而受之，曰："丘未達，不敢嘗。"

译文:

季康子赠药给孔子，**孔子拜谢**之后收下了，说："我还不了解这药的药性，不敢就服。"

注:

康子: 即季康子，姓季孙，名肥，鲁哀公时正卿。

英文:

When presented with some medicine by Ji Kangzi, Confucius accepted it with a deep bow, saying, "Sorry, I have no idea of its properties and dare not drink it."

17. 廄焚。子退朝，曰："傷人乎?"不問馬。

译文:

孔子从朝中回来知道马棚失了火，只问："伤人了吗?"并不问马匹怎么样。

英文:

The stable caught fire. Hurrying back from the court, Confucius asked, "Anyone hurt?" He did not ask about the horses.

18. 君賜食，必正席先嘗之。君賜腥，必熟而薦之。君賜生，必畜之。侍食於君，君祭，先飯。

译文:

国君赏赐熟食,一定正襟危坐只吃一点。赏赐生肉,带回去煮熟先供奉祖先。赏赐活物,一定要饲养起来。侍奉国君吃饭,要在君主举行祭礼前吃饭。

英文:

When the ruler gave him a gift of cooked food, he would first taste it in all seriousness. When given raw meat, he would first cook it and offer it to the ancestors. When given a live animal, he would keep it. When waiting on the ruler at table, he would taste the dishes before the ruler offering sacrifices.

19. 疾,君視之,東首,加朝服,拖紳。

译文:

孔子病了,国君来探问时,他虽不能站起来迎接,也一定头朝东,把朝服盖在身上,拖着大带以示恭敬。

英文:

When the King came to see Confucius, who was seriously ill, he was lying in bed with his head to the east and covered with the court dress and waistband in order to show his respect for the ruler.

20. 君命召，不俟駕行矣。

译文:

国君召见孔子，他不等套好车立即就走。

英文:

Hardly had the horses been yoked to the carriage when Confucius, summoned by the ruler, set off on foot.

21. 入太廟，每事問。

译文:

孔子进入周公庙，对每件不明白的事情都向别人请教。

英文:

Confucius would ask about everything whenever he entered the Temple of the Duke of Zhou.

22. 朋友死，無所歸，曰:"於我殯。"

译文:

朋友死了，没有人料理，孔子说:"由我负责办理丧事。"

When one of his friends died homeless, Confucius said, "I shall be in charge of his funeral."

23. 朋友之馈，虽车马，非祭肉，不拜。

译文:

对朋友赠送的礼品，即使是车马这样的重礼，只要不是祭肉，孔子接受的时候也不行礼。

英文:

Confucius would never bow when accepting gifts from a friend, even when he was given such gifts as a carriage and horses. The only exception was for sacrificial meat.

24. 寝不尸，居不容。

译文:

睡觉不能像死尸一样平躺，平时在家不必像参加祭祀或会客那样仪态庄重。

英文:

In bed, Confucius did not lie like a corpse; at home,

he did not look as solemn as did when he was making an offering or having an interview.

25. 見齊衰者，雖狎，必變。見冕者與瞽者，雖褻，必以貌。凶服者式之。式負版者。有盛饌，必變色而作。迅雷風烈必變。

译文：

孔子看见穿孝服的人，那怕是熟人，也一定上前表示同情。看见做官的和瞎子，即使常见面，也一定表示有礼貌。他坐车外出，碰上出丧的人和背负着图书的人，都要俯身以表示尊敬和同情。遇到丰盛的筵席，一定站起来，仪态庄重。碰上疾雷、大风时也会神色大变。

英文：

When he saw a man in mourning dress, whether he was an intimate friend or not, Confucius would walk over to him to show his sympathy. When seeing an official or a blind man, even if he often saw him, he would show his politeness. If out in his carriage, he saw a man in mourning dress or a man carrying books, he would lean forward with his hands on the crossbar to show his sympathy and respect. When invited to a sumptuous feast, he would rise to his feet with a solemn expression.

When suddenly there was a clap of thunder or a gust of wind, the Master would always change his countenance.

26. 升車，必正立，執綏。車中，不内顧，不疾言，不親指。

译文:

孔子上车时，一定先站得端端正正，然后攀着扶手带上去。坐在车上，不回头看，不大声喊叫，不指指划划。

英文:

Before getting into his carriage, Confucius would first stand straight and then hold the carriage band of supporting him to ascend. In the carriage he would not peer around. Nor would he shout or point.

27. 色斯舉矣，翔而後集。曰："山梁雌雉，時哉時哉!"子路共之，三嗅而作。

译文:

孔子乘车在山谷中行走，惊起山梁上几只野鸡飞向天空，盘旋一阵后又落在树上。孔子说："山梁上那几只野鸡一遇危险就飞走，也算识时务呀!"子路对它们拱拱手，野鸡又一齐飞走了。

注：

此段文字很费解，从来没有确切的译文。可能是由于脱误之故。

英文：

Confucius carriage was driving in the valley. Startled, some pheasants on the ridge flew up into the sky. After circling around for a while, they perched together on a tree. Confucius commented, "They fly away as soon as they see danger—how adaptable they are!" At this, Zi Lu cupped one hand on the other before his chest to show his respect for the birds. Flapping their wings the birds flew away.

先進篇第十一

1. 子曰："先進於禮樂，野人也；後進於禮樂，君子也。如用之，則吾從先進。"

译文：

孔子说："先学习礼乐而后做官的，是没有世袭特权的一般士人；先做官而后学习礼乐的，是有世袭特权的卿大夫子弟。如果要我选用人才，我就选用先学习礼乐而后做官的人。"

英文：

Confucius said, "Those who get on with the rites and music before taking office are from humble families; those who take office before getting on with the rites and music are from noble families. Were I to choose between the two, I would stand on the side of the former."

2. 子曰："從我於陳、蔡者，皆不及門也。"

译文：

孔子说："曾经跟随我在陈、蔡忍饥挨饿的人，现在都不在我这里了。"

陈、蔡: 国名。孔子周游列国时, 在陈、蔡之间被围困, 绝粮七日。当时跟随孔子的子路、子贡等回鲁国后相继离开了孔子。颜渊也死了。所以孔子说这句话表示怀念。

英文:

Confucius said, "None of those who endured the torments of hunger with me in Chen and Cai are here with me now."

Note: Chen and Cai are names of two states. While travelling in Chen and Cai, Confucius was besieged in the border area between Chen and Cai, and he ran out of food for seven days. Zi Lu, Zi Gong and the other disciples who were with Confucius at the time all left him one after another after returning to Lu. Yan Yuan died. So these words are said with nostalgia.

3. 德行: 颜淵, 閔子騫, 冉伯牛, 仲弓。言語: 宰我, 子貢。政事: 冉有, 季路。文學: 子游, 子夏。

译文:

孔子弟子各有所长, 德行好的有颜渊、闵子骞、冉伯牛、仲弓等。长于辞令的有宰我、子贡等。有办理政事才能的如冉有、季路等。熟悉古代文献的有子游、子夏等。

Confucius's disciples each had his own talent: Yan Yuan, Min Ziqian, Ran Boniu, and Zhong Gong were virtuous; those of eloquence were Zai Wo and Zi Gong; Those good at government were Ran You and Ji Lu; And Zi You and Zi Xia were familiar with ancient culture and literature.

4. 子曰:"回也非助我者也,於吾言無所不説。"

译文:

孔子说:"颜回对我讲的话无不心悦诚服地接受,从不提不同意见,这对我没有什么帮助。"

英文:

Confucius said, "Yan Hui always entirely accepts whatever I say. He has never disagreed with me, and this is of no help at all."

5. 子曰:"孝哉閔子騫! 人不間於其父母昆弟之言。"

译文:

孔子说:"闵子骞真孝顺! 使别人无法挑拨他父母兄弟之间的关系。"

Confucius said, "How filial Min Ziqian is! It is impossible to foment any discord between him and his parents and siblings."

6. 南容三復白圭，孔子以其兄之子妻之。

译文:

南容经常诵读关于白圭的诗，孔子认为他是一个谨小慎微的人，就把侄女嫁给他。

注:

南容: 孔子的学生南宫适，字子容。

白圭:《诗经·大雅》中一首诗。大意是: 白圭是一种珍贵而莹洁的玉器，如果上边沾有污点，还可以磨掉，如果说出的话有污点就没办法去掉了。

英文:

Nan Rong often repeated the verse about the white jade sceptre. Confucius thought him meticulous and conscientious and married his niece to him.

Note: White jade sceptre is a poem from *The Book of Songs*, the meaning of which is as follows: the sceptre of white jade was precious and pure. A stain on the sceptre may be removed. But it is impossible to remove the stain carried in words.

7. 季康子問: "弟子孰爲好學?" 孔子對曰: "有顏回者好學, 不幸短命死矣, 今也則亡。"

译文:

季康子问: "你学生中谁最爱学习?" 孔子回答说: "颜回最爱学习, 不幸早死, 现在没有这样的人了。"

注:

季康子: 姓季孙, 名肥, 鲁哀公时宰相。

英文:

Ji Kangzi asked, "Who is most eager to learn among your disciples?" Confucius answered, "Yan Hui was the one who loved learning most. Unfortunately, he died young. Now there is no one like this."

8. 顏淵死, 顏路請子之車以爲之椁, 子曰: "才不才, 亦各言其子也。鯉也死, 有棺而無椁。我不徒行以爲之椁。以吾從大夫之後, 不可徒行也。"

译文:

颜渊死后, 他父亲颜路请求孔子卖掉车子为颜渊办外椁。孔子说: "不管好坏, 都是自己的儿子, 我的儿子鲤死了, 也是只有棺而没有椁。我不能卖掉车子来给他买椁。因为我也算做过大夫的人，按礼是不可以没有车子的。"

注:

颜路：姓颜，名无繇，字路，颜渊的父亲，也是孔子的学生。

鲤：孔鲤，字伯鱼，孔子的儿子。

英文:

When Yan Yuan died, his father Yan Lu requested Confucius to sell his carriage in order to make an outer coffin for Yan Yuan. Confucius said, "Good or bad, he is your son. When my son Li died, he only had a coffin, no outer coffin at all. I did not sell my carriage to buy him an outer coffin. For, in accordance with the rites, it is improper for me, a former senior official, to go on foot."

9. 颜渊死，子曰："噫！天丧予！天丧予！"

译文:

颜渊死了，孔子仰天叹道："老天爷！你这是要我的命呀！"

英文:

When Yan Yuan died, Confucius heaved a deep

sigh, saying, "Alas, Heaven has bereaved me!"

10. 顏淵死, 子哭之慟。從者曰:"子慟矣!"曰:"有慟乎? 非夫人之爲慟而誰爲?"

译文:

颜渊死了, 孔子哭得很伤心。跟随的人劝道:"您太伤心了!"孔子说:"是吗? 我不为他伤心, 还有谁值得我伤心呢?"

英文:

When Yan Yuan died, Confucius wailed bitterly. His disciples said, "Master, you are grieving too much!" Confucius said, "Am I? If I didn't grieve for him, who else would deserve my grief?"

11. 顏淵死, 門人欲厚葬之, 子曰:"不可。"門人厚葬之。子曰:"回也視予猶父也, 予不得視猶子也。非我也, 夫二三子也。"

译文:

颜渊死后, 孔子的学生们打算厚葬他; 孔子说:"不能这样做。"结果学生们还是厚葬了颜渊。孔子知道后说:"颜回把我当父亲一样看待, 我却不能把他当儿子一样。厚葬不是我的主意, 是你这班同学们干的。"

孔子反对违礼厚葬，特别像颜渊那样的经济条件。孔子儿子鲤死时，也没有厚葬，所以孔子说："颜回把我当父亲一样，我却不能把他当儿子一样。"实是责备那些不听孔子教导的主张厚葬的学生。

英文:

When Yan Yuan died, Confucius' disciples wanted to give him a grand burial. Confucius said, "You must not do that." However, the disciples still gave him a grand burial. Knowing that, Confucius said, "Yan Yuan treated me as if I were his father. But I could not treat him as if he were my son. Such a grand burial was your idea, not mine."

Note: Confucius objected to the grand burial for Yan Yuan, especially because of Yan Yuan's economic condition. When his son had died, Confucius had buried him in a simple way. Therefore, he uttered the above remarks to reproach the disciples who had not listened to him and given Yan Yuan a grand burial.

12. 季路问事鬼神。子曰："未能事人，焉能事鬼?"曰："敢问死。"曰："未知生，焉知死。"

季路向老师请教服事鬼神的方法。孔子说: "不能服事人, 怎能服事鬼?" 季路又问: "请问死是怎么回事?" 孔子说: "不知道生, 怎么知道死?"

英文:

Zi Lu asked Confucius about how to serve the spirits. Confucius said, "How can one serve the spirits before one knows how to serve people?" Zi Lu went on asking, "What is death?" Confucius replied, "How can one understand death before understanding life?"

13. 闵子侍侧, 誾誾如也; 子路, 行行如也; 冉有、子贡, 侃侃如也。子乐。"若由也, 不得其死然。"

译文:

闵子骞在老师面前总是恭敬而正直的样子, 而子路则是一副刚强的样子; 冉有和子贡总是温和快乐的样子。孔子对学生很满意, 但又担心地说: "像仲由这样一味刚强好勇, 怕最后死不得其所呢。"

英文:

In attendance upon Confucius, Min Ziqian looked respectful and upright; Zi Lu looked unyielding; and Ran You and Zi Gong appeared mild and joyful. Whilst satis-

fied with his disciples, Confucius expressed his worries:
"Zhong You will not die a worthy death if he keeps being
unyielding and quick to fight as he has ever been."

14. 魯人爲長府。閔子騫曰: "仍舊貫,如之何? 何
必改作?"子曰: "夫人不言,言必有中。"

译文:

　　鲁国执政者决定翻建国库,闵子骞说: "旧库不是还
能用吗? 何必翻建呢?"孔子说: "这个人平时不爱多说
话,一说话必然说到点子上。"

英文:

　　The government of Lu decided to rebuild the state
treasury. Min Ziqian said, "Is the old treasury not adequate? Is it necessary to rebuild it?" Confucius said,
"That is a man of few words. But when he speaks he hits
the nail on the head."

15. 子曰: "由之瑟奚爲於丘之門?"門人不敬子路。
子曰: "由也升堂矣,未入於室也。"

译文:

　　孔子说: "仲由何必来我这里卖弄弹瑟呢?"由此孔子
的学生瞧不起子路。孔子又说道: "其实仲由的学问已经

不错了，只是还没有到家。"

注:
　　瑟: 古代乐器，和琴同类。

英文:

　　Confucius said, "Why did Zhong You come to play the *se* for me?" After that, Confucius' disciples began to look down upon Zi Lu. Confucius said, "In fact Zhong You is quite learned, only far from perfect."

　　Note: *Se* is an ancient Chinese musical instrument, similar to the zither.

　　16. 子貢問: "師與商也孰賢?"子曰: "師也過，商也不及。"曰: "然則師愈與?"子曰: "過猶不及。"

译文:

　　子贡问: "颛孙师和卜商，哪个好一些?"孔子说: "颛孙师办事好过头，卜商办事达不到。"子贡说: "那么还是颛孙师好一些了?"孔子说: "其实过头和达不到同样不好。"

注:
　　师: 颛孙师，即子张，孔子的学生。
　　商: 卜商，即子夏，孔子的学生。

Zi Gong asked," Who is preferable, Zhuansun Shi (a disciple of Confucius) or Bu Shang?" Confucius said, "Zhuansun Shi tends to go too far, but Bu Shang tends not to go far enough." Zi Gong said, "So is Zhuansun Shi preferable in fact?" Confucius said, "The fact is that going too far and not going far enough are equally bad."

17. 季氏富於周公，而求也爲之聚斂而附益之。子曰："非吾徒也，小子鳴鼓而攻之可也！"

译文:

季孙氏比周天子的卿士还富有，可是冉求还帮助他搜刮，以增加他的财富。孔子说："冉求已经不是我的学生了，你们可以大张旗鼓地攻击他。"

注:

季氏: 季孙氏，鲁国大夫。

周公: 泛指周天子左右卿士（一说专指周公旦）。孔子认为诸侯国（鲁）的大夫而财富多于周天子卿士，这是不合礼的。

求: 冉求，即子有，孔子的学生。当时是季孙氏家臣。季孙氏要用田赋制度增收赋税，派冉求征求孔子的意见，孔子明确表示反对对人民的过分剥削。可是冉求仍然听从季氏而实行田赋制度加重对人民的剥削，所以孔子不认他这个学生，并号召其他学生攻击冉求。

Jisun Shi possessed even more wealth than Zhou Gong. Nevertheless, Ran Qiu helped increase Jisun Shi's wealth through extortion. Confucius said, "Ran Qiu is no longer a disciple of mine. You may attack him openly on a large scale."

Note: Zhou Gong generally refers to the dukes serving the King of Zhou. (In another saying it refers to Ji Dan, the Duke of Zhou.) Confucius thought that it was against the rites that the senior officials under the Duke of Lu possessed more wealth than the senior officials in attendance upon the King of Zhou.

Ran Qiu, also known as Zi You, was then a steward of Jisun's Manor. Jisun Shi wanted to collect more land taxes and sent Ran You to ask for Confucius' advice. Confucius openly objected to it. But Ran Qiu still followed Jisun's instructions and carried out the practice of land taxes, which led to overexploitation of the common people. As a result, Confucius claimed that Ran Qiu was no longer his student and asked the other students to attack him.

18. 柴也愚，參也魯，師也辟，由也喭。

译文:

高柴愚笨，曾参迟钝，颛孙师偏激，仲由鲁莽。

注:

柴: 姓高，名柴，字子羔，孔子的学生。

英文:

Confucius said, "Gao Chai (a disciple of Confucius) is stupid; Zeng Shen is slow; Zhuansun Shi goes to extremes, Zhong You is rash and careless."

19. 子曰："回也其庶乎，屡空。赐不受命，而货殖焉，亿则屡中。"

译文:

孔子说："颜回的学问道德虽然已经很好，可是他却贫穷不堪。端木赐不安本分，而去经商，却每每能发财。"

英文:

Confucius said, "Yan Hui is quite learned and virtuous but he is extremely impoverished. Duanmu Ci is discontent with his lot. He engages in trade, and each time he turns out to be successful."

20. 子張問善人之道，子曰："不踐迹，亦不入於室。"

译文：

子张问怎样才能成为善人，孔子说："善人不必循别人走过的路，亦不必有很高的学问道德。"

英文：

Zi Zhang asked how to become a good man. Confucius said, "A good man neither has to follow in other people's tracks, nor has to be accomplished in learning or virtue."

21. 子曰："論篤是與，君子者乎？色莊者乎？"

译文：

孔子说："赞扬说话诚实的人，但要仔细观察他是真正的君子呢？还是伪装庄重的人呢？"

英文：

Confucius said, "Before praising a man who is honest in speech, one should observe: Is he a true gentleman or is his dignity just a pretence?"

22. 子路問："聞斯行諸？"子曰："有父兄在，如之何其聞斯行之？"冉有問："聞斯行諸？"子曰："聞斯行之。"公西華曰: "由也問'聞斯行諸', 子曰: '有父兄在'; 求也問'聞斯行諸', 子曰'聞斯行之'。赤也惑, 敢問。"子曰: "求也退, 故進之; 由也兼人, 故退之。"

译文:

子路问: "闻风而动对吗?"孔子说: "有父兄在, 怎么能闻风而动呢?"

冉有也问: "闻风而动对吗?"孔子说: "对。"

公西华大惑不解地问: "他们两个提出的问题相同, 而您的回答却相反, 我有些糊涂了, 敢问这是怎么回事。"

孔子说: "冉求做事好退缩, 所以我鼓励他大胆干; 仲由好勇胆大, 所以我有意压压他。"

英文:

Zi Lu asked, "Should one respond immediately to a call?" Confucius said, "How can you respond immediately to a call with your father and elder brothers alive?"

Ran You asked the same question, "Should one respond immediately to a call?" Confucius said, "Yes, one should."

Gongxi Hua was deeply perplexed, saying, "I am puzzled. May I know why you gave two different answers to the same question?"

Confucius said, "Ran You usually hangs back, so I

urge him on; Zhong You advances bravely and sometimes audaciously, so I hold him back."

23. 子畏於匡，顏淵後。子曰："吾以女爲死矣。" 曰："子在，回何敢死?"

译文:

孔子被囚禁在匡地，颜渊最后才来，孔子说："我以为你死了。"颜渊说："您还活着，我怎么敢死呢?"

英文:

Confucius was besieged in Kuang. Yan Yuan was the last to arrive to see him. Confucius said, "I thought you had died." Yan Yuan said, "How would I dare to die when you Master are alive?"

24. 季子然問："仲由、冉求可謂大臣與?"子曰："吾以子爲異之問，曾由與求之問。所謂大臣者，以道事君，不可則止。今由與求也，可謂具臣矣。"曰："然則從之者與?"子曰："弒父與君，亦不從也。"

译文:

季子然问："仲由、冉求能够作大臣吗?"孔子说："我以为您问什么人，原来是问仲由和冉求呀。所谓大臣，应以仁德来事奉君主，如行不通宁可辞职不干。在这方面可以说仲由和冉求都已具备了作大臣的条件。"季子然又问: "那他们会一切顺从上级吗?"孔子说: "杀父杀君主的事, 他们也不会顺从的。"

注:

季子然: 鲁国大夫季氏子弟。

英文:

Ji Ziran (a member of the Jisun's family) asked, "Can Zhong You and Ran Qiu be ministers?" Confucius said, "I had expected you to ask about others. You are only asking about Zhong and Ran. A minister should serve the ruler with benevolence. If he can't do this, he should rather resign his office. In view of this, Zhong You and Ran Qiu are already qualified to become ministers." Ji Ziran asked again, " So, do they always do what they are told to?" Confucius said, "No. They would not obey if they were asked to commit patricide or regicide."

25. 子路使子羔爲費宰。子曰: "賊夫人之子。"子路曰: "有民人焉, 有社稷焉, 何必讀書, 然後爲學?"子曰: "是故惡夫佞者。"

译文:

子路推荐子羔去费县当县长。孔子说: "子羔没经学习就去做官, 这是误人子弟。"子路不同意说: "那里有百姓，有管理机构，为什么一定要读书才算做学问呢?"孔子说："所以我讨厌狡辩的人。"

英文:

Zi Lu recommended Zi Gao to be the county magistrate of Fei. Confucius said, "You are doing harm to that young fellow. Because he takes office before acquiring any learning." Zi Lu disagreed, saying, "There are common people there and an administrative structure, why should he study books before being considered a man of knowledge?" Confucius said, "It is just what you have said that makes me dislike those who quibble."

26. 子路、曾皙、冉有、公西華侍坐。

子曰："以吾一日長乎爾，毋吾以也。居則曰：'不吾知也'！ 如或知爾，則何以哉?"

子路率爾而對曰："千乘之國，攝乎大國之間，加之以師旅，因之以饑饉；由也爲之，比及三年，可使有勇，且知方也。"

夫子哂之。

"求！爾何如?"

對曰："方六七十，如五六十，求也爲之，比及三年，可使足民。如其禮樂，以俟君子。"

"赤！爾何如?"

對曰："非曰能之，願學焉。宗廟之事，如會同，端章甫，願爲小相焉。”

“點！爾何如?”

鼓瑟希，鏗爾，舍瑟而作，對曰:“異乎三子者之撰。”

子曰:“何傷乎? 亦各言其志也。”

曰:“莫春者，春服既成，冠者五六人，童子六七人，浴乎沂，風乎舞雩，詠而歸。”

夫子喟然歎曰:“吾與點也!”

三子者出，曾皙後。曾皙曰:“夫三子者之言何如?”

子曰:“亦各言其志也已矣。”

曰:“夫子何哂由也?”

曰:“爲國以禮，其言不讓，是故哂之。”

“唯求則非邦也與?”

“安見方六七十如五六十而非邦也者?”

“唯赤則非邦也與?”

“宗廟會同，非諸侯而何? 赤也爲之小，孰能爲之大?”

译文:

子路、曾皙、冉有、公西华几个学生陪老师坐着说话。

孔子说:“我已经老了，不中用了。你们平时总埋怨没人了解你们，假如现在有人了解你们，打算重用你们，你们怎么样?”

子路不假思索地冲口而出:“如果让我去治理一个千

乘之国，尽管外面受几个大国的军队侵略，国内又闹灾荒，不出三年我能让人民勇敢善战，并且懂得礼义。"

孔子微微一笑。又问："冉求，你怎么样？"

冉求回答说："如果让我治理一个几十平方里的小国，三年时间，可以使人民富足，至于修明礼乐，我不行，只有等贤人君子来施行了。"

孔子问公西赤："你怎么样？"

公西赤回答说："在宗庙祭祀或诸侯会盟时，我希望能做个小傧相。这不是说我已经可以胜任了，只是愿意学习罢了。"

孔子又问："曾点，你怎么样？"

曾皙正在弹瑟，听老师问，赶紧把瑟放下站起来说："我可没有他们三位那么大的志向。"

孔子说："那有什么关系，我正想听听你们各自的志向。"

曾皙便道："我不过想在暮春三月，穿上春装，和一群年轻伙伴一起到沂水中游泳，躺在舞雩台上沐浴着和煦的春风，然后一路唱着歌回来。"

孔子听了长叹一声说："我和曾点想的一样。"

等子路、冉有、公西华出门，曾皙留在后面问："他们三个的话怎么样？"

孔子说："不过是各言其志罢了。"

曾皙说："那您为什么笑仲由呢？"

孔子说："治理国家要讲礼让，可是他却一点不谦虚，所以我笑他。"

曾皙又说："冉求和公西赤不是都说能治理国家吗?"

孔子说："我笑仲由不是说他不能治理国家,而是说他说话不够谦虚。譬如公西赤,他是个很懂礼仪的人,但他只说愿意学习做个小傧相。如果他只能做个小傧相,那谁能做大傧相呢?"

注:

曾皙:姓曾,名点,字子皙,曾参的父亲,孔子的学生。

英文:

In attendance upon Confucius were Zi Lu, Zeng Xi, Ran You, and Gongxi Hua. Confucius said, "I am old now and will no longer be useful soon. You often complain that few can understand you and appreciate your merits. Now, suppose someone did understand you and appreciate your merits, and he intended to put you in an important position, how would you go about things?"

Without a moment's thought, Zi Lu answered, "If I were to administrate a one-thousand-chariot state, which was under the invasion of several big states, and was hit repeatedly by famines, I could, in a period of three years, endue the people with bravery and fighting skills, and more importantly, teach them the rites and music."

Confucius smiled and turned to Ran Qiu, asking,

"What about you, Ran Qiu?"

Ran Qiu replied, "If I were to administrate a state of dozens of square, I could, within three years, help the people there become prosperous. As to the rites and music, they are beyond my ability. I would have to leave them to those virtuous gentlemen."

Confucius asked Gongxi Hua, "And you?" Gongxi Chi answered, "I would like to be an attendant during sacrificial ceremonies at the ancestral temple or at the alliances of dukes and princes. This does not mean that I am qualified for these activities. It only indicates that I am willing to learn."

Confucius asked, "Zeng Dian, what about you?" Zeng Xi was playing the zither. Hearing Confucius' question, he stopped playing and stood up, saying, "I am not at all as ambitious as they three." Confucius said, "That doesn't matter, I only want to know your respective wishes." Zeng Xi thus answered, "What I wish for is nothing but an outing in late spring. My friends and I, dressed in newly-made spring clothes, would go swimming in the Yi River, enjoy sun-bathing in the gentle breeze on the Rain Altar, and then, go home singing." With a deep sigh, Confucius said, "I am all for Zeng Dian."

After Zi Lu, Ran You, and Gongxi Hua had left,

Zeng Xi was left behind and he asked Confucius, "What do you think of what they said just now?"

Confucius answered, "They were only stating their respective wishes."

Zeng Xi asked, "Why did you laugh at Zhong You?"

Confucius answered, "Governing a state needs comity but Zhong You was far from modest, so I laughed at him." Zeng Xi asked again, "Didn't Ran You and Gongxi Hua also say they were able to administrate states?"

Confucius said, "I laughed at Zhong You not because he was not able to govern a state, but because he was far from modest. As to Gongxi Chi, he knows the rites and music very well, but he said he was willing to learn only to be a second—class attendant. Who could be the first—class attendant if he were to be a second—class attendant?"

顏淵篇第十二

1. 顏淵問仁，子曰："克己復禮爲仁。一日克己復禮，天下歸仁焉。爲仁由己，而由人乎哉?"顏淵曰："請問其目。"子曰："非禮勿視，非禮勿聽，非禮勿言，非禮勿動。"顏淵曰："回雖不敏，請事斯語矣。"

译文:

颜渊问什么是仁，孔子说："克制自己的言行合于礼就是仁。一旦能作到这样，人们就会承认你是仁人了。这完全要靠自己，靠别人是没有用的。"颜渊又问："怎样才能做到呢?"孔子说："不合于礼的东西不看，不合于礼的话不听，不合于礼的话不说，不合于礼的事不做。"颜渊说："我虽然迟钝，也要照您的话去做。"

英文:

Yan Yuan asked what benevolence was. Confucius said, "One who restrains himself in order to observe the rites is benevolent. Once you can do this, you will be unanimously considered a man of benevolence. Such a practice wholly depends on oneself, not on anybody else." Yan Yuan asked again, "How can one carry on such a practice?" Confucius answered, "Do not look at things that do not accord with the rites; do not listen to things that do not accord with the rites; do not say anything that does not accord with the rites; and do not do anything that does not accord with the rites." Yan Yuan said, "I will follow what you have said even though I am not gifted."

2. 仲弓問仁，子曰："出門如見大賓，使民如承大祭。己所不欲，勿施於人。在邦無怨，在家無怨。"仲弓曰："雍雖不敏，請事斯語矣。"

译文：

仲弓问什么是仁，孔子说："对待工作像接待贵宾一样严肃认真，役使老百姓像承当祭典一样小心谨慎。凡自己不喜欢的就不要强加于别人。不管在什么地方。都没有怨恨。"仲弓说："我虽然愚笨，也要照您说的话去做。"

注：

仲弓：姓冉，名雍，字仲弓，孔子的学生。

英文：

Zhong Gong asked what benevolence was. Confucius said, "Deal with your work as earnestly and conscientiously as you receive a distinguished guest; call up the common people for corvée labour as cautiously as if you were at a sacrificial ceremony; never impose upon others what you dislike yourself. By so doing, you will cause no resentment anywhere you go." Zhong Gong said, "I will follow what you have said even though I am not gifted."

3. 司馬牛問仁，子曰："仁者，其言也訒。"曰："其言也訒，斯謂之仁已乎?"子曰："爲之難，言之得無訒乎?"

译文：

司马牛问什么是仁，孔子说："仁人说话谨慎。"司马牛说："说话谨慎就是仁吗?"孔子说："知道做起来不容易，说话能不谨慎吗?"

注：

司马牛：姓司马，名耕，字子牛，孔子的学生。司马牛"多言而躁"。孔子的话是针对他的缺点说的。颜渊、冉雍、司马牛同问仁，孔子却因人施教，回答不一。

英文：

Sima Niu (a disciple of Confucius) asked what benevolence was. Confucius said, "A benevolent man is always careful in speech." Sima Niu asked, "Can a man be considered benevolent only because he is careful in speech?" Confucius said, "How can a man not be careful in speech as long as he knows it is difficult to act?"

Note: Confucius made these remarks in the light of Sima Niu's shortcomings of talkativeness and impetuousness. When Yan Yuan, Ran Yong, and Sima Niu asked the same question about benevolence, Confucius gave different answers in view of their different temperaments.

4. 司馬牛問君子，子曰："君子不憂不懼。"曰："不憂不懼，斯謂之君子已乎？"子曰："內省不疚，夫何憂何懼？"

译文:

司马牛问怎样才算君子，孔子说："君子不忧愁，不恐惧。"司马牛说："不忧愁，不恐惧，就可以算君子吗？"孔子说："能做到问心无愧的人，还会有忧愁和恐惧吗？"

英文:

Sima Niu asked about being a gentleman. Confucius said, "Gentlemen are free from worries and fears." Sima Niu asked again, "Can a person be called a gentleman just because he is free from worries and fears?" Confucius answered, "Can a man with a clear conscience ever have any worries and fears?"

5. 司馬牛憂曰："人皆有兄弟，我獨亡。"子夏曰："商聞之矣: '死生有命, 富貴在天。' 君子敬而無失, 與人恭而有禮。四海之內, 皆兄弟也。君子何患乎無兄弟也?"

译文:

司马牛忧愁地说: "别人都有亲兄弟, 唯独我没有。" 子夏劝慰道: "我听说: '死生听之命运, 富贵由天安排'。君子只要办事认真, 不出差错, 对人恭敬而有礼貌, 普天下人都是好兄弟, 你又何必忧虑没有亲兄弟呢?"

英文:

Sima Niu said sadly, "Everyone else has brothers, but I have none." Zi Xia consoled him by saying, "There is a saying that life and death is decided by destiny, and wealth and rank by Heaven. A gentleman only has to act earnestly, do nothing wrong, and be respectful and polite, and all men under Heaven are his brothers. Why should there be a need for you to worry about having no brothers?"

6. 子張問明。子曰: "浸潤之譖, 膚受之愬, 不行焉, 可謂明也已矣。浸潤之譖, 膚受之愬, 不行焉, 可謂遠也已矣。"

译文：

子张问怎样才算明智。孔子说："不信谗言，不怕诽谤。见事明白而有远见，也就算明智了。"

英文：

Zi Zhang asked what perspicacity was. Confucius said, "He who does not believe and is not afraid of slander, who sees things clearly and is far-sighted can be called perspicacious."

7. 子貢問政，子曰："足食，足兵，民信之矣。"子貢曰："必不得已而去，於斯三者何先？"曰："去兵。"子貢曰："必不得已而去，於斯二者何先？"曰："去食。自古皆有死，民無信不立。"

译文：

子贡问怎样治理国家，孔子说："粮食充足，军备充足，人民信任政府。"子贡说："如果迫不得已一定要去掉一项，在这三项中先去掉哪一项？"孔子说："去掉军备。"子贡又说："如果迫不得已还要去掉一项，在这二项中该去掉哪一项？"孔子说："去掉粮食。没有粮食，虽然会饿死，但自古以来，人都会死的。如果失去人民对政府的信任这一项，也就失去了立国之本了。"

Zi Gong asked what was needed for government. Confucius said, "Sufficient food, sufficient armaments, and common people's trust in the government." Zi Gong asked, "Suppose you were forced to get rid of one of the three, which one would you get rid of first?" Confucius said, "Armaments." Zi Gong went on asking, "Which one would you get rid of if you were to get rid of one of the remaining two?" Confucius answered, "The food. Although man will die of hunger without food, man has been destined to die since time immemorial. But if people lose their trust in the government then the country has lost its basis."

8. 棘子成曰: "君子質而已矣，何以文爲?"子貢曰: "惜乎，夫子之說君子也! 駟不及舌。文猶質也，質猶文也。虎豹之鞹猶犬羊之鞹。"

译文:

棘子成说: "君子只重本质就够了，何必再讲文彩(礼仪形式)?"子贡说: "很遗憾，您这样谈论君子。一言既出，驷马难追。其实本质和文彩对君子来说是同等重要的。假如把虎豹和犬羊皮上的毛 (文彩) 全刮掉，那这两类皮革就少有区别了。"

注:

棘子成: 卫国大夫。

英文:

Ji Zicheng (a minister of Wei) said, "It is enough for a gentleman to lay stress on his innate character. Why should he emphasize the ritual forms?" Zi Gong said, "It is a pity you talk about gentlemen in such a way. A team of four horses cannot overtake the words one has spoken. As a matter of fact, to a gentleman, innate character and ritual forms are of equal importance. Once their hair is all shaved off, there will be little difference between a tiger and a leopard and a dog and a sheep.

Note: The hair represents the ritual forms.

9. 哀公問於有若曰: "年饑，用不足，如之何?"有若對曰: "盍徹乎?"曰: "二，吾猶不足，如之何其徹也?"對曰: "百姓足，君孰與不足? 百姓不足，君孰與足?"

译文:

鲁哀公问有若: "年成不好，国家用度不够，应该怎么办?"有若说: "为什么不实行十分抽一的田税制度?"哀公说: "十分抽二，我还不够，怎么能实行十分抽一呢?"有若回答说: "如果老百姓用度够，您怎么会不够? 如果老百姓用度不够，您又怎么会够?"

有若：姓有，名若，孔子的学生。

英文：

Duke Ai of Lu asked You Ruo, "We've had a bad harvest, and I cannot collect enough taxes to cover the state expenditure. What should I do?" You Ruo said, "Why not reduce taxes to one in ten?" Duke Ai said, "Even to tax the people by two in ten falls far short of covering expenditure. There is no question of reducing taxes to one in ten!" You Ruo replied, "How can you fail to get enough when the people have enough? How can you get enough when the people do not have enough themselves?"

10. 子張問崇德辨惑。子曰："主忠信，徙義，崇德也。愛之欲其生，惡之欲其死。既欲其生，又欲其死，是惑也。'誠不以富，亦祇以異。'"

译文：

子张问怎样提高道德修养和辨别是非的能力。孔子说："亲近忠信诚实的人，一切从仁义出发，就能提高道德修养。对一个人爱起来，则希望他长寿；厌恶起来，恨不得他马上死去。既要他长寿，又要他短命，这就是不辨是非。"

"诚不以富，亦祇以异"。引自《诗经·小雅·我行其野》。孔子引于此，令历代注家费解，有人以为是错简，故不译。

英文:

Zi Zhang enquired how to cultivate virtue and the ability to distinguish between right and wrong. Confucius said, "He who makes friends with those trustworthy and honest, and is observant to benevolence can cultivate virtue. To love someone is to wish him longevity; to hate someone means to wish him an immediate death. To wish someone longevity and at the same time to wish them dead is to be unable to distinguish between right and wrong."

Note: In the original text, a verse follows the last sentence: "Not for her wealth, oh no! But merely for a change." (quotation from *The Book of Songs*) This has been a puzzle to generations of annotators, and it may be a textual error. Therefore it hasn't been translated here.

11. 齊景公問政於孔子，孔子對曰："君君，臣臣，父父，子子。"公曰："善哉! 信如君不君，臣不臣，父不父，子不子，雖有粟，吾得而食諸?"

译文:

齐景公问孔子怎样治理国家，孔子说: "君臣父子要各守其礼。"齐景公说: "对呀! 如果国君不像国君，臣不像臣，父亲不像父亲，儿子不像儿子，即使粮食很多，我能吃得到吗?"

注:

齐景公: 齐国国君，名杵臼。

英文:

Duke Jing of Qi asked Confucius how to govern a country. Confucius said, "Rulers, subjects, fathers, and sons should observe their respective rites." Duke Jing said, "How true! If the ruler is not a ruler, the subject not a subject, the father not a father, the son not a son, even if there is sufficient grain, will I be able to obtain it?"

12. 子曰: "片言可以折狱者，其由也與!"子路無宿諾。

译文:

孔子说: "根据一面之辞就可断案的，大概只有仲由吧! "

注:

孔子认为仲由为人直率、诚实，别人在他面前不会说假话，故说他"片言可以折狱。"文中后一句"子路无宿诺"，和上文没关系，故不译。

英文:

Confucius said, "It is probably only Zhong You that is able to settle a lawsuit according to the evidence of one party."

Note: Confucius thought that Zhong You was frank and honest, and people would not lie before him. That is why Confucius said Zhong You was able to settle a lawsuit on the evidence of one party. The last sentence in the original text, "Zi Lu always fulfills his promise", is probably a textual error and therefore has not been translated.

13. 子曰:"聽訟，吾猶人也。必也使無訟乎!"

译文:

孔子说:"我审理诉讼案件，和别人一样。目的是为了不发生诉讼案件。"

注:

孔子说这话时任鲁国司寇 (治理刑事的官)。

英文:

Confucius said, "The way I settle a lawsuit is not different from others. I am trying, however, to prevent any lawsuit from being started."

Note: Confucius made the above remarks when he was the minister of criminal jurisdiction in Lu.

14. 子張問政，子曰："居之無倦，行之以忠。"

译文：

子张向孔子请教如何从政，孔子说："身居官位不懈怠，执行政策不走样。"

英文：

Zi Zhang asked about government. Confucius said, "Never slack off in your position and fulfill your responsibility loyally."

15. 子曰："博學於文，約之以禮，亦可以弗畔矣夫！"

译文：

孔子说："君子广泛地学习文化典籍，并用礼来约束自己，就可避免离经叛道了。"

英文：

Confucius said, "A gentleman will not go astray so long as he studies extensively and regulates himself with the rites."

16. 子曰: "君子成人之美，不成人之恶。小人反是。"

译文:

孔子说: "君子成全别人的好事，不去促成别人的坏事。小人却和这相反。"

英文:

Confucius said, "A gentleman helps others fulfill good deeds and never helps them in bad deeds. A petty man just does the opposite."

17. 季康子問政於孔子，孔子對曰: "政者，正也。子帥以正，孰敢不正?"

译文:

季康子向孔子问政治之道，孔子说: "政就是端正。您自己行为端正，谁敢不端正呢?"

英文:

Ji Kangzi asked Confucius about the way to govern. Confucius said, "To govern is to be upright. Who dares not to be upright if you yourself are upright?"

18. 季康子患盜，問於孔子。孔子對曰: "苟子之不欲，雖賞之不竊。"

译文:

季康子忧虑盗贼太多，向孔子请教怎么办。孔子对曰: "如果您不贪求太多的财货，就是奖励盗窃，也没人会干的。"

英文:

Ji Kangzi was worried that there were too many thieves. He asked Confucius for advice. Confucius answered, "If you were not greedy for exorbitant wealth, no one would commit burglary even if they got rewarded to do so."

19. 季康子問政於孔子曰: "如殺無道，以就有道，何如?"孔子對曰: "子爲政，焉用殺? 子欲善而民善矣。君子之德風，小人之德草，草上之風，必偃。"

译文:

季康子向孔子请教治理政事时说: "如果用杀掉坏人，重用好人的方法来治理国家，你觉得怎么样?"孔子说: "治理政事，何必一定要杀人呢? 您想把国家搞好，老百姓也想把国家搞好。执政者好比风，老百姓好比草。风往哪边吹，草向哪边倒。"

英文:

Ji Kangzi asked Confucius about government, saying, "What do you think of governing a state by taking away the lives of villains and promoting good people?" Confucius said, "Why should one slay in order to govern? You want the country to be good, and so do the common people. The ruler is like the wind, the common people are like the grass. Whichever way the wind blows, the grass can not help but bend."

20. 子張問: "士何如斯可謂之達矣?" 子曰: "何哉, 爾所謂達者?" 子張對曰: "在邦必聞, 在家必聞。" 子曰: "是聞也, 非達也。夫達也者, 質直而好義, 察言而觀色, 慮以下人。在邦必達, 在家必達。夫聞也者, 色取仁而行違, 居之不疑。在邦必聞, 在家必聞。"

译文:

子张问: "读书人怎样做才可以通达呢?" 孔子反问: "你所说的通达指什么?" 子张回答说: "不管是在国家做官还是在大夫家做事都一定要有名望。" 孔子说: "这叫名望, 不是通达。所谓通达的人, 品质正直, 爱好礼仪, 善于察言观色, 对人礼让。这种人无论在国家做官或在大夫家做事都一定通达。至于你所说的有名望的人, 只不过表面上好讲仁德，而实际行动又违背仁德，就自以为是仁人了，这种人不管在国家做官还是在大夫家做事只不过是会骗取名望罢了。"

英文:

Zi Zhang asked, "What should an intellectual do to become knowledgeable?" Confucius asked, "What do you mean by 'knowledgeable'?" Zi Zhang answered, "I mean having a good reputation no matter whether one serves the court or a ruling family." Confucius said, "That is called being known, not being knowledgeable. In order to be knowledgeable, one must be frank and upright by nature, and be lover of the rites. One must carefully weigh up a person's words and closely watch his expression. He must give precedence to others out of courtesy. Such a person is sure to be knowledgeable no matter whether he serves the court or a ruling family. The known person you mentioned is one who only talks about benevolence but goes back on benevolence in practice. He considers himself benevolent. As a matter of fact, such a person wins his fame only through tricks whether he serves the court or a ruling family."

21. 樊遲從遊於舞雩之下，曰："敢問崇德、修慝、辨惑。"子曰："善哉問！先事後得，非崇德與？攻其惡，無攻人之惡，非修慝與？一朝之忿，忘其身，以及其親，非惑與？"

译文：

樊迟陪老师在祭天台下游玩，说："请问怎样提高品德，消除别人对自己的怨恨和辨别是非。"孔子说："问得好！工作争先，享受在后，不是提高品德了吗？凡事多作自我批评，不去指责别人，不就可以消除别人对自己的怨恨了吗？仅凭一时气愤，不考虑个人安危，甚至自己的父母，这不是糊涂吗？"

英文：

Fan Chi accompanied Confucius on an outing to the Rain Altar. Fan Chi asked, "May I know how to cultivate virtue, to clear up resentment, and to distinguish between right and wrong?" "What a good question! Is a man not cultivating virtue when he works first but gets rewards afterwards? Can a man not clear up resentment by criticising himself and not criticising others? Is not a man muddle-headed if he lets sudden anger make him forget his own safety and even the safety of his parents?"

22. 樊遲問仁，子曰："愛人。"問知，子曰："知人"。樊遲未達。子曰："舉直錯諸枉，能使枉者直。"樊遲退，見子夏，曰："鄉也，吾見於夫子而問知，子曰：'舉直錯諸枉，能使枉者直。'何謂也?"子夏曰:"富哉言乎! 舜有天下，選於眾，舉皋陶，不仁者遠矣。湯有天下，選於眾，舉伊尹，不仁者遠矣。"

译文:

樊迟问什么是仁，孔子说: "仁就是爱人。"樊迟又问什么是智，孔子说: "善于识别人就叫智。"见樊迟仍不理解，孔子又说: "选拔重用正直的人，邪恶的人就没有市场。"樊迟退出来找到子夏，说: "我刚才向老师请教什么是智，老师说: '选拔重用正直的人，邪恶的人就没有市场。'这是什么意思?"子夏说: "这话含意相当深刻，舜有天下，在众人中选用了皋陶，那些坏人只得远远避开了。汤有天下，在众人中选用了伊尹，那些坏人只得远远避开了。"

注:

皋陶: 传说舜时贤相。

伊尹: 商汤时贤相，曾辅佐汤灭夏兴商。

英文:

Fan Chi asked what benevolence was. Confucius answered, "To be benevolent is to love." Again Fan Chi asked what wisdom was. Confucius answered, "To know others well is to be wise." Seeing that Fan Chi was unable to understand, Confucius added, "To put those who are straight and upright in important positions makes the wicked become straight and upright." Fan Chi left and went to see Zi Xia. He told Zi Xia, "Just now I asked the Master about wisdom. He said, 'To put those who are straight and upright in important positions makes the wicked become straight and upright.' What did he mean?" Zi Xia answered, "He meant a lot! When Shun was ruling his empire, he chose Gao Yao from the multitude. By so doing, he kept the wicked at bay; when Tang was ruling his empire, he chose Yi Yin from the multitude. By so doing, he kept the wicked at bay."

23. 子貢問友，子曰："忠告而善道之，不可則止，毋自辱焉。"

译文:

子贡问如何对待朋友，孔子说："对朋友要诚恳劝告和引导，如不听从也就作罢，不必自讨没趣。"

英文:

Zi Gong asked how to treat friends. Confucius said, "Advise earnestly and guide properly, stop doing so if they don't follow. Do not get vexed."

24. 曾子曰："君子以文會友，以友輔仁。"

译文:

曾子说:"君子用文章学问聚会朋友,藉朋友帮助培养仁德。"

英文:

Zeng Zi said, "A gentleman makes friends through his learning and cultivates virtue and benevolence through those friends."

子路篇第十三

1. 子路問政，子曰："先之勞之。"請益，曰："無倦。"

译文:

子路请教管理政事，孔子说："自己以身作则带领百姓工作。"子路请再讲一些，孔子说："办事不要懈怠。"

英文:

Zi Lu asked about government. Confucius said, "Urge the common people to work hard by setting an example yourself." Zi Lu requested for more advice. Confucius said, "Do not slack on your duties."

2. 仲弓爲季氏宰，問政，子曰："先有司，赦小過，舉賢才。"曰："焉知賢才而舉之?"子曰："舉爾所知，爾所不知，人其舍諸?"

译文:

仲弓做了鲁国大夫季氏的家臣，向老师请教如何管理政事，孔子说："凡事带头去做，不计较别人的小过失，提拔优秀的人才。"仲弓问："怎样识别优秀人才呢?"孔子说："提拔你所了解的；你不了解的人，难道别人不会提拔吗?"

While serving as a steward of the Jisun's Family (who were high officials in Lu), Zhong Gong asked how to govern. Confucius said, "Set an example for others to follow, be lenient to minor mistakes, and promote men of talent." Zhong Gong went on asking, "How to distinguish men of talent?" Confucius said, "Promote those you know well. Will others then fail to promote those you do not know well?"

3. 子路曰:"衛君待子而爲政,子將奚先?"子曰:"必也正名乎!"子路曰:"有是哉,子之迂也!奚其正?"子曰:"野哉,由也!君子於其所不知,蓋闕如也。名不正則言不順,言不順則事不成,事不成則禮樂不興,禮樂不興則刑罰不中,刑罰不中則民無所錯手足。故君子名之必可言也,言之必可行也。君子於其言,無所苟而已矣。"

译文:

子路说:"卫国国君等您去治理政事,您打算首先干什么事?"孔子说:"先正名分!"子路说:"您竟迂腐到这种地步!何必一定要正名分呢?"孔子说:"你真不懂事!君子对自己不懂的事,是不乱说的。名分不正,说话就不能顺理成章；不能顺理成章，事情就办不成；事情办不成，礼乐就不能兴起；礼乐不兴，刑罚就不能得当；刑罚不当，老百姓就无所适从。所以，治理政事者必须言出合于礼，能够实行，而不能随随便便。"

注：

卫君：卫国国君。当时卫国经过父子争夺君位，搞乱了"君、臣、父、子"的名分，所以孔子提出要先正名。

英文：

Zi Lu said, "The King of Wei is waiting for you to go to administrate his country. What are you going to do first?" Confucius said, "To rectify names." Zi Lu said, "Why be so pedantic? Why should there be a need to rectify names?" Confucius said, "You don't understand! A gentleman will never be in a haste to present his opinions as to what he does not understand. If names are not rectified, what is said will not sound reasonable; if what is said does not sound reasonable, efforts cannot culminate in success; if efforts cannot culminate in success, the rites and music will not thrive; if the rites and music do not thrive, crimes cannot be punished properly; if crimes are not punished properly, the common people will have nothing to go by. Therefore, whatever a ruler says must be in accordance with the rites. He must be practical, and never be casual."

Note: There was a royal family of struggle for power going on in the Wei. In the course of the struggle, the distinctions between father and son, ruler and minister had been lost. So Confucius advocated that the first measure to be taken should be the rectification of names.

4. 樊遲請學稼，子曰："吾不如老農。"請學爲圃，曰："吾不如老圃。"樊遲出。子曰："小人哉，樊須也！"上好禮，則民莫敢不敬；上好義，則民莫敢不服；上好信，則民莫敢不用情。夫如是，則四方之民襁負其子而至矣，焉用稼？"

译文：

樊迟向老师请教怎样种庄稼，孔子说："我不如老农。"又请教种菜，孔子说："我不如菜农。"樊迟退出后，孔子说："樊迟真是小人见识！治人者讲究礼节，老百姓就不敢不尊敬；治人者行为端正，老百姓就不敢不服从；治人者讲信用，老百姓就不敢讲假话。能做到这样的话，四方百姓就会携子女来归附，用得着自己种庄稼吗？"

英文：

Fan Chi asked Confucius about how to grow crops. Confucius answered, "I am not as good as a peasant." Then Fan Chi asked about how to grow vegetables.

Confucius said, "I am not as good as a gardener." After Fan Chi left, Confucius said, "How narrow-minded Fan Chi is! When rulers observe the rites, the common people will not dare to show disrespect; when rulers act properly, the common people will not dare to show disobedience; when rulers keep their promises, the common people will not dare to tell lies. If they are able to do this, people from all directions will come to submit themselves to the authority of such rulers. What need is there for a ruler to grow crops himself?"

5. 子曰:"誦《詩》三百, 授之以政, 不達; 使於四方, 不能專對; 雖多, 亦奚以爲?"

译文:

孔子说:"熟读了《诗经》三百篇的人, 处理政务, 却行不通; 出使外国, 又不能随机应变, 独立行事。这种人读书虽多, 又有什么用呢?"

英文:

Confucius said, "If a man knows the three hundred poems of *The Book of Songs*, but fails when given administrative responsibilities; and if he fails to act according to circumstances and to deal with affairs independently when sent on diplomatic missions, what is the use of so much learning?"

6. 子曰："其身正，不令而行；其身不正，雖令不從。"

译文:

孔子说："执政者行为端正，不发命令老百姓也会跟着走；执政者行为不端正，纵三令五申老百姓也不会听从。"

英文:

Confucius said, "If the ruler acts properly, the common people will obey him without being ordered to; if the ruler does not act properly, the common people will not obey him even after repeated injunctions."

7. 子曰："鲁、衞之政，兄弟也。"

译文:

孔子说："鲁国和卫国的政治差不多。"

注:

鲁国是周公旦封地，卫国是康叔封地，周公旦和康叔是兄弟。当时，鲁国和卫国相处和睦如兄弟。所以孔子的话有双重意思。

英文:

Confucius said, "In terms of government, the State of Lu and the State of Wei are brothers."

Note: The State of Lu was the fief of Ji Dan, the Duke of Zhou, while the State of Wei was that of Kangshu, Ji Dan's brother. At that time, Lu and Wei were on brotherly terms and were governed in a similar fashion. Thus what Confucius said carries the double mearing.

8. 子謂衛公子荊: "善居室。始有，曰:'苟合矣。'少有，曰:'苟完矣。'富有，曰:'苟美矣。'"

译文:

孔子谈到卫国公子荆时说: "他对居住房舍的要求以节俭为美德，开始居室很简陋，他说:'差不多已经够用了'。后来增加一点，他说:'这已经很完备了。'房舍建得大一些，他就说:'这就太富丽堂皇了。'"

注:

公子荆: 卫国大夫，字南楚，卫献公的儿子。当时的卿大夫，不但贪污成风，而且奢侈成风，所以孔子很称赞公子荆的廉洁节俭的行为。

英文:

Confucius talked about Duke Jing of Wei, saying,

"He takes frugality as a merit with regard to a house to live in. When he first had a house, he said, 'It is more or less big enough!' Then a little more space was added to it, and he said, ' It already has everything.' When the house was further extended, he said, 'It is too sumptuous!'"

Note: Duke Jing of Wei was a senior official of Wei. Among the ministers and other senior officials, embezzlement and extravagance were common practices. Therefore Confucius appreciated very much Prince Jing's simple and frugal life style.

9. 子适卫，冉有仆。子曰：“庶矣哉！”冉有曰：“既庶矣，又何加焉？”曰：“富之”。曰：“既富矣，又何加焉？”曰：“教之。”

译文：

孔子到卫国去，冉有给他赶车。孔子说：“卫国的人口真多呀！”冉有说：“人口已经多了，怎么办？”孔子说：“使他们富足起来。”冉有又问：“富足之后又该怎么办？”孔子说：“教育他们。”

注：

孔子主张先使民富裕然后教育，故有此话。

英文：

When Confucius went to the State of Wei, Ran You

drove the carriage for him. Confucius said, "What a large population Wei has!" Ran You asked, " What should be done with such a large population?" Confucius answered, "Enrich the people." Ran You went on asking. "What should be done when they have become rich?" Confucius answered, "Educate them!"

10. 子曰: "苟有用我者，期月而已可也，三年有成。"

译文:

孔子说: "如果让我治理国家，一年就差不多了，三年之后能大见成效。"

英文:

Confucius said, "If I were given the opportunity, it would only take me a single year to administrate a country well; and remarkable achievements could be made in three years."

11. 子曰: "'善人爲邦百年，亦可以勝殘去殺矣。'誠哉是言也!"

译文:

孔子说: "有人说: '善良的人治理国家连续百年，就可以克服残暴免除虐杀了。'这话说得很对。"

英文:

Confucius said, "It has been said, 'Cruelty and killing would be no more if good people were to govern a country for a hundred successive years.' How true that is!"

12. 子曰: "如有王者，必世而後仁。"

译文:

孔子说: "既使有圣明君主兴起，也要经过三十年之后才能实现仁政。"

英文:

Confucius said, "Even with the rise of a sagacious ruler, it will still take him thirty years to realise benevolent government."

13. 子曰: "苟正其身矣，於從政乎何有? 不能正其身，如正人何?"

孔子说:"执政者如果自己端正,治理国家还有什么困难? 如果自身不端正,又怎能匡正别人?"

英文:

Confucius said, "Why should a ruler have any difficulty in administrating his country if he himself is upright? How could a ruler correct others if he himself is not upright?"

14. 冉子退朝,子曰:"何晏也?"對曰:"有政。"子曰:"其事也。如有政,雖不吾以,吾其與聞之。"

译文:

冉有从办公的地方回来,孔子说:"怎么回来这么晚?"冉有回答说:"有政务。"孔子说:"那是事务,不能说政务。如果有政务,虽然不用我了,我也会知道的。"

注:

冉子:冉有,孔子的学生。当时任鲁国大夫季氏家臣。此章是孔子指出冉有把事务说成政务,用词不当。

英文:

Ran You came back from court. Confucius asked, "Why so late?" Ran You answered, "There were government affairs." Confucius said, "They weren't government affairs, they were actually routine affairs. If there were government affairs, I would be informed even if I were not involved."

Note: Ran You was retainer of the Jisun's Family of Lu. In this chapter. Confucius points out the improper use of words.

15. 定公問: "一言而可以興邦,' 有諸?"孔子對曰: "言不可以若是其幾也。人之言曰: '爲君難, 爲臣不易。'如知爲君之難也, 不幾乎一言而興邦乎?"曰: "一言而喪邦, 有諸?"孔子對曰: "言不可以若是其幾也。人之言曰: '予無樂乎爲君, 唯其言而莫予違也。'如其善而莫之違也, 不亦善乎? 如不善而莫之違也, 不幾乎一言而喪邦乎?"

译文:
鲁定公问: "一句话可以使国家兴旺, 有这事吗?"孔子说: "话不能这样简单机械的理解。有人说: '做君主难, 做臣子不容易'。如果知道艰难而君臣兢兢业业地工作, 这不近于一句话就使国家兴旺了吗?"鲁定公又问: "一句话可以使国家丧亡, 有这事吗?"孔子回答说: "话也不能这样说。有人说: '我做君主唯一高兴的是没人敢违抗我的话。'如果你说的话正确, 没人违抗是对的, 但如果你说的话是错的, 而没有人敢违抗, 这不也近于一句话可以使国家丧亡了吗?"

定公: 名宋, 鲁国国君。

英文:

Duke Ding of Lu asked, "Is it true that one saying can make a country flourish?" Confucius answered, "It cannot be understood in such a simple way. Some say, 'To be a ruler is difficult, and to be a minister is not easy, either.' If the ruler and the minister understand the difficulty and work conscientiously, is it not true that a saying can make a country flourish?"

Again, Duke Ding asked, "Is it true that one saying can ruin a country?" Confucius replied, "It is hard to say. Someone once said 'The only thing that pleases me is that nobody disobeys what I say.' If what he says is correct, and nobody disobeys him, that is good; if what he says is not correct, and still nobody disobeys him, is it not true that a saying can ruin a country?"

16. 葉公問政, 子曰: "近者説, 遠者來。"

译文:

叶公向孔子请教管理政事, 孔子说: "使您管区内的百姓高兴, 管区外的人纷纷来投奔您。"

注:

叶公: 姓沈, 名诸梁, 楚国大夫。

英文:

Duke She asked about government. Confucius said, "If people under your reign are happy, people will be attracted to come from afar ."

17. 子夏爲莒父宰, 問政。子曰:"無欲速, 無見小利。欲速則不達, 見小利則大事不成。"

译文:

子夏做了莒父县县长, 向孔子请教如何管理政事, 孔子说:"做事不要图快, 不要贪图小利。图快反而达不到目的, 贪图小利就办不成大事。"

英文:

When Zi Xia became county magistrate of Jufu County, he asked Confucius about government. Confucius said, "Do not make haste, do not covet small gains. If you make haste, you cannot reach your goal; if you covet small gains, your efforts will not culminate in great achievements."

18. 葉公語孔子曰:"吾黨有直躬者, 其父攘羊而子證之。"孔子曰："吾黨之直者異於是：父爲子隱，子爲父隱，直在其中矣。"

译文:

叶公对孔子说："我家乡有个正直的人，他父亲偷了人家的羊他亲自去告发。"孔子说："我家乡正直的人与此不同：父亲为儿子隐瞒，儿子为父亲隐瞒，正直就表现在这里面。"

注:

孔子的伦理哲学基础是父慈、子孝，所以有此议论。

英文:

Duke She said to Confucius, "In my hometown, there is a straight and upright man. When his father stole a sheep, that man accused his father of theft." Confucius said. "The straight and upright men in my hometown are of a quite different type: the father will conceal the son's mistake, and the son will conceal the father's too. This is an expression of straightness and uprightness."

Note: Confucius' philosophy of ethics is based on the principle of paternal love and filial piety.

19. 樊遲問仁，子曰："居處恭，執事敬，與人忠。雖之夷狄，不可棄也。"

译文:

樊迟问什么是仁,孔子说:"侍父母态度恭敬,办事情严肃认真,对朋友忠诚老实。这三种品德到什么地方都不能背弃。"

英文:

Fan Chi asked about benevolence. Confucius said, "Be respectful to parents, be conscientious in official affairs. Be loyal and honest to friends. These three moral principles can never be defied anywhere."

20. 子貢問曰:"何如斯可謂之士矣?"子曰:"行己有耻,使於四方不辱君命,可謂士矣。"曰:"敢問其次?"曰:"宗族稱孝焉,鄉黨稱弟焉。"曰:"敢問其次?"曰:"言必信,行必果,硜硜然小人哉!抑亦可以爲次矣。"曰:"今之從政者何如?"子曰:"噫!斗筲之人,何足算也!"

译文:

子贡问孔子:"什么样的人可以称士?"孔子说:"常怀羞愧之心来约束自己的行为,出使外国能不辜负君主的委托,这样的人可以称为士。"子贡问:"比这差一等的呢?"孔子说:"宗族中称赞他孝顺父母,乡里人称赞他恭敬尊长。"子贡又问:"请问比这再差一等的呢?"孔子说:"说话诚信,办事果断,虽然这些人不分是非黑白,只知贯彻执行,是些浅薄固执的小人,不过也可以算作最下等的士了。"子贡说:"您看现在,那些执政者怎样?"孔子说:"这帮器量狭小的人,又能算得什么呢?"

英文:

Zi Gong asked Confucius, "What man can be called a *Shi* (educated man)?" Confucius answered, "A man who restrains himself with a good sense of shame and who always lives up to the ruler's expectations when he is sent on diplomatic missions can be called a *Shi*." Zi Gong went on asking, "What about the grade below?" Confucius answered," Someone who is praised for being filial to his parents in his clan, and for being respectful to the elders in the neighbourhood. "Zi Gong asked again, "What about the next?" Confucius said, "One who keeps his promises and acts resolutely. Even though he is unable to distinguish between right and wrong, and he is such a stubborn and shallow petty person that he acts as he is told to, he can be called a *Shi* of the lowest grade." Zi Gong asked then, "What do you think about today's rulers?" Confucius said, "Oh, they are so narrow-minded that they count for very little."

21. 子曰:"不得中行而與之,必也狂狷乎! 狂者進取,狷者有所不爲也。"

译文:

孔子说:"如果没有能循规蹈矩的人为友,却宁愿和行为激进性格耿直的人交往。行为激进的人勇于进取,性格耿直的人不肯做坏事。"

英文:

Confucius said, "If one is unable to make friends with those who conform to conventions, one had better associate with those who are progressive and straight. Those who are progressive keep forging ahead, those who are straight are never willing to do any evil deeds."

22. 子曰:"南人有言曰:'人而無恒,不可以作巫醫。'善夫!'不恒其德,或承之羞!'"子曰:"不占而已矣。"

译文:

孔子说:"南方人有句话:'人无恒心,不能当巫医。'这话是不错的。《易经》上也说:'三心二意的人,难免会受羞辱。'这些话的意思都是说无恒心的人,什么事也做不成。"

注:

巫医:中国古代以卜筮治病的人。

Confucius said, "There is a saying among southerners: 'Without constancy, one cannot become a healer.' This is quite true! *The Book of Changes* says, ' If one does not show constancy in one's virtue, one will, perhaps, suffer shame.' All these sayings tell us that a man without constancy accomplishes nothing."

23. 子曰："君子和而不同，小人同而不和。"

译文：

孔子说："君子讲有原则的团结而不盲从附和，小人只是盲从附和而不讲原则。"

英文：

Confucius said, "A gentleman unites with people of principle and never follows others blindly. A petty man follows others blindly without regard to principle."

24. 子貢問曰："鄉人皆好之，何如？"子曰："未可也。""鄉人皆惡之，何如？"子曰："未可也。不如鄉人之善者好之，其不善者惡之。"

译文：

子贡问："全乡人都喜欢他，这个人怎么样？"孔子说:"难说。"子贡又问:"要是全乡人都厌恶他,这个人怎么样?"孔子说:"也难说。最好是全乡的好人都喜欢他,全乡的坏人都厌恶他,这才是好人。"

英文:

Zi Gong asked, "What do you think of a person who is liked by everyone in the village?" Confucius said, "It is difficult to say." Zi Gong then asked, "What if everyone in the village hates him?" Confucius said, "That is also difficult to say. Only if all the good people in the village like him and all the bad people in the village hate him can he be called a virtuous man."

25. 子曰:"君子易事而難説也。説之不以道,不説也。及其使人也,器之。小人難事而易説也。説之雖不以道,説也。及其使人也,求備焉。"

译文:

孔子说:"在君子手下工作容易而要讨他喜欢却很难。如果用不正当的手段讨他喜欢,他是不会喜欢的。他使用人是根据各人的才德合理使用。相反,在小人手下工作很难而要讨他喜欢却很容易。即使用不正当的手段讨他喜欢,他也会喜欢的。而他使用人却要求全责备。"

英文:

Confucius said, "It is easy to work under a gentleman, but it is not easy to please him. He dislikes anyone who tries to please him by unscrupulous means. He appreciates talent and chooses people for different jobs according to their talent. On the contrary, it is not easy to work under a petty man, but it is easy to please him. He likes anyone who tries to please him by unscrupulous means. When he chooses people for jobs, he is over demanding."

26. 子曰:"君子泰而不骄,小人骄而不泰。"

译文:

孔子说:"君子心情平和而不傲慢,小人傲慢而心情不平和。"

英文:

Confucius said, "A gentleman always keeps even-tempered without being arrogant while a petty man is arrogant without being even-tempered."

27. 子曰:"刚、毅、木、讷,近仁。"

译文:

孔子说:"刚强、果断、质朴、言语谨慎,具有这四种品德的人差不多就是仁人了。"

英文:

Confucius said, "The four qualities of unyieldingness, resoluteness, modesty, and cautiousness in speech can make a person almost benevolent."

28. 子路問曰:"何如斯可謂之士矣?"子曰:"切切偲偲,怡怡如也,可謂士矣。朋友切切偲偲,兄弟怡怡。"

译文:

子路问:"怎样才可以称做士呢?"孔子说:"互相勉励,和睦相处,可以称作士了。朋友间互相勉励,兄弟间和睦相处。"

英文:

Zi Lu asked, "What should a man do before he can be called a gentleman?" Confucius answered, "Encouraging others and getting along well with others, one can be called an educated man. Friends should encourage each other; brothers should get along well with each other."

29. 子曰："善人教民七年，亦可以即戎矣。"

译文：

孔子说："经过善人七年训练，老百姓也可以参军作战。"

英文：

Confucius said," The common people will be ready to fight any battles after seven years' training by a good man."

30. 子曰："以不教民戰，是謂棄之。"

译文：

孔子说："让没有经过训练的人民去作战，这实际上是让人民去送死。"

英文：

Confucius said, "To send those who have no military training at all to the battle field is to send them to the grave yard."

憲問篇第十四

1. 憲問恥，子曰："邦有道，穀；邦無道，穀，恥也。""克、伐、怨、欲不行焉，可以爲仁矣？"子曰："可以爲難矣，仁則吾不知也。"

译文:

原宪问老师什么叫耻辱，孔子说："国家政治清明的时候，就可以安心做官领俸禄；如果在国家政治黑暗的时候，也去做官领俸禄，这就叫耻辱。"原宪又问："如果好胜、自夸、怨恨和贪欲这四种毛病都不曾表现过，是否可以说他已经做到仁了呢？"孔子说："恐怕只能说这已经难能可贵了。"

注:

宪: 姓原名宪，字子思，孔子的学生。

英文:

Yuan Xian asked what shameful was. Confucius said," Under wise and honest government, it is right that one takes office and lives on the salary at ease. But it is shameful that under dark and corrupt government, one still takes office and lives on the salary at ease." Again Yuan Xian asked, "Can a man be called benevolent who has never done others down, bragged about himself, had a grudge against others, or been covetous?" Confucius answered, "I am afraid what he has accomplished can only be said to be difficult and worthy of praise. But I do not know for sure whether or not he has become benevolent."

2. 子曰: "士而懷居，不足以爲士矣。"

译文:

孔子说: "如果留恋安逸的生活，就不配做士了。"

英文:

Confucius said, "It is not befitting to an educated man to indulge in an easy and comfortable life."

3. 子曰: "邦有道，危言危行; 邦無道，危行言孫。"

译文:

孔子说: "国家政治清明，说话正直，行为也正直; 国家政治黑暗，行为要正直，说话却要随和谨慎。"

英文:

Confucius said, "Under wise and honest government, speak and act in a straight and upright fashion; under dark and corrupt government, act in a straight and upright fashion but in speech be affable and cautious."

4. 子曰："有德者必有言，有言者不必有德。仁者必有勇，勇者不必有仁。"

译文：

孔子说："道德高尚的人一定有名言，但有名言的人不一定道德高尚。仁人一定勇敢，勇敢的人却不一定是仁人。"

英文：

Confucius said, "A virtuous man must have said something of note; but someone who has said something of note is not necessarily a man of virtue. A benevolent man is surely courageous, but a courageous man is not necessarily a man of benevolence."

5. 南宫适問於孔子曰："羿善射，奡盪舟，俱不得其死然。禹、稷躬稼而有天下。"夫子不答。南宫适出，子曰："君子哉若人！尚德哉若人！"

译文：

南宫适问孔子："羿擅长射箭，奡擅长水战，都不得善终。禹、稷亲自下田耕种而得到了天下。怎么解释这些历史呢?"孔子没有正面回答他,等他退出去以后,孔子才称赞说:"这是个崇尚道德的君子呀!"

注:

南宫适:姓南宫,名适,字子容,孔子的学生。

羿:传说是夏代有穷国君主,善射,曾夺夏太康的王位,后被其臣寒浞所杀。

奡:传说是寒浞之子,大力士,善水战,后被少康所杀。

禹:传说中的远古圣君,治水有功,重视农业。

稷:传说是周朝祖先,教民种植庄稼,被后世尊为谷神。

南宫适主张德治而反对暴力,所以向孔子提出羿、奡好勇而不得善终,禹、稷躬耕而有天下这样的问题,孔子才称赞他。

英文:

Nangong Kuo (a disciple of Confucius) asked Confucius, "Yi was good at archery, and Ao was good at water battle. Both came to an untimely end. Yu and Ji who planted crops in the fields themselves won the empire. How should we understand this?" Confucius did not answer. When Kuo had left, Confucius praised him, saying, "What a gentleman! How he upholds virtue!"

Note: Yi: In folk legend, he was the monarch of the State of You Qiong in the Xia Dynasty. He was good at archery, and took over the reign of Emperor Tai Kang by force. He was killed by his subject Han Zhuo.

Ao: In folk legend, he was the son of Han Zhuo, and had unusual strength. He was good at water battle. He was killed by Emperor Shao Kang.

Yu: In folk legend, he was a wise Emperor of ancient times. He made great achievements in water control, and laid great emphasis on agriculture.

Ji: The legendary ancestor of the Zhou Dynasty. He taught the people to grow crops, and was worshipped as the God of Grains.

Nangong Kuo advocated government by virtue, and opposed government by force. That is why Confucius praised Nangong Kuo.

6. 子曰: "君子而不仁者有矣夫, 未有小人而仁者也。"

译文:

孔子说: "君子之中有不仁的人, 小人之中却绝没有仁人。"

英文:

Confucius said, "It is true that some gentlemen are not benevolent, but it will never be true that a petty man is benevolent."

7. 子曰:"愛之，能勿勞乎? 忠焉，能勿誨乎?"

译文:

孔子说:"爱他，就不能让他贪图安逸。忠于他，就不能不对他进行教诲。"

英文:

Confucius said, "To love him means not to let him indulge in comfort; to be loyal to him means to teach him."

8. 子曰:"爲命，裨諶草創之，世叔討論之，行人子羽修飾之，東里子産潤色之。"

译文:

孔子说:"郑国政策法令的制定，通常由裨谌起草，世叔提出具体意见，再交给外交官子羽进行修改，最后由子产作文字上润色加工。由这四位贤大夫共同完成的文件，很少出差错。"

注:

裨谌: 郑国大夫。

世叔: 名游吉，郑国大夫。

子羽: 姓公孙，名挥，字子羽，郑国大夫。

子产: 姓公孙，名侨，字子产，郑国大夫。

Confucius said, "When it comes to formulating a document of law or decree in the State of Zheng, usually it is Pi Chen that would work out the draft; Shi Shu that would put forward specific suggestions; Zi Yu that would revise it; and finally, it is Zi Chan that would polish it. The documents worked out through the common efforts of the four wise senior officials seldom suffers flaws."

9. 或問子産，子曰："惠人也。"問子西，曰："彼哉！彼哉！"問管仲，曰："人也。奪伯氏駢邑三百，飯疏食，沒齒無怨言。"

译文:

有人问孔子子产这个人怎样，孔子说："这是一个宽厚仁慈的人。"问子西，孔子不肖正面回答。又问到管仲，孔子说："这是个人才，他剥夺了伯氏三百户封地，使他的生活很困难，但却至死不怨恨。"

注:

子产：郑国的大夫。

子西：即公孙夏，郑国大夫，子产的同宗兄弟。

管仲：名夷吾，齐桓公时宰相。

伯氏：齐国大夫。

Someone asked about Zi Chan. Confucius said, "He was generous and kind." Then the man asked about Zi Xi, but Confucius did not answer directly. The man then asked about Guan Zhong. Confucius said, "He was a genius. He took three hundred households from the fief of the Bo Family, which led to the deterioration of living standards in the Bo Family. However, Bo never complained right until his last day."

10. 子曰:"貧而無怨難, 富而無驕易。"

译文:

孔子说:"做到贫穷而无怨言很难, 做到富贵而不骄傲较容易。"

英文:

Confucius said, "It is difficult for one to make no complaints when poor; but it is easy for one to show no arrogance when rich."

11. 子曰:"孟公綽爲趙、魏老則優, 不可以爲滕、薛大夫。"

孔子说:"让孟公绰做晋国赵氏、魏氏的家臣,才力有馀,却不能胜任滕国、薛国这些小国的大夫之职。

注:

孟公绰:鲁国大夫,性寡欲,为孔子所尊敬。

赵、魏:晋国最有权势的大夫赵氏、魏氏。

滕、薛:鲁国附近的两个小国。

英文:

Confucius said, "Meng Gongchuo (a senior official of Lu) is adequate to be a steward of the Zhao and Wei families but is not adequate to be a minister of such small states as Teng and Xue."

12. 子路問成人,子曰:"若臧武仲之知,公綽之不欲,卞莊子之勇,冉求之藝,文之以禮樂,亦可以爲成人矣。"曰:"今之成人者何必然? 見利思義,見危授命,久要不忘平生之言,亦可以爲成人矣。"

译文:

子路问怎样才算一个完美无缺的人,孔子说:"智慧像臧武仲那样,清心寡欲如孟公绰,勇敢像卞莊子,多才多艺像冉求,再用礼乐制度约束自己的行为,就可以算是一个完善无缺的人了。"又说:"现在的所谓完人并非如此,能够不取不义之财,危急时不惜生命和安贫乐道，也就可以算作完善的人了。"

注：

    臧武仲：鲁国大夫。在齐国时，因能预料齐庄公被杀而设法辞去庄公给他的封田，因而不受牵连，人们认为他智慧过人。

    公绰：即孟公绰，鲁国大夫。以性寡欲有名。

    卞庄子：鲁国大夫，以勇敢著称。

    冉求：孔子的学生，以多才多艺受孔子赞赏。

英文：

    Zi Lu asked what one had to do to be a perfect man. Confucius said, "A perfect man should be as wise as Zang Wuzhong, as ascetic as Meng Gongchuo, as brave as Bian Zhuangzi, as talented as Ran You, and he should keep himself within the bounds of the rites and music." Then he went on, "What is called a perfect man nowadays does not have to do all this. If he can resist the temptation of ill—gotten profits, if he is ready to sacrifice his life in face of danger, if he still feels at ease when poor, he may be said to be a perfect man."

    Note: Zang Wuzhong was a senior official of Lu. When in the State of Qi, he managed to decline the fief of Duke Zhuang of Qi because he predicted that the Duke would be killed before long. Thus he kept himself out of trouble, and gained a reputation of great wisdom.

    Gongchuo, also known as Meng Gongchou, was a

senior official of Lu, respected by Confucius for his ascetic way of life.

Bian Zhuangzi, a senior official of Lu, was famous for his bravery.

Ran Qiu: Confucius' disciple, was famous for his talents.

13. 子問公叔文子於公明賈曰: "信乎! 夫子不言, 不笑, 不取乎?" 公明賈對曰: "以告者過也。夫子時然後言, 人不厭其言; 樂然後笑, 人不厭其笑; 義然後取, 人不厭其取。" 子曰: "其然? 豈其然乎?"

译文:

孔子向公明贾问公叔文子, 说: "听说这老先生不说, 不笑, 不取, 这是真的吗?" 公明贾回答说: "这是传话的人传错了。他老人家只是该说的时候才说, 该笑的时候才笑, 该取的时候才取, 所以别人都不讨厌他。" 孔子说: "原来如此, 真是这样吗?

注:

公叔文子: 卫国大夫, 卫献公之孙。

公明贾: 姓公明, 名贾, 公叔文子的使臣。

英文:

Confucius asked Gongming Jia about Gongshu Wenzi (the former was a steward of the latter and the latter was a minister of Wei), saying, "Is it true that that old gentleman never speaks, never laughs, and never takes anything?" Gongming Jia answered, "Whoever told you that has passed the message on wrong. My old Master speaks only when it is necessary for him to; he laughs only when he feels happy; he takes only when he should take his right share. Therefore, people never grow tired of him." Confucius said, "Is it true? I wonder if your explanation is true."

14. 子曰："臧武仲以防求爲後於魯，雖曰不要君，吾不信也。"

译文:

孔子说："臧武仲凭借自己的封地要求鲁君立自己后代为鲁国卿大夫，有人说这不是要挟君主，我不相信。"

英文:

Confucius said, "Zang Wuzhong used his fief to coerce the Duke of Lu into letting his successors take his position. Someone said it was not coercion. I do not believe it."

15. 子曰："晉文公譎而不正，齊桓公正而不譎。"

译文:

孔子说:"晋文公诡诈而不正派,齐桓公正派而不诡诈。"

注:

晋文公: 姓姬,名重耳,晋国国君。春秋霸主之一,因曾召周天子而使诸侯朝之,故孔子认为他"谲而不正"。

齐桓公: 姓姜,名小白,齐国国君。春秋霸主之一,曾以周天子名义讨伐不向周入贡的楚国,故孔子称他"正而不谲。"

英文:

Confucius said, "Duke Wen of Jin was not upright but crafty while Duke Huan of Qi was not crafty but upright."

Note: Duke Wen of the Jin: the ruler of the State of Jin, and one of the powerful chiefs of the Spring and Autumn Period. He made the other dukes worship the King of Zhou. That is why Confucius thought he was not upright but crafty.

Duke Huan of Qi: the ruler of Qi, another powerful chief of the Spring and Autumn Period. In the name of the King of Zhou, he sent a punitive expedition against the State of Chu, for it refused to pay tribute to the Zhou Kingdom. That is why Confucius said that he was not crafty but upright.

16. 子路曰："桓公殺公子糾，召忽死之，管仲不死。"曰："未仁乎？"子曰："桓公九合諸侯，不以兵車，管仲之力也。如其仁，如其仁。"

译文：

子路说："齐桓公杀了他的哥哥公子纠，召忽自杀以殉，而管仲也是公子纠的家臣，却不跟着死，反而归附桓公，这能算是仁人吗？"孔子说："齐桓公多次主持天下诸侯会盟，避免了战争，这都是管仲的力量，他当然是仁人了。"

注：

召忽：公子纠家臣，和管仲一起辅佐公子纠争夺君位，公子纠被杀后，他也自杀。

管仲：公子纠家臣，和召忽一起辅佐公子纠争夺君位，公子纠被杀后，他归附齐桓公。

英文：

Zi Lu said, "Duke Huan of Qi killed his elder brother, Prince Jiu. Zhao Hu committed suicide as a sacrifice. Guan Zhong was also Prince Jiu's retainer, but he did not sacrifice his life for his lord. On the contrary he went to serve Duke Huan. Should he be said to be benevolent?" Confucius said, "Duke Huan held a number of meetings of all the dukes, which prevented war among the states. All these should be attributed to Guan

Zhong's efforts. He should of course be called a benevolent man."

Note : Zhao Hu: one of Prince Jiu's retainers. Together with Guan Zhong he helped Prince Jiu to seize the throne. When Prince Jiu was killed, Zhao Hu committed suicide.

Guan Zhong: another retainer of Prince Jiu, who helped Prince Jiu to seize the throne. When Prince Jiu was killed, Guan Zhong submitted to Duke Huan of Qi.

17. 子貢曰："管仲非仁者與? 桓公殺公子糾, 不能死, 又相之。"子曰："管仲相桓公, 霸諸侯, 一匡天下, 民到于今受其賜。微管仲, 吾其被髮左衽矣。豈若匹夫匹婦之爲諒也, 自經於溝瀆而莫之知也?

译文：

子贡说："管仲不能算仁人吧? 齐桓公杀了公子纠, 而他做为公子纠的家臣, 不但不自杀殉主, 反而去辅佐齐桓公。"孔子说："管仲辅佐齐桓公, 称霸诸侯, 匡正天下, 人民到今天还受到他的好处。假如没有管仲, 我们恐怕早已沦为落后民族, 披散着头发, 衣襟向左边开。难道一定要他像普通百姓那样为着小节小信而自杀在山沟里没有人知道吗?"

注：
被发左衽: 披散着头发, 衣襟左开。是当时少数民族装束。

Zi Gong said, "Should Guan Zhong be said to be benevolent? When Duke Huan of Qi killed Prince Jiu, Guan Zhong, one of Prince Jiu's retainers, became a retainer to Duke Huan of Qi instead of sacrificing his life for his lord." Confucius said, "That is true. Guan Zhong assisted Duke Huan in gaining dominance over the other dukes, and in consolidating all the states under heaven. Today, we still enjoy the benefits he brought us. Without Guan Zhong, we would have been reduced to barbarians with our hair down and robes folded to the left (the dressing style of the minorities at that time). Why should he have followed the common people who would commit suicide and lie dead in the bleak mountain valley without being noticed?"

18. 公叔文子之臣大夫僎與文子同升諸公。子聞之，曰："可以爲'文'矣。"

译文:

公叔文子的家臣僎，由于文子的推荐，和文子一道做了卫国的大臣。孔子听说这件事后，说："他不愧谥为'文'了。"

公叔文子: 卫国大夫。谥号"文", 故称。"文"有顺理成章之意, 故孔子有此说。

傁: 原为公叔文子家臣, 由于公叔文子推荐, 做子卫国大夫。

英文:

On the recommendation of Wenzi, Xun, Wenzi's steward, was promoted to be a minister of the Wei as Wenzi was. Hearing about that, Confucius said, "Now he deserves the epithet *wen.*"

Note: *Wen* means having a grasp of the principles of government.

19. 子言衛靈公之無道也, 康子曰: "夫如是, 奚而不喪?"孔子曰: "仲叔圉治賓客, 祝鮀治宗廟, 王孫賈治軍旅。夫如是, 奚其喪?"

译文:

孔子谈到卫灵公的昏庸无道时, 季康子说: "既然如此, 为什么卫国没有败亡?"孔子说: "卫国有仲叔圉主持外交, 祝鮀主管祭祀, 王孙贾统率军队, 像这样, 怎么会败亡?"

注:

卫灵公: 卫国国君。

康子：季康子，鲁国大夫。

仲叔圉：即孔文子，他和祝鮀、王孙贾都是卫国大夫。

英文：

When Confucius talked about the benightedness of Duke Ling of Wei, Ji Kangzi asked, "That being the case, why did the State of Wei not collapse?" Confucius said, "The State of Wei had Zhong Shuyu in charge of foreign relations, Zhu Tuo in charge of ancestral sacrifice, Wangsun Jia in charge of military forces. That being the case, how could the State of Wei have collapsed?"

20. 子曰："其言之不怍，则为之也难。"

译文：

孔子说："说起来大言不惭，做起来就不容易了。"

英文：

Confucius said, "It is difficult to keep a promise one has made in boast."

21. 陈成子弑简公。孔子沐浴而朝，告於哀公曰："陈恒弑其君，请讨之。"公曰："告夫三子。"孔子曰："以吾從大夫之後，不敢不告也。君曰：'告夫三子'者！"之三子告，不可。孔子曰："以吾從大夫之後，不敢不告也。”

译文:

　　齐国大夫陈恒杀了齐简公。孔子沐浴斋戒后朝见鲁哀公，说:“陈恒杀了他的君主，请你出兵讨伐他。”哀公说:“你去向季孙、仲孙、孟孙三位大夫报告吧。”孔子退朝后说:“因为我曾经做过大夫，不敢不来向君主报告这件事，君主却让我去报告三位大夫。”

　　孔子又去报告三位大夫，果然不肯出兵。孔子说:“因为我曾经做过大夫，所以不敢不来报告。”

注:

　　陈成子: 即陈恒，齐国大夫。

　　简公: 姓姜，名壬，齐国国君。

　　三子: 指鲁国最有权势的三家大夫，即季孙、仲孙、孟孙。当时他们把持了鲁国大权。

英文:

　　Chen Heng, a senior official of Qi, killed Duke Jian of Qi. Having taken a ceremonial bath and gone on fast, Confucius presented himself to Duke Ai of Lu, saying, "Chen Heng killed his lord. Please send a punitive expedition against him." Duke Ai said, "You go and report to Jisun, Zhongsun, and Mengsun." After quitting court, Confucius said, "I once was a senior official. So I did not dare not to report the case to the lord. But the lord asked me to tell the three senior officials." So, Confucius reported the request to the three senior officials. Just as Confucius had expected, the three senior officials refused to take any action. Confucius said, "Just because I was once a senior official, I had to report the case."

22. 子路問事君，子曰："勿欺也，而犯之。"

译文：

子路问怎样事奉君主，孔子回答说："不可阳奉阴违，可以当面规劝。"

英文：

Zi Lu asked about how to serve a lord. Confucius answered, "Do not feign compliance but advise him with honesty."

23. 子曰："君子上達，小人下達。"

译文：

孔子说："君子通达于仁义，小人通达于财利。"

英文：

Confucius said, "The gentleman achieves benevolence while the petty man achieves material gains."

24. 子曰:"古之學者爲己,今之學者爲人。"

译文:

孔子说:"古人学习为了**充实提高自己**的学问道德,现在的人学习是为了**装饰自己给别人看**。"

英文:

Confucius said, "People in ancient times studied to enrich their knowledge and improve themselves; people today study to decorate themselves and impress others."

25. 蘧伯玉使人於孔子,孔子與之坐而問焉,曰:"夫子何爲?"對曰:"夫子欲寡其過而未能也。"使者出,子曰:"使乎! 使乎!"

译文:

卫国大夫蘧伯玉派一位使者去拜访孔子,孔子让坐后问:"大夫在家做什么呢?"使者回答说:"他老人家总想少犯过错而还没有做到。"使者出去后,孔子连说:"这是一位好使者! 这是一位好使者!"

注:

蘧伯玉:名瑗,卫国大夫。

Qu Boyu (a senior official of Lu) sent a messenger to Confucius. Having made him take a seat, Confucius asked, "What does your lord do at home?" The messenger answered, "My lord always tries to reduce errors, but he has not been able to do that." When the messenger left, Confucius said, "What a good messenger! What a good messenger!"

26. 子曰:"不在其位，不謀其政。"曾子曰:"君子思不出其位。"

译文:

孔子说:"不在那个职位，就不谋划那方面的政事。"曾子说:"这就是说君子思考问题不超出他的职务范围。"

英文:

Confucius said, "Do not get involved in the government affairs that are not your responsibility." Zengzi explained, "That is to say that a genlteman never gives any thought to the affairs beyond his office."

27. 子曰:"君子耻其言而過其行。"

译文:

孔子说:"君子以说得多,做得少为耻辱。"

英文:

Confucius said, "A gentleman takes it as a disgrace to let his words outstrip his deeds."

28. 子曰:"君子道者三,我無能焉:仁者不憂,知者不惑,勇者不懼。"子貢曰:"夫子自道也。"

译文:

孔子说:"君子所行的三件事,我一件也没有做到:仁德的人不忧愁,智慧的人不迷惑,勇敢的人不畏惧。"子贡说:"这正是老师的自我表述。"

英文:

Confucius said, "I fail to do any of the following three things that a gentleman should do: a man of benevolence never worries; a man of wisdom never gets confused; a man of courage never fears." Zi Gong commented, "That is just the Master's self-image."

29. 子貢方人,子曰:"賜也賢乎哉? 夫我則不暇。"

子贡讥评别人的短处，孔子说: "你端木赐就那么好吗? 我就没有闲功夫议人短长。"

注:

赐: 端木赐，即子贡。

英文:

Zi Gong sneered at others' shortcomings. Confucius said, "Are you, Duanmu Ci, that perfect? I personally do not have any time for such gossip."

30. 子曰: "不患人之不己知，患其不能也。"

译文:

孔子说: "不怕别人不了解自己，就怕自己没有真才实学。"

英文:

Confucius said, "Do not worry that your abilities are not appreciated. Just make sure that you possess them."

31. 子曰: "不逆詐，不億不信，抑亦先覺者，是賢乎!"

译文:

孔子说: "不凭空怀疑别人是否欺诈, 也不随意猜测别人是否讲信用, 这一切如能凭感觉发现, 才算贤者。"

英文:

Confucius said, "A man may be said to be virtuous if he never suspects groundlessly others' honesty and credit, but judges it all correctly by intuition."

32. 微生畝謂孔子曰: "丘何爲是栖栖者與? 無乃爲佞乎?" 孔子曰: "非敢爲佞也, 疾固也。"

译文:

微生亩对孔子说: "你为什么这样东奔西跑到处游说呢? 是否为了卖弄自己的才能呢?" 孔子说: "不敢卖弄自己的才能, 只是讨厌那些顽固不化的人。"

注:

微生亩: 姓微生, 名亩。

英文:

Weisheng Mu said to Confucius, "Why do you rush preaching all over the place? Are you showing off your talent?" Confucius said, "I am not so impertinent as to show off my talent. I just detest those with incorrigible obstinacy."

33. 子曰: "驥不稱其力，稱其德也。"

译文:

孔子说: "千里马值得称赞的不是它的气力，而是它的品德。"

英文:

Confucius said, "With regard to a horse that covers a thousand li a day, it is not its strength but its virtue that is worth praising."

34. 或曰: "以德報怨，何如?"子曰: "何以報德? 以直報怨，以德報德。"

译文:

有人对孔子说: "以恩德来报答怨恨，怎么样?"孔子说: "那以什么来报答恩德呢? 应该用公平正直来对待怨恨，以恩德来报答恩德。"

英文:

Someone asked Confucius, "What do you think of repaying resentment with virture?" Confucius said, "Then, what do you repay virtue with? Just repay resentment with fairness and justice, and repay virtue with virtue."

35. 子曰："莫我知也夫！"子貢曰："何爲其莫知子也?"子曰："不怨天，不尤人，下學而上達。知我者其天乎！"

译文:

孔子说："没有人能够了解我！"子贡说："为什么没有人了解您呢?"孔子说："不了解我，我也不怨天尤人，因为我是通过学习一些平常的知识而悟出了根本的道理。所以，大概只有天了解我吧！"

英文:

Confucius said, "Nobody is able to understand me." Zi Gong asked, "Why is there nobody who is able to understand you?" Confucius explained, "Though not understood, I still do not blame Heaven and the multitude. For I have understood quite a lot fundamental truth through studying ordinary knowledge. So, perhaps, only Heaven understands me!"

36. 公伯寮愬子路於季孫。子服景伯以告，曰："夫子固有惑志於公伯寮，吾力猶能肆諸市朝。"子曰："道之將行也與，命也；道之將廢也與，命也。公伯寮其如命何！"

公伯寮向季孙氏诽谤子路。子服景伯把这事告诉了孔子，并说："季孙氏已经相信了公伯寮的话，但我有力量将公伯寮置于死地。"孔子说："我的主张能否实行，完全由命运来决定。公伯寮能对命运怎样！"

注:

公伯寮：字子周，孔子的学生。

季孙：鲁国最有权势的大夫之一。

子服景伯：鲁国大夫。

英文:

Gongbo Liao spoke ill of Zi Lu before Jisun Shi. Zifu Jingbo told Confucius, saying, "Jisun Shi has believed what Gongbo Liao said, but I still have power to make Gongbo Liao ruined." Confucius said," Whether or not my propositions may be adopted and practised depends totally upon destiny. What can Gongbo Liao do in face of destiny?"

37. 子曰："賢者辟世，其次辟地，其次辟色，其次辟言。"子曰："作者七人矣。"

译文:

孔子说："有才德的人为躲避恶浊的社会现实而隐居

不出，差一等的也要择地而居，再差一等的则避免看某些人难看的脸色，或者避免听到某些难听的话。"孔子又说: "像这样的人已经有七位了。"

注:

作者七人: 指伯夷、叔齐、虞仲、夷逸、朱张、柳下惠、少连等。

英文:

Confucius said, "People of virtue live in seclusion in order to shun the foul secular world; those who come next choose a place to live in with care; those who come last shun unpleasant looks and words." Confucius went on, "There have already been seven such men."

Note: "Seven such men" refer to Bo Yi, Shu Qi, Yu Zhong, Yi Yi, Zhu Zhang, Liu Xiahui, and Shao Lian.

38. 子路宿於石門。晨門曰: "奚自?"子路曰: "自孔氏。"曰: "是知其不可而爲之者與?"

译文:

子路在石门住了一夜。第二天清早进城时，看城门的人问他: "从哪里来?"子路说: "从孔子那里来。"看门人说: "就是那个明明知道做不到却硬要去做的人吗?"

Zi Lu stayed for the night at Stone Gate. Early next morning when Zi Lu was to enter the city gate, the gatekeeper asked him, "Where have you come from?" Zi Lu answered, "From the Master Confucius." The gatekeeper said, "Is that Confucius who persists in working hard at what he has realised to be hopeless?"

39. 子擊磬於衛，有荷蕢而過孔氏之門者，曰："有心哉，擊磬乎!"既而曰："鄙哉；硜硜乎! 莫己知也，斯己而已矣。深則厲，淺則揭。"子曰："果哉! 末之難矣。"

译文:

孔子在卫国时，有一天正在敲磬演习礼仪，恰巧一个挑草筐的汉子在门前走过，说："这个敲磬的人好像有很深沉的心思。"就停下来听了一会儿又说："从低沉的磬声里听得出这个人见识未免太狭小了? 好象一直在说没有人了解自己，没有人了解自己就独善其身罢了。这好比过河，水深了就脱下衣服，水浅就把衣裳提起来。"孔子听后说："这个人涉世很深。我也没办法说服他。"

英文:

One day in the State or Wei, Confucius was playing the chime stone in a rehearsal of the rites. A man carrying baskets happened to pass by, saying, "The man playing the chime stone seems to be deeply troubled in his mind." After listening for a while, he said again, "How narrow-minded that man is! The low-deep sound of the chime stone betrays all this. He seems to have been complaining that he is not understood. If you are not understood then you should just pay attention to your own morality, regardless of others. It is like crossing a river. When the river is deep, just take off your clothes; when the river is shallow, lift your clothes." Hearing that, Confucius said, "This man is quite experienced. I have no way to convince him."

40. 子張曰："《書》云：'高宗諒陰，三年不言。'何謂也?"子曰："何必高宗，古之人皆然。君薨，百官總己以聽於冢宰三年。"

译文:

子张问："《尚书》上说：'殷高宗守孝，三年不谈政事。'这是什么意思呢?"孔子说："不只是高宗，古人都这样。国君死了，继位的国君三年不问政事，各部门的官员听命于宰相。"

英文:

Zi Zhang asked, "*The Book of Historical Documents* says, 'Gao Zong did not hold court for three

years to mourn his predecessor.' What does this mean?"
Confucius said, "It was not only Gao Zong who did that.
Ancient people all had the same practice. When the emperor passed away, the successor would not hold court for three years. All the officials in court would be under the premier's command."

41. 子曰: "上好禮，則民易使也。"

译文:

孔子说: "在上位的人凡事依礼而行，就容易使老百姓听从指使。"

英文:

Confucius said, "When the superiors observe the rites, the common people will be easy to command."

42. 子路問君子，子曰: "修己以敬。"曰: "如斯而已乎?"曰: "修己以安人。"曰: "如斯而已乎?"曰: "修己以安百姓。修己以安百姓，堯舜其猶病諸!"

译文:

子路问怎样才能算是君子，孔子说: "加强自身修养，严肃认真的工作。"子路问: "这样就够了吗?"孔子说: "修养自己，使亲友得安乐。"子路又问: "这样做就够了吗?"孔子说:"还要能使老百姓都得到安乐,这一点连尧、舜都还没有完全做到哩!"

英文:

Zi Lu asked how to be a gentleman. Confucius said, "A gentleman cultivates himself virtuously and works earnestly." Zi Lu asked again, "Is that enough?" Confucius explained, "To cultivate oneself brings peace and happiness to the people close to one." Zi Lu then asked, "Is that enough?" Confucius said, "To bring peace and happiness to the common people, even Yao and Shun did not realize that!"

43. 原壤夷俟。子曰:"幼而不孫弟,長而無述焉,老而不死,是爲賊。"以杖叩其脛。

译文:

孔子去看老朋友原壤,他却傲慢无理的叉开双腿坐着不动。孔子用拐杖敲着他的腿说:"你这家伙从小不知礼节,长大又毫无贡献,老了还不死,白糟蹋粮食,真是个害人精。"

注:

原壤:鲁国人,孔子的老朋友。

Confucius went to see his old friend, Yuan Xiang. The latter sat arrogantly with his legs spread wide. Confucius tapped him on the leg with his walking stick, saying, "You were defiant to the rites when young, and accomplished little when grown up. Now you refuse to die when old, but just eat up food. You are a real waster!"

44. 闕黨童子將命。或問之曰:"益者與?"子曰:"吾見其居於位也,見其與先生並行也。非求益者也,欲速成者也。"

译文:

阙党一位少年奉命来见孔子。有人问孔子说:"这个少年是求上进的人吗?"孔子说:"我看见过他的行为多不合礼节,这不是一个求上进的人,是一个急于求成的人。"

英文:

A boy from Que Dang came to see Confucius as ordered. After the boy left, someone asked Confucius, "Is that a boy who is eager to strive for progress?" Confucius answered, "I noticed that his behaviour was not in accordance with the rites. He is not one who is eager to strive for progress but one who is impatient for success."

衛靈公篇第十五

1. 衛靈公問陳於孔子，孔子對曰："俎豆之事，則嘗聞之矣；軍旅之事，未之學也。"明日遂行。

译文:

　　卫灵公问孔子军队布阵之法，孔子说："礼仪方面的事情，我曾经听到过一些；打仗方面的事情，我没有学过。"第二天孔子便离开了卫国。

注:

　　卫灵公: 卫国国君。

英文:

　　Duke Ling of Wei asked Confucius about military formations. Confucius said, "I have heard about the rites, but I have never studied anything about warfare." The next day Confucius left the State of Wei.

2. 在陳絕糧，從者病，莫能興。子路慍見曰："君子亦有窮乎?"子曰："君子固窮，小人窮斯濫矣。"

译文:

　　孔子周游列国时在陈国断绝了粮食，跟随他的人都饿病了，不能起床。子路来见孔子埋怨说："君子也有穷困的时候吗？"孔子说："君子虽遇穷困，但能坚持，小人一遇穷困便胡作非为了。"

英文：

When Confucius was travelling in the states, his provisions ran out in the State of Chen. His travelling companions fell too ill from hunger to rise to their feet. Zi Lu went to see Confucius, complaining, "Are there times when gentlemen become impoverished?" Confucius answered, "When gentlemen become impoverished, they can still persevere in virtue; when petty men are impoverished, they will act in defiance of virtue."

3. 子曰："賜也，女以予爲多學而識之者與？"對曰："然，非與？"曰："非也，予一以貫之。"

译文：

孔子说："端木赐，你以为我是博学强记吗？"子贡回答说："是呀！难道不是这样吗？"孔子说："不是这样，我只是用一个基本观念来贯串起来。"

注：

赐：端木赐，即子贡，孔子的学生。

Confucius said, "Duanmu Ci, do you think I am a man with wide range of knowledge and a good memory?" Zi Gong replied, "Yes I do. Is that not true?" Confucius said, "No. I just use a fundamental concept to bind it all together."

4. 子曰:"由，知德者鮮矣。"

译文:

孔子对子路说:"仲由，真正懂得德的人是很少的。"

注:

由: 仲由，即子路，孔子的学生。

英文:

Confucius said to Zi Lu, "Zhong You, only few understand virtue."

5. 子曰:"無爲而治者，其舜也與? 夫何爲哉? 恭己正南面而已矣。"

译文:

孔子说:"一切顺其自然，自己不做了什么而能使天下太平的人，大概只有舜吧? 他做了什么呢? 他只是从容安祥地坐在王位上罢了。"

英文:

Confucius said, "It was, perhaps, only Shun who brought peace to the multitude without taking any action against natural order. What did he actually do? What he did was only to sit on the throne with composure."

6. 子張問行，子曰："言忠信，行篤敬，雖蠻貊之邦，行矣。言不忠信，行不篤敬，雖州里，行乎哉？立則見其參於前也，在輿則見其倚於衡也，夫然後行。"子張書諸紳。

译文:

子张问怎样使自己的主张行得通，孔子说："说话忠诚老实，行为忠厚严肃，即使在落后野蛮地区也行得通。言语欺诈无信，行为刻薄轻浮，即便在本乡本土，能行得通吗？只要你随时随地牢记'忠诚老实，忠厚严肃'几个字，就到处行得通。"于是子张把这几个字写在自己的衣带上。

英文:

Zi Zhang asked about how to get his proposals carried through. Confucius said, "If you speak with trustworthiness and earnesty and act with honesty and conscience, you could get them through even in back-

—286—

ward and barbarian land. On the contrary, if you lie and slander, and act crudely and frivolously, could you get through even in your own neighbourhood? As long as you always remember the following dictum: Be trustworthy and earnest, conscientious and honest, and you shall get through at all times." Zi Zhang wrote the dictum down on his sash.

7. 子曰:"直哉,史魚! 邦有道如矢;邦無道如矢。君子哉,蘧伯玉! 邦有道則仕;邦無道則可卷而懷之。

译文:

孔子赞叹说:"好一个刚正不阿的史鱼! 国家政治清明时,他像射出的箭一样刚直;国家政治黑暗时,他仍像射出的箭一样刚直。好一位君子蘧伯玉! 国家政治清明时,他就出来做官;国家政治黑暗时,他就退隐下来。"

注:

史鱼:姓史,名鳅,字子鱼,卫国大夫。

蘧伯玉:名瑗,卫国大夫。

英文:

Confucius said, "How straight Shi Yu is! When the government is enlightened, he is as straight as an arrow; when the government is benighted, he is as straight as an arrow, too. **What** a gentleman Qu Boyu is! When the government is enlightened, he takes office; when the government is benighted, he resigns from office and lives in seclusion."

8. 子曰: "可與言而不與之言，失人；不可與言而與之言，失言。知者不失人，亦不失言。"

译文:

孔子说: "对可以交往的人而不与之交往，是错失了人；对不可以交谈的人与之交谈，是失言。聪明人不会失人，也不会失言。"

英文:

Confucius said, "To fail to speak to a man who is worth contacting is to let a man slip into uselessness; to speak to a man who is not worth communicating with is to waste words. A wise man shall not let a man slip into uselessness, nor shall he waste his words."

9. 子曰: "志士仁人，無求生以害仁，有殺身以成仁。"

译文:

孔子说: "志士仁人，没有贪生怕死而损害仁德的，只有牺牲自己而成全仁德。"

英文:

Confucius said, "A man of benevolence and lofty ideals should not, at the expense of benevolence, cling cravenly to life instead of braving death. He will, on the contrary, lay down his life for the accomplishment of benevolence."

10. 子貢問爲仁，子曰："工欲善其事，必先利其器。居是邦也，事其大夫之賢者，友其士之仁者。"

译文:

子贡问怎样实行仁德，孔子说："工匠要想做好他的工作，一定要先准备好他的工具。住在一个国家，就要事奉大夫中的贤人，交往士人中的仁人。"

英文:

Zi Gong asked how to practise benevolence. Confucius said, "A craftsman must prepare his tools beforehand in order to do his work well. Similarly, in a country, one must serve those among the senior officials who are virtuous, and make friends with those among the educated who are benevolent."

11. 顏淵問爲邦，子曰："行夏之時，乘殷之輅，服周之冕，樂則《韶》、《舞》，放鄭聲，遠佞人。鄭聲淫，佞人殆。"

译文:

颜渊问如何治理国家，孔子说："用夏代的历法，坐殷朝的车子，戴周朝的礼帽，音乐演奏《韶》乐和《舞》乐，舍弃郑国的乐曲，疏远谄媚的小人。郑国的乐曲淫荡，谄媚的小人很危险。"

注:

孔子认为夏历便于指导农业生产，殷朝的车子自然质朴，周代礼帽礼服华美，故有此说。

英文:

Yan Yuan asked how to govern. Confucius said, "Use the calendar of Xia, take the carriage of Yin, wear the ceremonial hat of Zhou, and play Shao and Wu music. Abandon the music of Zheng and keep your distance from cunning men. The music of Zheng is lascivious and cunning men are dangerous."

Note: Confucius recommended the Xia calendar because it was suitable for agriculture, the Yin carriage because it was simple, and the ceremonial dress of Zhou because it was grand.

12. 子曰："人無遠慮，必有近憂。"

译文：

孔子说："一个人如果没有长远打算，忧患很快就会出现。"

英文：

Confucius said, "Worries will soon appear if one gives no thought to a long-term plan."

13. 子曰："已矣乎！吾未見好德如好色者也。"

译文：

孔子说："算了吧！我没见过有像爱好美色那样爱好美德的人。"

英文：

Confucius said, "That's enough! I have never met a man who loves benevolence more than woman's beauty."

14. 子曰："臧文仲其竊位者與，知柳下惠之賢而不與立也。"

译文:

孔子说:"臧文仲大约是个做官不管事的人,他明明知道柳下惠贤良而不举荐他。"

注:

臧文仲: 鲁国大夫。

柳下惠: 姓展,名禽,鲁国的贤人。

英文:

Confucius said, "Zang Wenzhong was, perhaps, a man who only took office without taking the responsibility of it. He knew well about Liu Xiahui's ability and virtue, but he failed to promote him to an important position."

15. 子曰:"躬自厚而薄責於人,則遠怨矣。"

译文:

孔子说:"多自责而少责备人,自然就可以避免怨恨了。"

英文:

Confucius said, "Being strict with oneself and lenient to others is sure to save one from ill will."

16. 子曰:"不曰'如之何,如之何'者,吾末如之何也已矣。"

译文:

孔子说: "遇事不多想想'怎么办'的人,我对他们也不知怎么办了。"

英文:

Confucius said, "There is nothing that I can do about those who never ask themselves what they should do when they are to set about things."

17. 子曰: "群居終日,言不及義,好行小慧,難矣哉!"

译文:

孔子说: "整天聚在一起闲聊,说话不合道理,好卖弄小聪明,这种人很难有什么成就。

英文:

Confucius said, "Those who spend the whole day long merely chatting idly, saying unreasonable things and parading their cleverness will accomplish little."

18. 子曰: "君子義以爲質,禮以行之,孫以出之,信以成之。君子哉!"

译文:

　　孔子说: "以公正为做人的根本，行为合礼，语言谦逊，态度忠诚，这才是真正的君子。"

英文:

　　Confucius said, "A man may be said to be a true gentleman only if he takes fairness as his basic life principle, observes the rites in his behaviour, speaks with modesty, and acts with earnesty."

　　19. 子曰: "君子病無能焉，不病人之不己知也。"

译文:

　　孔子说: "君子只怕自己没有才能，不怕别人不了解自己。"

英文:

　　Confucius said, "A gentleman fears his own lack of talent more than others′ failure to understand him."

　　20. 子曰: "君子疾没世而名不稱焉。"

译文:

　　孔子说: "君子遗憾的是死后无名。"

Confucius said, "A gentleman regrets leaving no name when he is gone."

21. 子曰："君子求諸己，小人求諸人。"

译文:

孔子说："君子严格要求自己，小人苛刻要求别人。"

英文:

Confucius said, "A gentleman sets strict demands on himself while a petty man sets strict demands on others."

22. 子曰：君子矜而不争，群而不黨。"

译文:

孔子说："君子庄重而不与人争，讲和睦相处而不闹宗派。"

英文:

Confucius said, "A gentleman is grave without being contentious, and keeps harmonious relationships with others without forming cliques."

23. 子曰："君子不以言舉人，不以人廢言。"

译文:

孔子说："君子不因人说好听的话就提拔他们，也不因他是坏人就鄙弃他说过的正确的话。"

英文:

Confucius said, "A gentleman does not promote a man whose words are pleasant to his ear, neither does he disdain his correct words, for he is an unpleasant man."

24. 子貢問曰："有一言而可以終身行之者乎?"子曰："其恕乎! 己所不欲，勿施於人。"

译文:

子贡问："有没有可以终身奉行的一句话?"孔子说："就是恕吧! 自己不想做的事情，就不要加给别人。"

英文:

Zi Gong asked, "Is there a single word that a man can follow as his life guide?" Confucius said, "Yes. It is, perhaps, the word 'forbearance'. Do not impose upon others what you do not desire yourself."

25. 子曰："吾之於人也，誰毀誰譽? 如有所譽者，其有所試矣。斯民也，三代之所以直道而行也。"

译文:

孔子说: "我对于别人，从不轻易诋毁或称赞，如果有所称赞，那也一定是经过考察验证的。夏、商、周三代的人都如此，所以一直走在正道上。"

英文:

Confucius said, "I have seldom condemned or praised anyone. If I ever praised someone, he must have been put on test and his deeds must have been proved. The sage kings of the three dynasties of Xia, Shang, and Zhou followed the same principle so that they were always on the right path."

26. 子曰: "吾猶及史之闕文也。有馬者，借人乘之，今亡矣夫! "

译文:

孔子说: "我还能够看到史书中存疑的地方。有马的人，先借给别人使用。今天就没有这种事了。"

注:

此段文字很难理解。历代注家莫衷一是。

英文:

Confucius said, "I am still able to detect ambiguities in history books. Those who had horses would let others use them. Nowadays, there are not such people any longer."

Note: This chapter is very difficult to understand. Annotators at different times have given different explanations to it.

27. 子曰: "巧言亂德。小不忍，則亂大謀。"

译文:

孔子说: "花言巧语足以败坏道德。小事上不忍耐，就会坏了大事。"

英文:

Confucius said, "Sweet words will ruin one's virtue; lack of patience in small matters will bring destruction to overall plans."

28. 子曰: "衆惡之，必察焉，衆好之，必察焉。"

译文:

孔子说: "大家都讨厌他，一定要考察一番；大家都喜欢他，也一定要考察一番。"

Confucius said, "Be sure to look into the case if a man is disliked by all the people around him. Be sure, too, to look into the case if he is liked by all the people around him."

29. 子曰: "人能弘道, 非道弘人。"

译文:

孔子说: "人的才能可以把道光大, 不是道可以把人的才能光大。"

英文:

Confucius said, "It is man's ability that enhances *Tao*; it is not *Tao* that enhances man's ability."

30. 子曰: "過而不改, 是謂過矣。"

译文:

孔子说: "有过错不改正, 才是真错。"

英文:

Confucius said, "Not to correct the mistake one has made is to err indeed."

31. 子曰："吾嘗終日不食，終夜不寢，以思，無益，不如學也。"

译文:

孔子说："我曾经废寝忘食的整天苦思冥想，结果没有收益，不如踏踏实实去学习。"

英文:

Confucius said, "I once spent day and night in cudgelling my brains without taking meals and sleep. But all my efforts turned out to be of little effect. I should have spent all that time learning steadily."

32. 子曰："君子謀道不謀食。耕也，餒在其中矣；學也，禄在其中矣。君子憂道不憂貧。"

译文:

孔子说："君子用心力于学术思想体系的研究，不用心力于谋求衣食。耕田，常常饿肚子，而学习则能得到俸禄。故君子担忧的是学问，而不是贫穷。"

英文:

Confucius said, "A gentleman devotes himself to studying the academic system of ideology instead of seeking food and clothing. If one is engaged in tilling the land, he may often be hungry. If one is engaged in learning, he may be rewarded with an official salary. Therefore, it is not poverty but learning that a gentleman worries about."

33. 子曰："知及之，仁不能守之，雖得之，必失之。知及之，仁能守之，不莊以涖之，則民不敬。知及之，仁能守之，莊以涖之，動之不以禮，未善也。" 位

译文：

孔子说："用才智可以取得权位，但如果不能用仁德去保持它，即使得到了，也一定会失去。用才智取得权位，也能够用仁德保持它，但如果不能以负责的态度去治理百姓，就不会得到老百姓的拥护。如果用才智取得了权位，又能用仁德保持它，也能以负责的态度去治理百姓，但如果不能依礼役使百姓，这政权也就不是十全十美的。"

英文：

Confucius said, "Without benevolence, one will lose the position of power that one has attained through wisdom and talent. With benevolence, one can keep the position. But one cannot gain the support of the multitude if one does not command the multitude with conscience.

If one can attain a position of power with wisdom and talent, keep it with benevolence, and at the same time, can command the multitude with conscience, still such a regime can not be called a perfect regime if one does not command the multitude according to the rites."

34. 子曰: "君子不可小知而可大受也，小人不可大受而可小知也。"

译文:

孔子说: "君子不可以用小事考验却能担当大任; 小人不能担当大任却能经受小事的考验。"

英文:

Confucius said, "A gentleman can be entrusted to great responsibilities without being tested in small matters. A petty man can stand the test of small matters, but he can never be entrusted to great responsibilities."

35. 子曰: "民之於仁也，甚於水火。水火，吾見蹈而死者矣，未見蹈仁而死者也。"

译文:

孔子说: "老百姓对于仁德的需要，比对水火的需要更迫切。我看见过有人在水火之中丧命，却从未见过因实行仁德而丧命的。"

Confucius said, "Benevolence is more vital to the common people than water and fire. I have seen people die in water and fire, but I have never seen anyone die of practising benevolence."

36. 子曰: "當仁，不讓於師。"

译文:

孔子说: "面临仁德时，不必让老师先行。"

英文:

Confucius said, "In the face of benevolence, do not give precedence even to your teacher."

37. 子曰: "君子貞而不諒。"

译文:

孔子说: "君子重信义而不拘小节。"

英文:

Confucius said, "A gentleman pays attention to faithfulness rather than small matters."

38. 子曰:"事君,敬其事而後其食。"

译文:

孔子说:"在朝为官,应该认真办事而不计报酬。"

英文:

Confucius said, "Being an official in court, a man should give priority to his office responsibilities over the reward of his job."

39. 子曰:"有教無類。"

译文:

孔子说:"我对人无区别地都加以教育。"(也可译为:"人人都有受教育的权利。")

英文:

Confucius said, "In educating people, I treat everyone the same."

Note: This could also be translated as: "Everyone is entitled to be educated."

40. 子曰:"道不同,不相爲謀。"

译文:

孔子说: "政治主张不同, 不互相探讨。"

英文:

Confucius said, "People who follow different political paths do not take counsel with one another."

41. 子曰: "辭達而已矣。"

译文:

孔子说: "言辞能把意思表达清楚也就可以了。"

英文:

Confucius said, "It is enough that one's words get the ideas across."

42. 師冕見, 及階, 子曰: "階也。"及席, 子曰: "席也。"皆坐, 子告之曰: "某在斯, 某在斯。"師冕出。子張問曰: "與師言之道與?"子曰: "然, 固相師之道也。"

译文:

师冕来见孔子, 走到台阶边, 孔子说: "这是台阶。"走到坐席边, 孔子又说: "这是坐席。"等大家坐下来, 孔子又把某人坐在哪里——告诉师冕。师冕告辞后, 子张问孔子: "这是同乐师讲话的方式吗?"孔子说: "是的, 这是帮助乐师的方式。"

注:

师冕: 姓冕的乐师, 古时乐师多是盲人。

英文:

Shi Mian (a musician) went to see Confucius. Approaching the steps Confucius said, "Here are the steps." When they came to the mat, Confucius said again, "Here is the mat." When everyone was seated, Confucius told Shi Mian where everyone was seated one by one. After Shi Mian left, Zi Zhang asked Confucius, "Is that the way to talk to a musician?" Confucius answered, "Yes. That is the way to help a musician."

Note: In ancient times, many musicians were blind.

季氏篇第十六

1. 季氏將伐顓臾。冉有、季路見於孔子曰："季氏將有事於顓臾。"

孔子曰："求！無乃爾是過與？夫顓臾，昔者先王以爲東蒙主，且在邦域之中矣，是社稷之臣也。何以伐爲？"

冉有曰："夫子欲之，吾二臣者皆不欲也。"

孔子曰："求！周任有言曰：'陳力就列，不能者止。'危而不持，顛而不扶，則將焉用彼相矣？且爾言過矣，虎兕出於柙，龜玉毁於櫝中，是誰之過與？"

冉有曰："今夫顓臾，固而近於費。今不取，後世必爲子孫憂。"

孔子曰："求！君子疾夫舍曰欲之而必爲之辭。丘也聞有國有家者，不患貧而患不均，不患寡而患不安。蓋均無貧，和無寡，安無傾。夫如是，故遠人不服，則修文德以來之。既來之，則安之。今由與求也，相夫子，遠人不服，而不能來也；邦分崩離析，而不能守也；而謀動干戈於邦內。吾恐季孫之憂，不在顓臾，而在蕭牆之內也。"

译文：
　　鲁国大夫季孙氏准备攻打顓臾。当时在季氏家作家臣的冉有、子路两人去谒见孔子，说："季氏准备对颛臾用兵。"

孔子说："冉求！这不应该责备你们吗？颛臾，是上代君主让它主办东蒙山的祭祀，而且是在鲁国疆域之内，是鲁国的藩属，为什么要去攻打它呢？"

冉求解释说："是季孙大夫要这样干，我们两个都不同意的。"

孔子说："冉求！周任曾说过：'任其职就尽其责，如果行不通就辞职不干。'这譬如看着瞎子行路遇到了危险，不去扶持，那又何必要你们这些助手呢？而且你的话也不对。老虎、犀牛从笼子里跑出来伤人，龟甲、美玉毁坏在匣子里无人知道，这是谁的过错呢？这难道不是你们这些作家臣的责任吗？"

冉有辩解说："现在颛臾城墙坚固，而且又离季孙大夫的采邑费地很近。现在不夺取它，必然会给后世子孙留下祸患。"

孔子说："冉求！君子最讨厌为掩饰自己的贪心而寻找各种藉口的人。我只听说过不管诸侯还是大夫治理国家，不怕贫穷就怕财富分配不均，不怕人口稀少，就怕不安定。只要财富分配均匀便不觉得穷困，境内和平安定便不会觉得人口稀少，局势稳定，政权就不会有倾覆的危险。做到这样，远方民族还不归服，也不必动武，只需修治仁义礼乐的政教来招致他们。他们归服后，就要使他们安心住下去。现在你和仲由辅助季孙大夫，远方民族不来归服，而不能以仁义礼乐招致他们；现在鲁国四分五裂，又不能保全，反而策划着攻打颛臾。恐怕季孙氏所忧患的不在颛臾，而在鲁君那里。"

注:

颛臾：鲁国的附属国。

季氏：鲁国把持政权的季孙氏。和鲁国国君矛盾很大，他怕颛臾利用有利地势帮助鲁国国君收回主权，因此找借口先下手对颛臾用兵。

周任：古代一位史官。

英文:

Jisun Shi, a senior official of Lu, was going to launch an attack on Duan Yu. Ran You and Zi Lu, who were then stewards of the Jisun's Family, went to see Confucius and told him, "Jisun Shi is going to attack Duan Yu."

Confucius said, "Ran Qiu! Is it not you that are to blame? The last duke of Lu let Duan Yu host the sacrifice to our ancestors at Dong Meng Mountains. Furthermore, its territory lies within the boundary of Lu and is a vassal State to Lu. What should there be the reason for Jisun to attack Duan Yu?"

Ran Qiu explained, "It is Jisun Shi who insists on the attack. We two actually disagreed." Confucius said, "Ran You! Zhou Ren once said: 'Fulfill your duties when you take office.' If you can't see something through, you'd better resign. What use to a blind man is an assistant who does not support and help him when he is in danger? Besides, what you said is wrong. Whose fault is it if tigers and rhinoceros escape from their cages and hurt people, and if tortoise shell and jade are damaged in their caskets without anyone knowing it? Shouldn't you, the stewards, take the responsibility?"

Ran Qiu explained, "Now Duan Yu is strongly fortified. Moreover, he is quite close to the fief of the Jisun's Family. If he is not taken over now, it would be a source of trouble to our coming generations."

Confucius said, "Ran Qiu! A gentleman most detests the man who makes various excuses for his avarice. There is a saying: No matter who administrates the state, the duke or senior official, he does not worry about poverty but unfair distribution; he does not worry about underpopulation but instability of the state. As long as wealth is fairly distributed, the common people will not feel the poverty; as long as the state is stable within its territory, the common people will not realize the underpopulation. Politically stable, the government will never be under the threat of collapse. Instead of resorting to arms, the government only needs to cultivate benevolence, the rites and music in order to attract the minorities in the remote areas. Once they are attracted, the government should make sure that they live peacefully. Now you and Zhong You are assisting Jisun Shi, but people in the remote areas do not submit themselves to your authority. The only resason is that you fail to attract them with benevolence and the rites and music. The State of Lu has now fallen to pieces. Instead of making efforts to keep it whole, you are plotting an attack on Duan Yu. I am afraid Jisun Shi's touble does not come from Duan Yu, but from the Duke of Lu."

Note: Duan Yu is a dependency of Lu. The Jisun's Family had actually seized power in Lu, and were in discord with the Duke of Lu. Jisun Shi was afraid that Duan Yu would use its advantageous location to help the Duke of Lu to regain the throne. This is why Jisun was trying to find an excuse to attack Duan Yu.

2. 孔子曰: "天下有道, 則禮樂征伐自天子出; 天下無道, 則禮樂征伐自諸侯出。自諸侯出, 蓋十世希不失矣; 自大夫出, 五世希不失矣; 陪臣執國命, 三世希不失矣。天下有道, 則政不在大夫。天下有道, 則庶人不議。"

译文:

孔子说: "天下政治清明, 制礼作乐和出兵征伐等大事都由天子决定; 天下政治昏乱, 制礼作乐和出兵征伐便决定于诸侯。由诸侯专权，很少有传到十代不垮台的；由大夫专权，很少有传到五代不垮台的；卿、大夫家臣把持国家政权，很少有传三代不垮台的。天下政治清明，国家政权就不会落在大夫手中，老百姓也不会诽议朝廷。"

英文:

Confucius said, "When the government is honest, major issues such as the rites, music and military affairs are decided by the Emperor. When the government is not honest, all these matters will be decided by dukes. If that happens, the sovereignty seldom lasts more than ten generations; if the decisive power falls into the hands of senior officials, the sovereignty will never last more than five generations; if retainers dominate the state, it will not be a surprise that the sovereignty does not last more than three generations. With honest government, the sovereignty of a state will not fall into the hands of senior officials, and the common people will not make any critical comments."

3. 孔子曰："禄之去公室五世矣，政逮於大夫四世矣，故夫三桓之子孫微矣。"

译文:

孔子说:"国家政权离开鲁君已经五代了,政权落到季氏手中也已经四代了,所以鲁桓公的三房子孙现在也衰微了。

注:

五世、四世:鲁国政权自鲁君丧失到孔子说这段话时,已经历了宣公、成公、襄公、昭公、定公五代;自季氏把持鲁国政权也已经历了文子、武子、平子、桓子四代。

三桓:指鲁国的三卿,仲孙、叔孙、季孙皆出于鲁桓公,故称"三桓"。

英文:

Confucius said, "It is five generations since the sovereignty passed from the Duke of Lu. And it is four generations since the state came under the control of the Jisun's Family. So the three descendents of Duke Huan of Lu are on the decline."

Note: Five generations: When Confucius made the above remarks, the sovereignty of the State of Lu had already passed through the following five generations since the Duke of Lu lost his power: Duke Xuan, Duke Cheng, Duke Xiang, Duke Zhao, and Duke Ding.

Four generations: The Jisun Family had held the dominant power of Lu for the following Wenzi, Wuzi, Pingzi, Huanzi four generations.

Three descendants of Duke Huan: This refers to the three senior officials of Lu under Duke Huan: Zhongsun, Shusun, Jisun.

4. 孔子曰：“益者三友，损者三友。友直，友谅，友多闻，益矣。友便辟，友善柔，友便佞，损矣。”

译文：

孔子说：“交朋友有三种人可以交，有三种人不可以交。同正直的人、诚实的人、广见博闻的人交朋友，是有益的。同谄媚奉承的人、当面恭维背后毁谤的人、夸夸其谈并无真才实学的人交朋友，是有害的。”

英文：

Confucius said, "There are three kinds of people one may make friends with. Equally, there are three kinds of people one should not make friends with. It is beneficial for one to make friends with those who are upright, honest, and erudite. It is harmful for one to make friends with those who toady, those who flatter people but slander them behind their backs, those who brag but are not erudite at all."

5. 孔子曰：“益者三樂，損者三樂。樂節禮樂，樂道人之善，樂多賢友，益矣。樂驕樂，樂佚遊，樂宴樂，损矣。"

译文：

孔子说："有益的快乐有三种，有害的快乐也有三种。以得到礼乐的调节为快乐，以宣扬别人的长处为快乐，以多交贤良的朋友为快乐，这是有益的快乐。以尊贵骄傲为快乐，以尽情游荡为快乐，以吃吃喝喝为快乐，这是有害的快乐。

英文：

Confucius said, "There are three kinds of beneficial pleasure. Equally there are three kinds of harmful pleasure. The three beneficial kinds include: to prepare for the rites and music; to give publicity to others' good qualities; to make friends with those who are virtuous. The three harmful kinds are as follows: to be arrogant about one's position; to loiter to one's heart's content; and to indulge in food and drink."

6. 孔子曰："侍於君子有三愆：言未及之而言謂之躁，言及之而不言謂之隱，未見顏色而言謂之瞽。"

译文：

孔子说："陪着君子说话切忌犯三种毛病：不该说话时抢着说这叫做急躁，该说话时却不说这叫隐瞒，不先看人家的脸色便贸然说话这叫做瞎子。"

英文:

Confucius said, "In attendance on a gentleman, one should avoid three errors: to speak when it is not necessary is to be rash; not to speak when it is necessary is to be evasive; and to speak without observing someone's facial expression is to be blind."

7. 孔子曰: "君子有三戒: 少之時，血氣未定，戒之在色；及其壯也，血氣方剛，戒之在鬭；及其老也，血氣既衰，戒之在得。"

译文:

孔子说: "君子有三件事要警惕: 年少时，血气还没有稳定，要警惕贪恋女色；到了壮年，血气正旺盛，要警惕争强好斗；到了老年，血气已经衰竭，要警惕贪得无厌。"

英文:

Confucius said, "A gentleman should maintain vigilance against three things: In youth when the vital spirits are not yet settled, he should be on guard against lusting for feminine beauty; in the prime of life when the vital spirits are exuberant, he should be on guard against being bellicose; in old age when the vital spirits are on the decline, he should be on guard against insatiable avarice."

8. 孔子曰："君子有三畏：畏天命，畏大人，畏聖人之言。小人不知天命而不畏也，狎大人，侮聖人之言。"

译文：

孔子说："君子有三怕：怕天命，怕王公大人，怕圣人的言论。小人不懂天命而不怕，不知尊重王公大人，轻慢圣人的言论。"

英文：

Confucius said, "A gentleman stands in awe of three things. He is in awe of the mandate of Heaven, he is in awe of great men, and he is in awe of the words of wise men. Being ignorant, the petty man is not in awe of the mandate of Heaven. He does not treat great men with respect and he despises the words of wise men."

9. 孔子曰："生而知之者，上也；學而知之者，次也；困而學之，又其次也；困而不學，民斯為下矣。"

译文：

孔子说："生来就有知识的人，是上等人；经过学习得知识的人，是次等人；遇到困难再去学习的人，是又次一等的人；遇到困难也不学习的人，是最下等的人了。"

英文：

Confucius said, "Those who are born with knowledge are the highest; those who obtain knowledge through learning are the next; those who learn in the face of difficulty are lower, and those who do not learn even in the face of difficulty are the lowest."

10. 孔子曰："君子有九思：视思明，聽思聰，色思温，貌思恭，言思忠，事思敬，疑思問，忿思難，見得思義。"

译文：

孔子说："君子要考虑九件事：看的时候，要考虑是否看明白了。听的时候，要考虑是否听清楚了。脸上的颜色，要考虑是否温和。容貌态度，要考虑是否端庄。与人交谈，要考虑是否诚恳。对待工作，要考虑是否认真。遇到疑难，要考虑如何向人请教。将要发怒时，要考虑会有什么后患。要得到什么，先要考虑是否应该得到。"

Confucius said, "A gentleman concentrates on the following nine things: seeing clearly when he uses his eyes; hearing acutely when he uses his ears; looking mild when it comes to facial expression; appearing sedate when it comes to demeanour; being sincere when he speaks; being conscientious when it comes to his office responsibility; seeking advice when he is in the face of difficulty; foreseeing the consequences when he gets angry; asking himself whether it is right when he wants to gain something."

11. 孔子曰: "見善如不及, 見不善如探湯。吾見其人矣, 吾聞其語矣。隱居以求其志, 行義以達其道。吾聞其語矣, 未見其人也。"

译文:

孔子说: "追求善良, 要争先恐后; 避开邪恶, 要像开水烫手一样急迫。我见过这样的人, 也听过这样的话。避世隐居来保全自己的志向, 实行礼义来贯彻自己的主张。我听到过这样的话; 却没有见过这样的人。"

英文:

Confucius said, "Striving to be the first and fearing to lag behind when seeking goodness; retreating as quickly as if hurt by boiling water when avoiding vices. I have met such persons and I have heard such a claim. Living in seclusion in order to attain their will; practising righteousness in order to carry out their political ideals. I have heard such a claim, but I have never met such persons."

12. 齊景公有馬千駟，死之日，民無德而稱焉。伯夷、叔齊餓于首陽之下，民到于今稱之。其斯之謂與?

译文:

齐景公有四千匹马，死了以后，老百姓不知道他有什么值得称颂的德行。伯夷、叔齐饿死在首阳山下，老百姓至今称颂他们。

注:

齐景公: 名析臼，齐国国君。

伯夷、叔齐: 商朝末年孤竹君的两个儿子。父亲死后，他兄弟二人因互让君位而同时出走。周灭商后，他们不食周粟，最后饿死在首阳山。

其斯之谓与: 此句和上文不相衔接，可能有断续或有阙文，故不译。

英文:

Duke Jing of Qi owned four thousand horses. When he died, the common people did not know what qualities that he possessed were worth praising. Bo Yi and Shu Qi died of hunger at the foot of Shouyang Mountains. The common people have heen praising their deeds ever since.

Note: The last sentence in the Chinese version is not related to the rest of the chapter, and may be a textual error, therefore it is not translated here.

13. 陳亢問於伯魚曰：“子亦有異聞乎？”對曰：“未也。嘗獨立，鯉趨而過庭。曰：‘學詩乎？’對曰：‘未也。’‘不學詩，無以言。’鯉退而學詩。他日，又獨立，鯉趨而過庭。曰：‘學禮乎？’對曰：‘未也。’‘不學禮，無以立。’鯉退而學禮。聞斯二者。”陳亢退而喜曰：“問一得三：聞詩，聞禮，又聞君子之遠其子也。”

译文：

陈亢问孔子的儿子的伯鱼道：“你整天和先生在一起，是否得到特别的教导？”伯鱼回答说：“没有。有一天我父亲一个人站在院子里，我想紧走几步过去，他叫住我问：‘学过《诗》没有？’我说：‘还没有。’他说：‘不学《诗》，就不知道如何说话。’我回去后学习《诗》。又有一天，我又在院子里碰见父亲。他问我：‘学习过《礼》吗？’我回答说：‘还没有。’他说：‘不学《礼》，就不能立身处世。’我又回去学《礼》。就这两件事算是我受到的特别教导吧。”陈亢回去后高兴地说：“我问一个问题，却知道了三件事：知道了学《诗》的意义，学《礼》的意义，也知道了君子不偏爱自己的儿子。”

注：

陈亢：姓陈，名亢，字子禽。

伯鱼：姓孔，名鲤，字伯鱼，孔子的儿子。

英文：

Chen Kang asked Bo Yu, the son of Confucius, "You are with the Master all day long. Do you receive any special instruction?" "No, I do not," answered Bo Yu. "One day my father was standing in the courtyard and I quickened my steps to cross over. He stopped me and asked, 'Have you studied *The Book of Songs?*' I answered, 'Not yet.' He said, 'you will not know how to speak properly unless you study it .' After that, I began to study the book. Another day, again I came across my father in the courtyard. He asked, 'Have you studied *The Book of Rites?*' I answered, 'Not yet.' He said, 'You will not know how to conduct yourself unless you study it.' After that, I began to study the book. Those two things may be said to be the special instruction I have received from my father." Chen Kang went away delighted, saying, "I asked only one question, but I learnt three things: I learnt about the *The Book of Songs;* I learnt about *The Book of Rites;* and I also learnt that a gentleman never shows any favour to his son."

14. 邦君之妻，君稱之曰夫人，夫人自稱曰小童；邦人稱之曰君夫人，稱諸異邦曰寡小君；異邦人稱之亦曰君夫人。

译文:

国君的妻子，国君称她为夫人，夫人自称为小童；国内人尊称她为君夫人，但对外国人说话则称她为寡小君；外国人也称她为君夫人。

英文:

The ruler of a state calls his wife "Lady"; and the wife will call herself "the little child". People of the state refer to her respectfully by the term "the lady of the ruler". But when abroad, she called herself "the little lord". People of other states refer to her by the term "the lady of the ruler".

陽貨篇第十七

1. 陽貨欲見孔子，孔子不見，歸孔子豚。孔子時其亡也，而往拜之。遇諸塗。謂孔子曰："來! 予與爾言。"曰："懷其寶而迷其邦，可謂仁乎?"曰："不可。""好從事而亟失時，可謂知乎?"曰："不可。""日月逝矣，歲不我與。"孔子曰："諾，吾將仕矣。"

译文:

阳货想见孔子，孔子却不想见他，他便趁孔子不在家时派人送去一只蒸熟的乳猪。使孔子不得不去向他道谢。孔子也探听阳货不在家时去致谢。不想两个人在路上碰见了。阳货叫住孔子说："来! 我同你说话。"孔子只好走过去，阳货说："把自己的本事藏起来而听任国家混乱不堪，这可以说是仁吗?"孔子不作声，阳货自己说："不可以。"他又说："一个人喜欢参与政事而屡次错失机会，这可以叫做聪明吗?"孔子仍不作声，阳货仍自己回答说："不可以。况且日月如梭，岁月不待人呀。"孔子只好应付说："好吧，我打算出来做官。"

注:

阳货: 又称阳虎，鲁国大夫季氏家臣。季氏已几代把持鲁国政权，这时阳货又把持了季氏的权柄。孔子说他是"陪臣执国命"。他想拉拢孔子做官，孔子实际上并未在阳货当权时出仕。

Yang Huo went to see Confucius. Confucius declined his visit. One day, Yang Huo sent Confucius a present of steamed suckling pig when he knew that Confucius was not in. That meant that Confucius had to go and express his gratitute to Yang Huo in person. In the same way, Confucius having someone keep watch on Yang Huo's house, went to express his thanks during Yang Huo's absence. It so happened that they met on the way. Yang Huo stopped Confucius and said, "Come over, I want to speak to you." Confucius had to go over. Yang Huo said to him, "Can a man be called benevolent who hides his talent and allows the country to be thrown into chaos?" Confucius did not answer. Yang Huo answered himself, "No, he cannot." He went on saying, "Can a man be called wise who is eager to take part in government affairs but misses the chance each time?" Again, Confucius did not answer. Yang Huo answered himself again, "No, he cannot, either. The days and months slip by, and time waits for no man." Confucius had to answer in a perfunctory way, "All right, I shall take office."

Note: Yang Huo, also known as Yang Hu, was a retainer of the Jisun's Family. For several generations, the

State of Lu had been under the control of the Jisun Family, and the Jisun Family was under the control of Yang Huo at that time. Yang Huo wanted to persuade Confucius to take office. But Confucius did not take any official post when Yang Huo was in power.

2. 子曰：“性相近也，習相遠也。”

译文：

孔子说：“人的本性都差不多，只是由于习俗不同，便相距越来越远了。”

英文：

Confucius said, "Men are similar to one another by nature. They diverge gradually as a result of different customs."

3. 子曰：“唯上知與下愚不移。”

译文：

孔子说：“只有天生的聪明人和下等愚人是习俗所改变不了的。”

英文：

Confucius said, "Only those who are born wise and

those who are born foolish are not susceptible to changes in customs."

4. 子之武城，聞弦歌之聲。夫子莞爾而笑，曰："割鷄焉用牛刀?"子游對曰："昔者偃也聞諸夫子曰:'君子學道則愛人，小人學道則易使也。'"子曰："二三子! 偃之言是也。前言戲之耳。"

译文:

孔子在学生们陪同下来到武城，听到演习礼乐的弦歌之声。他微微一笑说："治理武城这样的小城用不着礼乐教化（杀鸡何必用宰牛的刀呢?）。"子游说："我以前听老师讲过:'做官的学习了礼乐的道理就会有仁爱之心，老百姓学习了礼乐的道理就会听从使唤。'教育总是有用的吧。"孔子便对随行的学生们说："学生们，言偃的话是对的，我刚才那句话只是和他开个玩笑罢了。"

注:

子游: 姓言，名偃，字子游，孔子的学生，当时任武城县长。

英文:

Accompanied by his disciples, Confucius went to the town of Wu Cheng. Hearing the rehearsal of the rites and music, he smiled and said, "To administrate a small town like this does not need the rites and music." Zi You said,

"Once I heard you Master say: ' Those in office will develop benevolence when they have studied the rites and music. The common people will be easy to command when they have studied the rites and music'. Education is useful after all!" Confucius then said to the disciples present: "Disciples, Yan Yan is right. What I said to you just now was just a joke."

Note: Zi You is Confucius' disciple. He was county magistrate of Wucheng at that time.

5. 公山弗擾以費畔，召，子欲往。子路不說，曰："末之也已，何必公山氏之之也?"子曰："夫召我者，而豈徒哉? 如有用我者，吾其爲東周乎!"

译文:

公山弗扰以费邑为据点图谋背叛季氏，召孔子去，孔子打算走一趟。子路很不高兴，说："没地方去就算了，何必一定去公山氏那里呢?"孔子说："那个召我去的人，难道会让我白跑一趟吗? 如果有人用我，我要在鲁国复兴西周的礼乐制度。"

注:

公山弗扰: 鲁国大夫季氏家臣。

英文:

Gongshan Furao used the city of Fei as a stronghold to stage a revolt against the Jisun's Family. Confucius planned to see him when he was summoned. Zi Lu was unhappy about it, saying, "If you have nowhere else to go, you just stay. Why must you go to Gongshan?" Confucius answered, "Do you think the man who summoned me wants me to go for nothing? Whenever there is someone who needs me, I will try to revive the rites and music of West Zhou in Lu."

6. 子張問仁於孔子，孔子曰："能行五者於天下，爲仁矣。""請問之。"曰："恭，寬，信，敏，惠。恭則不侮，寬則得衆，信則人任焉，敏則有功，惠則足以使人。"

译文:

子张问孔子怎样做才是仁，孔子说："能够处处实行五种品德，就是仁人了。"子张问："请问哪五种品德?"孔子说："庄重，宽厚，诚信，勤敏，慈惠。庄重就不会招致侮辱，宽厚就能得到众人拥护，诚信就能得到别人任用，勤敏就能取得成功，慈惠就能很好地使唤人。"

英文:

Zi Zhang asked Confucius how to be benevolent. Confucius said, "To embrace five qualities at once is benevolent." Zi Zhang asked, "What are the five qualities?"

Confucius said, "They are gravity, tolerance, trustworthiness, diligence, and generosity. With gravity you will not be humiliated; tolerance brings the support of the multitude; trustworthiness wins the trust of others; diligence paves the way to success; and generosity makes it easy to exercise control over others."

7. 佛肸召，子欲往。子路曰："昔者由也聞諸夫子曰：'親於其身爲不善者，君子不入也。'佛肸以中牟畔，子之往也，如之何？"子曰："然，有是言也。不曰堅乎，磨而不磷？不曰白乎，涅而不緇？吾豈匏瓜也哉？焉能繫而不食？"

译文：

佛肸召孔子，孔子想去。子路说："过去我听老师讲过：'君子不去坏人那里做事。'现在佛肸以中牟为据点图谋造反，您却到那里去，怎么能这样呢？"孔子说："是的，我讲过这样的话。但是，你没听说过吗？最坚硬的东西是磨不薄的，洁白的东西是染不黑的。难道我是只葫芦只能挂着让人看而不能吃吗？"

注：

佛肸：晋国大夫范中行的家臣，中牟县长。赵简子以晋侯的名义攻打范中行，佛肸便以中牟为据点反叛，所以召孔子去。孔子认为赵简子如果灭掉范中行，就会形成晋国的分裂，所以想去帮助佛肸对抗赵简子。

Confucius wanted to go when Bi Xi summoned him. Zi Lu said, "Some time ago, I heard you, Master, say, 'A gentleman should never serve those who are not good.' Now Bi Xi is using Zhongmo as a stronghold to stage a revolt. But you are going there. How do you explain this?" Confucius said, "Yes. I did say what you mentioned just now. However, have you ever heard the following saying: That which is hardest can never be worn thin; that which is pure white can never be dyed black. How can I allow myself to be treated like a gourd which can only hang on the wall without being eaten?"

Note: Bi Xi was a retainer of Fan Zhongxing, a senior official of Jin, and the county magistrate of Zhongmo. Zhao Jianzi staged an attack on Fan Zhongxing in the name of the Duke of Jin. Therefore, Bi Xi used Zhongmo as a stronghold to launch a revolt and summoned Confucius. Confucius thought that the State of Jin would break up if Zhao Jianzi were to defeat Fan Zhongxing. So Confucius wanted to help Bi Xi to fight against Zhao Jianzi.

8. 子曰: "由也, 女聞六言六蔽矣乎? 對曰: "未也。" "居! 吾語女。好仁不好學, 其蔽也愚; 好知不好學,

其蔽也蕩；好信不好學，其蔽也賊；好直不好學，其蔽
也絞；好勇不好學，其蔽也亂；好剛不好學，其蔽也
狂。"

译文：

孔子问："仲由！你听说过六种品德和六种弊病的关
系吗？"子路回答说："没听说过。"孔子说："坐下来！我告
诉你。爱好仁德而不好学习，它的弊病是容易被人愚
弄；爱耍聪明而不好学习，它的弊病是容易放荡不羁；
诚实而不好学习，它的弊病是容易被别人利用，反害了
自身；耿直而不好学习，它的弊病是容易说话尖刻伤
人；勇敢而不好学习，它的弊病是容易出乱子；好刚强
而不好学习，它的弊病是容易产生胆大妄为的心理。"

英文：

Confucius asked, "Zhong You, have you heard
about the relationship between the six qualities and the
six faults?" Zi Lu answered, "No, I have not. "Confucius
said, "Come and sit down! I shall tell you. To love benevolence without loving learning is to be liable to be
fooled; to believe in wisdom without loving learning is to
be liable to dissoluteness; to be honest without loving
learning is to be liable to being made use of and self—destruction; to be straight without loving learning is to be
liable to harmful and biting speech; to be courageous

without loving learning is to be liable to disobedience; to be unyielding without loving learning is to be liable to recklessness."

9. 子曰: "小子何莫學夫詩? 詩, 可以興, 可以觀, 可以群, 可以怨; 邇之事父, 遠之事君; 多識於鳥獸草木之名。"

译文:

孔子对学生们说: "你们为什么不学诗呢? 学诗, 可以丰富想象力, 可以提高观察事物的能力, 可以融恰同志间的关系, 可以学会讽刺的方法。近则可以用诗中的道理事奉父母, 远则可以用诗中的道理和方法事奉君主。还可以多掌握一些鸟兽草木的名称。"

英文:

Confucius said to his disciples, "Why do none of you study *The Book of Songs*? Studying *The Book of Songs* can enrich the imagination, enhance the powers of observation, smooth the relations among one's fellow men, and help master the art of satire. On one hand, the teachings presented in *The Book of Songs* can help one serve one's parents well; on the other hand, the knowledge and methods provided in *The Book of Songs* can help one serve one's lord well. Morever, one can learn a lot of names of birds, beasts, plants, and trees."

10. 子謂伯魚曰: "女爲《周南》、《召南》矣乎? 人而不爲《周南》、《召南》, 其猶正墻面而立也與! "

译文:

孔子对伯鱼说: "你学习《周南》、《召南》了吗? 一个人如果不学习《周南》、《召南》, 那就好比对墙站着寸步难行了! "

注:

《周南》、《召南》:《诗经》国风开头两部分篇名。儒家认为这两部分诗歌是合乎礼义的。

英文:

Confucius said to Bo Yu, "Have you studied *Zhou Nan* and *Zhao Nan*? If a man does not study *Zhou Nan* and *Zhao Nan*, he will be as unable to make any progress as if he were facing directly towards a wall."

Note: *Zhou Nan* and *Zhao Nan* are the first two chapters of *Guo Feng* in *The Book of Songs*. Confucians thought that the poems in these two chapters were in accordance with the rites and music.

11. 子曰: "禮云禮云, 玉帛云乎哉? 樂云樂云, 鐘鼓云乎哉?"

译文:

孔子说: "礼, 并非仅指玉帛等礼器而言。乐, 也并非仅指钟鼓乐器而言。"

英文:

Confucius said, "'The rites' does not only refer to the presents of jade and silk in the rites. 'The music' does not only refer to musical instruments like bells and drums, either."

12. 子曰: "色厉而内荏, 譬诸小人, 其犹穿窬之盗也与! "

译文:

孔子说: "外表严厉而内心怯弱的人, 如果用坏人作比喻, 大概像个挖洞跳墙的小偷而已。

英文:

Confucius said, "Compared to a bad man, a coward who pretends to be brave is like a thief who gets in through a hole in the wall or climbs over walls."

13. 子曰: "乡愿, 德之贼也。"

译文:

孔子说: "没有是非的好好先生, 是道德的败坏者。"

英文:

Confucius said, "A man who is unable to distinguish between right and wrong is the one who ruins virtue."

14. 子曰: "道聽而塗説, 德之棄也。"

译文:

孔子说: "热衷于传播小道消息的行为, 是对道德的背弃。"

英文:

Confucius said, "To indulge in gossip and spreading rumours is to abandon virtue."

15. 子曰: "鄙夫可與事君也與哉? 其未得之也, 患得之。既得之, 患失之。苟患失之, 無所不至矣。"

译文:

孔子说: "不可与品德低下的人共事, 因为这种患得患失的人为保住自己的既得利益, 是无所不用其及的。"

Confucius said, "Do not work with those of little virtue. For such people, who, swayed by the considerations of their personal gains and losses, will resort to every conceivable means in order to maintain their vested interest."

16. 子曰："古者民有三疾，今也或是之亡也。古之狂也肆，今之狂也荡；古之矜也廉，今之矜也忿戾；古之愚也直，今之愚也詐而已矣。"

译文:

孔子说："古代人和现代人不一样。古时狂妄的人不过是肆意直言，而现在狂妄的人则是放荡不羁了；古时矜持的人不过是不容侵犯，现在矜持的人则是凶恶蛮横；古时愚笨的人还直率，现在愚笨的人只是欺诈罢了。"

英文:

Confucius said, "People in ancient times were quite different from those in modern times. In ancient times, arrogant men were just recklessly unrestrained in speech while arrogant men in modern times have become dissolute; in ancient times, imperious men were just hard to challenge while imperious men in modern times are rude and fiendish; in ancient times, stupid men were still straight while in modern times they are but tricky and unscrupulous."

17. 子曰: "巧言令色, 鲜矣仁!"

译文:

孔子说: "一贯花言巧语, 伪装和善的人, 不会有什么仁德。"

英文:

Confucius said, "A man who speaks with honeyed words and pretends to be kind cannot be benevolent."

18. 子曰: "恶紫之夺朱也, 恶郑声之乱雅樂也, 恶利口之覆邦家者。"

译文:

孔子说: "我憎恶用紫色代替大红色; 憎恶以郑国的民间音乐扰乱典雅的正统音乐; 憎恶用花言巧语颠覆国家的人。"

注:

紫之夺朱: 古代以朱色 (大红色) 为正色。但春秋时代有些君主喜穿紫色衣服, 以紫色取代朱色的正色地位, 所以遭孔子非议。

英文:

Confucius said, "I detest replacing vermillion with purple. I detest the confusion of the folk music of Zheng with classic conventional music. I detest those who try to subvert the state with clever words."

Note: Replacing vermillion with purple: In ancient times, vermillion was considered the pure colour. During the Spring and Autumn Period, some lords turned to dressing in purple. As a result, the colour purple replaced vermillion and became the pure colour. Hence Confucius' reproach.

19. 子曰:"予欲無言"。子貢曰:"子如不言,則小子何述焉?"子曰:"天何言哉? 四時行焉, 百物生焉, 天何言哉?"

译文:

孔子说:"我不想说话了。"子贡说:"您如果不说话,我们这些学生传述什么呢?"孔子说:"天说了什么呢? 春夏秋冬四时照样有规律地运行, 万物照样生长, 天说话了吗?"

英文:

Confucius said, "I am not going to speak any more."

Zi Gong said, "If you do not speak any more, what should we, your disciples, transmit?" Confucius answered, "What speech has Heaven ever made? Spring, summer, autumn, and winter still rotate as regularly as ever. All things on earth keep growing. Does Heaven say anything?"

20. 孺悲欲見孔子，孔子辭以疾。將命者出户，取瑟而歌，使之聞之。"

译文:

孺悲来见孔子，孔子以生病为理由推辞不见。传话的人刚出房门，孔子便取下瑟来边弹边唱，故意让孺悲听见。不见他并非因为生病，而是怪他不懂拜见长者之礼。

注:

孺悲: 鲁国人，鲁哀公曾派他向孔子学习士丧礼。

英文:

Ru Bei wanted to see Confucius, but Confucius declined to see him with the excuse that he had been ill. As soon as the messenger had quit the room, Confucius took his zither and began to play and sing, making sure that Ru Bei heard it.

Note: Confucius declined to see Ru Bei not because

he was ill, but because Ru Bei did not observe the rites when he met his elders.

21. 宰我問："三年之喪，期已久矣。君子三年不爲禮，禮必壞；三年不爲樂，樂必崩。舊穀既没，新穀既升，鑽燧改火，期可已矣。"子曰："食夫稻，衣夫錦，於女安乎？"曰："安。""女安，則爲之！夫君子之居喪，食旨不甘，聞樂不樂，居處不安，故不爲也。今女安，則爲之！"宰我出，子曰："予之不仁也！子生三年，然後免於父母之懷。夫三年之喪，天下之通喪也。予也有三年之愛於其父母乎？"

译文：

宰我问："父母死后，守孝三年，为期也太长了。君子三年不习礼仪，礼仪就会败坏，三年不演习音乐，音乐就会失传。旧谷已吃完，新谷又已登场，服丧一周年也就可以了。"孔子说："父母去世不满三年便吃白米饭，穿锦衣，你心安吗？"宰我说："心安。"孔子说："你只要心安，就可以去干！君子在服丧期间吃美味不觉香甜，听音乐不觉得快乐，住在家里不觉安适，所以，才坚持服丧三年。现在你感到心安理得，便去守一年好了！"宰我退出之后，孔子说："宰我真不讲仁德！儿女生下来，三年以后才能离开父母的怀抱。为父母服丧三年，是天下通行的丧礼，难道他就没有从父母那里得到过三年怀抱的爱抚吗？"

宰我: 又称宰予, 字子我。孔子的学生。

英文:

Zai Wo said, "Three years is too long for a gentleman to be in mourning for his parents. The rites will be ruined if the gentleman does not practise them for three years; the music will lose its tune if the gentleman does not play it for three years. After the old grain has been used up, and the new grains are about to be harvested, a year has passed and mourning has gone on long enough." Confucius said, "Would you be at ease enjoying white rice and wearing finery during the three years mourning?" "Yes, I would." Zai Wo answered. Confucius said, "All right! If you can be at ease doing all that, do as you please. A gentleman in mourning finds no relish for eating delicious food, no pleasure in music, and no ease in his comfortable home. That is why a gentleman insists on being in mourning for three years. Since you feel at ease doing all that, do as you please." When Zai Wo left, Confucius said, "Zai Wo is not benevolent at all! Parents do not stop nursing their baby until he is three years old. Three years' mourning for parent's death is the common practice throughout the Empire. Has Zai Wo not had such a love from his parents for three years?"

22. 子曰:"飽食終日，無所用心，難矣哉! 不有博奕者乎? 爲之，猶賢乎已。"

译文:

孔子说:"整天吃饱饭没事干，这种人不会有出息。不是有下棋的游戏吗? 就是下下棋也比闲着没事强。"

英文:

Confucius said, "He who always has a full stomach but does nothing meaningful is simply a good-for-nothing. Is there not a game of chess? Even playing chess is better than idling the time away."

23. 子路曰:"君子尚勇乎?"子曰:"君子義以爲上。君子有勇而無義爲亂，小人有勇而無義爲盗。"

译文:

子路问:"君子崇尚勇敢吗?"孔子说:"君子以义为最高尚的品德。君子有勇无义就会造反作乱，小人有勇无义就会做强盗。"

英文:

Zi Lu asked, "Does a gentleman regard bravery as a

virtue?" Confucius said, "A gentleman regards morality as the supreme virtue. Possessed with bravery but devoid of morality, a gentleman will stage a revolt while a petty man will become a bandit."

24. 子貢曰："君子亦有惡乎？"子曰："有惡：惡稱人之惡者，惡居下流而訕上者，惡勇而無禮者，惡果敢而窒者。"曰："賜也亦有惡乎？""惡徼以爲知者，惡不孫以爲勇者，惡訐以爲直者。"

译文:

子贡问："君子也有憎恨的事吗？"孔子说："有的，憎恨一味说别人坏话的人，憎恨处在下位而毁谤上级的人，憎恨勇武而无礼的人，憎恨刚愎自用而顽固不化的人。"孔子反问子贡说："赐，你憎恨什么？"子贡回答说："我憎恨把抄袭别人的成果当作聪明的人，憎恨把逞强当作勇敢的人，憎恨好发人阴私却自以为正直的人。"

英文:

Zi Gong asked, "Is there anything that a gentleman detests?" Confucius answered, "Yes, there is. He detests those who publicise the misdeeds of others; he detests those subordinates who slander their superiors; he detests brave men who lack the spirit of the rites; and he detests those who are self-willed and incorrigibly

obstinate." Then Confucius asked Zi Gong, "Zi G
what do you detest?" Zi Gong answered, "I detest those
who consider plagiarism wisdom, those who take impet-
uosity for bravery, and those who expose others' secrets
and consider themselves upright."

25. 子曰："唯女子與小人爲難養也。近之則不孫，
遠之則怨。"

译文:

孔子说："只有女人和小人是很难相处的。亲近了，
他们会无礼；疏远了，他们又会埋怨。"

英文:

Confucius said, "Only women and petty men are difficult to deal with. When you let them get close, they are
insolent; when you keep them at a distance, they complain."

26. 子曰："年四十而見惡焉，其終也已。"

译文:

孔子说："一个人到四十岁还被人厌恶，他这一辈子
也就完了。"

英文:

Confucius said, "There are no prospects for a man who is still disliked by the age of forty."

微子篇第十八

1. 微子去之，箕子爲之奴，比干諫而死。孔子曰："殷有三仁焉！"

译文：

殷纣王昏暴无道，微子只好离开了他，箕子做了他的奴隶，比干因谏劝而被杀死。孔子说："殷朝末年有这三位仁人。"

注：

微子：名启，殷纣王同母兄长。

箕子：名胥徐，殷纣王叔父。

比干：殷纣王叔父。

英文：

King Zhou of the Yin Dynasty became a self–indulgent despot during the last days of his sovereignty. Wei Zi left him, Ji Zi became a slave, and Bi Gan was killed for remonstrating with him. Confucius said, "They were three benevolent men at the end of the Yin Dynasty."

2. 柳下惠爲士師，三黜。人曰："子未可以去乎？"曰："直道而事人，焉往而不三黜？枉道而事人，何必去父母之邦?"

译文:

柳下惠担任鲁国的法官,多次被撤职。有人劝他说:"你不会离开鲁国吗?"他回答说:"秉公执法到哪里去不会被撤职呢? 如果不秉公办事,又何必要离开自己的国家呢?"

注:

柳下惠: 姓展, 名获, 又名禽, 鲁国大夫。

英文:

Liu Xiahui was a judge of Lu, but had been removed from office several times. Someone said to him, "Why do you not leave Lu?" Liu answered, "Can one avoid being removed from office elsewhere if one does one's duty impartially? If not impartial, what is the point of leaving one's own country?"

3. 齊景公待孔子曰:"若季氏, 則吾不能, 以季、孟之間待之。"曰:"吾老矣, 不能用也。"孔子行。

译文:

齐景公讲到怎样对待孔子时说:"我不能像鲁国国君对待季氏那样对待孔子,我可以按季氏以下,孟氏以上的礼遇对待他。"后来又说:"我已经老了,不能用他了。"

孔子便离开了齐国。

注:

齐景公: 齐国国君。

季氏: 季孙氏, 鲁国大夫。

孟氏: 孟孙氏, 鲁国大夫。

英文:

Duke Jing of Qi once talked about how to treat Confucius, saying, "I am unable to treat Confucius as the Duke of Lu treats Jisun Shi. I can only place him below Jisun Shi but above Mengsun Shi." Afterwards, he explained, "I am old and unable to make full use of his talent." On hearing that, Confucius left the State of Qi.

4. 齊人歸女樂, 季桓子受之, 三日不朝, 孔子行。

译文:

齐国派人送来一班歌姬舞女, 季桓子接受了, 于是数日不上朝听政, 孔子见如此便离开了鲁国。

注:

季桓子: 季孙斯, 鲁国的宰相。

英文:

The State of Qi sent a group of singing and dancing girls. Ji Huanzi (Jisun Si, the Premier of Lu) accepted them. He stayed with them and did not go to court for several days. On seeing that, Confucius left Lu.

5. 楚狂接輿歌而過孔子曰:"鳳兮，鳳兮，何德之衰？往者不可諫，來者猶可追。已而，已而，今之從政者殆而!"孔子下，欲與之言。趨而辟之，不得與之言。

译文:

楚国狂士接輿唱着歌经过孔子车前，唱道:"凤凰，凤凰呀! 您生不逢时，过去的已不可挽回，未来的尚来得及改正。算了，算了吧! 现在的执政者可不好接近。"孔子下车，想同他交谈，接輿却赶快避开了。

注:

接輿: 楚国隐士。

英文:

Jie Yu, the Madman of Chu, went past Confucius' carriage, singing,

"Phoenix, oh phoenix!

How thy virtue has declined!

What is past is beyond help;

What is to come is not yet lost.

Perilous is the lot of those in office today."

Intending to speak to him, Confucius got out of the carriage. But the Madman avoided him in a hurry.

Note: Translation of song from *Confucius, The Analects*, D.C.Lau, P.311.

6. 長沮、桀溺耦而耕，孔子過之，使子路問津焉。長沮曰："夫執輿者爲誰?"子路曰："爲孔丘。"曰："是魯孔丘與?"曰："是也。"曰："是知津矣。"問於桀溺。桀溺曰："子爲誰?"曰："爲仲由。"曰："是魯孔丘之徒與?"對曰："然。"曰："滔滔者天下皆是也，而誰以易之? 且而與其從辟人之士也，豈若從辟世之士哉?"耰而不輟。子路行以告。夫子憮然曰："鳥獸不可與同群，吾非斯人之徒與而誰與? 天下有道，丘不與易也。"

译文:

长沮、桀溺二人一起耕田，孔子路过那里，让子路去问渡口在什么地方。长沮问子路："那个驾车的人是谁?"子路说："是孔丘。"长沮说："是鲁国的那位孔丘吗?"子路说："就是他。"长沮说："那么，他应该早就知道渡口在哪里了。"子路只好又去问桀溺。桀溺说："您是谁?"子路回答："我是仲由。"桀溺说："您是鲁国孔丘的学生吗?"子路回答："是的。"桀溺说："现在天下像洪水泛滥一样混乱不堪，你们能改变它吗? 你与其跟着孔丘到处逃避无道君主，还不如跟着我们逃避现实。"说着，仍旧不停地干活。

子路只得回来报告孔子。孔子听后怅然若失地说："我们不能躲进山林和鸟兽在一起生活，不同世人在一

起又跟谁在一起呢？如果天下政治清明，我们也用不着
参与改革了。”
注：
　　长沮、桀溺：两位隐士。

英文：

Chang Ju and Jie Ni were ploughing. Confucius was
passing them and sent Zi Lu to ask where the ferry was.
Chang Ju asked Zi Lu, "Who is that man driving the carriage?" Zi Lu answered, "It is Confucius." Chang Ju said,
"Is it that Confucius of Lu?" Zi Lu answered, "Yes, it is
him." Chang Ju said, "Then, he should know where the
ferry is." Zi Lu had to turn to Jie Ni. Jie Ni asked, "Who
are you?" Zi Lu answered, "I am Zhong You." Jie Ni
said, "Then, are you a disciple of Confucius' of Lu?" Zi
Lu said, "Yes, I am." Jie Ni said, "At present, the world
is as turbulent as a flooding river. Can you change it?
You have been following your Master to escape a bad
ruler. Why do you not, like us, withdraw yourself from
reality." After saying that, he went on harrowing without
a pause.

　　Zi Lu had to go back to Confucius. Hearing Zi Lu's
story, Confucius looked lost in thought. He said, "Since
we are unable to live in deep mountains with birds and
beasts, who else can we live with but secular men? We do

not have to do anything if there is a wise government under Heaven."

7. 子路從而後，遇丈人，以杖荷蓧。子路問曰："子見夫子乎？"丈人曰："四體不勤，五穀不分，孰爲夫子？"植其杖而芸。子路拱而立。止子路宿，殺鷄爲黍而食之，見其二子焉。明日，子路行以告。子曰："隱者也。"使子路反見之，至，則行矣。子路曰："不仕無義。長幼之節，不可廢也；君臣之義，如之何其廢之？欲潔其身而亂大倫。君子之仕也，行其義也。道之不行，已知之矣。"

译文：

子路跟随孔子**周游列**国时有一次落在后面，遇到一位老人用拐杖扛着除草用的工具。子路上前问道："您看见我的老师了吗？"老人说："四肢不动，五谷不分的人怎么能称作老师呢？"老人说完把拐杖插在田头，锄草去了。子路只好恭敬地站在一边。

老人留子路住宿，又杀鸡做饭招待子路，还叫自己的两个儿子出来和子路相见。

第二天，子路赶上孔子，把这件事告诉他，孔子说："这肯定是一位隐士。"于是叫子路再回去看看。子路赶回去，老人却已经走了。子路对孔子说："宁肯作隐士也不出去做官是不对的。长幼之间的礼节都不可废弃，那君臣之间的义理就更不能废弃呀！为了自己清白，隐居不出，这实际上是破坏了君臣之间的根本伦理关系。做官正是为了实行君臣之义理呀。我早就知道，我们的政治主张实行不了。"

英文:

Zi Lu was lagging behind as he accompanied Confucius travelling in the states. On the way, he met an old man carrying a hoe on a walking stick over his shoulder. Zi Lu went up and asked, "Have you met my Master?" The old man said, "How can a man be called a Master if he does not toil with his four limbs and if he can not tell one grain from another?" After saying that, the old man planted his walking stick in the field, and began to hoe up the weeds. Zi Lu had to stand aside with respect.

The old man invited Zi Lu to stay for the night. He killed a chicken and cooked rice for the guest to eat. And he introduced his two sons to the guest.

The next day, Zi Lu caught up with Confucius. He told his Master about what he had experienced. Confucius said, "That old man must be a recluse." He sent Zi Lu to see the old man again. The old man had already gone when Zi Lu got there. Zi Lu said to Confucius, "It is not right to be a recluse rather than take office. Since the etiquette of the old and young should not be abandoned, then there is no question of abandoning the loyalty of the ministers to the ruler. Withdrawig from reality to keep one s character unsullied is just abandoning the fundamental moral relationship between the ruler and the subjects. To take office is just to fulfill one´s loyal duties to the ruler. I have known for a long time that our political ideal can not be carried out."

8. 逸民：伯夷、叔齊、虞仲、夷逸、朱張、柳下惠、少連。子曰："不降其志，不辱其身，伯夷、叔齊與！"謂柳下惠、少連："降志辱身矣，言中倫，行中慮，其斯而已矣。"謂虞仲、夷逸："隱居放言，身中清，廢中權。我則異於是，無可無不可。"

译文：

古今隐逸的人才有：伯夷、叔齐、虞仲、夷逸、朱张、柳下惠、少连等。孔子说："不改变自己的意志，不辱没自己的身份，是伯夷和叔齐两个。"说柳下惠、少连两个"改变了自己的意志，辱没了自己的身份。但他们言语合于法度，行为谨慎。"又说虞仲、夷逸是"避世隐居，言语正直，洁身自好，与世无争。"孔子又说："我和这些人不同，没有什么可以，也没有什么不可以。"

英文:

Up till then, there had been several men who had withdrawn from society, Bo Yi, Shu Qi, Yu Zhong, Yi Yi, Zhu Zhang, Liu Xiahui, and Shao Lian. Confucius said, "Only Bo Yi and Shu Qi did not bend their own will, and never did any disgrace to their own names." He meant that Liu Xiahui and Shao Lian bent their own will and disgracd their names. "But their speech was up to moral standards and their behaviour was circumspect." Confucius also thought that Yu Zhong and Yi Yi "withdrew from society, spoke with uprightness, preserved their purity and stood aloof from worldly success." Confucius also said, "I, however, am different, not seeing anything permissible nor impermissible."

9. 大師摯適齊，亞飯干適楚，三飯繚適蔡，四飯缺適秦，鼓方叔入於河，播鼗武入於漢，少師陽、擊磬襄入於海。

译文:

鲁国礼崩乐坏，乐师流亡四方。太师挚跑到了齐国，二饭乐师干跑到了楚国，三饭乐师缭跑到了蔡国，四饭乐师缺跑到了秦国，打鼓的方叔隐居在黄河地区，摇小鼓的武隐居在汉水之涯，少师阳和击磬的襄跑到了海边住下来。

古代天子诸侯吃饭时均奏乐，所以乐师有"亚饭"、"三饭"、"四饭"之称。

英文:

In Lu, the rites collapsed and the music was ruined. The musicians had to leave Lu. Zhi, the grand musician, left for Qi; Gan, musician for the second course, left for Chu; Liao, musician for the third course, left for Cai; Que, musician for the fourth course, left for Qin. Fan Shu, the drummer, lived in seclusion in the Yellow River valley; Wu, player of the hand drum, settled in the Han River valley; Yang, the grand musician's deputy, and Xiang, player of the chime stone, fled to settle by the sea.

Note: in ancient times, the mealtimes of emperors and lords were accompanied by music. Hence the "musician for the second course, the third course", etc.

10. 周公謂魯公曰:"君子不施其親，不使大臣怨乎不以。故舊無大故則不棄也，無求備於一人。"

译文:

周公对鲁公说:"执政者不疏远自己的亲族，不使大臣怨恨没有被重用。老臣旧友没有犯大错误就不要轻易抛弃他们，用人不能求全责备。"

周公: 周公旦, 周文王之子, 武王弟。西周初杰出的政治家。传他创立了周朝的典章制度。孔子心中的圣人。

鲁公: 周公长子, 字伯禽, 鲁国始祖。

英文:

The Duke of Zhou said to the Duke of Lu(the former's son), "Those in power should not become estranged from their relatives, nor should they leave any opportunity for ministers to complain that they are not put in important positions. Do not cast aside old ministers and friends unless they make serious mistakes. Do not demand perfection."

Note: The Duke of Zhou, Dan by name, was son of Duke Wen of Zhou and brother of King Wu of Zhou. The Duke of Zhou was an outstanding statesman of the Western Zhou Period. It is said that he established the system of dress and the regulations of the Zhou Dynasty. Confucius looked on him as a sage.

11. 周有八士: 伯達, 伯适, 仲突, 仲忽, 叔夜, 叔夏, 季隨, 季騧。

译文:

周朝有八位著名读书人, 他们是: 伯达, 伯适, 仲突，仲忽，叔夜，叔夏，季随，季骗。

注:

这八个人生平事迹不详。

英文:

There were eight great scholars in the Zhou Dynasty: Bo Da, Bo Kuo, Zhong Tu, Zhong Hu, Shu Ye, Shu Xia, Ji Sui, and Ji Gua.

Note: Little is known about the eight men mentioned above.

子張篇第十九

1. 子張曰: "士見危致命，見得思義，祭思敬，喪思哀，其可已矣。"

译文:

子张说: "读书人遇到国家危难时肯献出生命，不轻取不义之财，祭祀时要考虑态度严肃恭敬，居丧时要考虑悲痛哀伤。能做到这样，也就可以了。"

英文:

Zi Zhang said, "It is satisfactory for a gentleman to lay down his life when his country is in danger, to keep in mind what is right in the face of gain, to show his reverence during a sacrifice, and to express his sorrow in mourning."

2. 子張曰: "執德不弘，信道不篤，焉能爲有? 焉能爲亡?"

译文:

子张说: "不能固守仁德，信仰又不忠实，这种人有他不多，没他不少。"

英文:

Zi Zhang said, "He is a nobody, who does not stick to benevolence, nor to his belief."

3. 子夏之門人問交於子張。子張曰:"子夏云何?"對曰:"子夏曰:'可者與之,其不可者拒之。'"子張曰:"異乎吾所聞:君子尊賢而容衆,嘉善而矜不能。我之大賢與,於人何所不容? 我之不賢與,人將拒我,如之何其拒人也?"

译文:

子夏的学生问子张交朋友的原则。子张问:"子夏怎么说?"子夏的学生回答说:"子夏说:'可以交往的就交,不可以交往的就拒绝他。'"子张说:"这和我听到的不一样,君子尊敬贤人也能容纳普通的人。赞扬才华出众的人也应该同情没有才能的人。我如果是个贤人,那就什么人都可以交往,我如果是个坏人,别人就不会和我交往,我还谈得上去拒绝别人吗?"

英文:

One of Zi Xia's disciples asked Zi Zhang about friendship. Zi Zhang asked, "What has Zi Xia said?" Zi Xia's disciple answered, "Zi Xia said, 'Make friends with those who are adequate and dismiss those who are not.'

Zi Zhang said, "What I have been taught is quite different. A gentleman respects virtuous men, and tolerates common people. He praises the talented and sympathises with the talentless. If I am a virtuous man, I will make friends with all sorts of people; if I am not, others will not make friends with me. Then what is the point of talking about dismissing others?"

4. 子夏曰："雖小道，必有可觀者焉，致遠恐泥，是以君子不爲也。"

译文：

子夏说："即使是些小技艺，也一定有可取的地方，只是不能成为远大事业，故君子不肖为。"

英文：

Zi Xia said, "Even the small crafts have their worthwhile aspects. The gentleman does not use them only because they do not help accomplish great causes."

5. 子夏曰："日知其所亡，月無忘其所能，可謂好學也已矣。"

译文：

子夏说："每天都能学得新知识，每月温习已学得的知识，日积月累这就算好学了。”

英文:

Zi Xia said, "One can be said to have mastered what one has learned if one learns new knowledge every day, and reviews what one has learned every month."

6. 子夏曰: "博學而篤志，切問而近思，仁在其中矣。"

译文:

子夏说: "博闻强记，多请教，善思考，仁德就在其中了。"

英文:

Zi Xia said, "There is no need for one to look for benevolence if one has learned widely, inquired earnestly, and dealt with things thoughtfully."

7. 子夏曰: "百工居肆以成其事，君子學以致其道。"

译文:

子夏说:"工匠在作坊里完成自己的工作，读书人则通过学习来掌握道理。"

Zi Xia said, "The craftsman practises his trade in his workshop while the gentleman masters truth through learning."

8. 子夏曰:"小人之過也必文。"

译文:

子夏说:"小人对过错一定百般掩饰。"

英文:

Zi Xia said, "The petty man tries his best to cover up his errors."

9. 子夏曰:"君子有三變: 望之儼然,即之也温,聽其言也厲。"

译文:

子夏说:"君子给人的印象: 外表庄重严肃,性情温和可亲,讲话严厉不苟。"

英文:

Zi Xia said, "The gentleman impresses people in the following three ways: he seems grave at a distance, cordial when approached, and stern in speech."

10. 子夏曰: "君子信而後勞其民，未信，則以爲厲己也; 信而後諫，未信，則以爲謗己也。"

译文:

子夏说: "君子必须得到百姓信任以后才可以使唤他们，否则百姓会以为是虐待他们; 君子必须得到君主信任以后才可以进谏，否则君主会以为是诽谤自己。"

英文:

Zi Xia said, "The gentleman must gain the trust of the common people before he gives orders to them. Otherwise, they will feel abused. The gentleman must gain the trust of the ruler before he remonstrates with him. Otherwise, the ruler will feel slandered."

11. 子夏曰: "大德不踰閑，小德出入可也。"

译文:

子夏说: "人在大节上不能超越界限，在小节上有些出入是应当允许的。

英文:

Zi Xia said, "As long as one does not step out of bounds in big matters, it is permissible for one not to be meticulous."

12. 子游曰:"子夏之門人小子, 當灑掃應對進退則可矣, 抑末也。本之則無, 如之何?"子夏聞之, 曰:"噫! 言游過矣! 君子之道, 孰先傳焉, 孰後倦焉, 譬諸草木, 區以別矣。君子之道, 焉可誣也? 有始有卒者, 其惟聖人乎!"

译文:

子游说:"子夏的学生做些洒水扫地和迎送宾客的末节小事是可以的, 礼乐大道却没有学到, 这怎么行呢?"子夏听了这话, 说:"咳! 言游的话说错了, 君子的学术, 哪些先讲, 哪些后授, 这也和草木分类一样有所区别, 怎么可以随意歪曲呢? 循序渐进而且有始有终地教育学生, 大概只有圣人吧!"

英文:

Zi You said, "It is all right that Zi Xia's disciples are engaged in sweeping, cleaning, and receiving guests. However, those are small matters. They have not learned the rites and music yet. What should one do about it?" On hearing all that, Zi Xia said, "What Yan You said is wrong. In terms of a gentleman's learning, what is to be taught first, what is to be taught last is similar to the categorization of plants. How can one disrupt the order at will? It is probably a sage alone that can teach his followers in the proper order and see it through to the end."

13. 子夏曰: "仕而優則學, 學而優則仕。"

译文:

　　子夏说: "做官有馀力就去学习, 学习有馀力就去做官。"

注:

　　这是传统注释, 我以为应该译为: "做官不能决断就去学习, 学习优良就可去做官。"

英文:

　　Zi Xia said, "A man studies when he is not decisive in his office responsibilities; a man takes office when he does well in his studies."

14. 子游曰: "喪致乎哀而止。"

译文:

　　子游说: "居丧, 以充分表现悲哀就可以了。"

英文:

　　Zi Xia said, "Nothing more is required if mourning has given full expression to sorrow."

15. 子游曰:"吾友張也爲難能也,然而未仁。"

译文:

子游说:"我的朋友子张可以说已是难得的人才,但他还不能称为仁人。"

英文:

Zi You said, "Zi Zhang, my friend, is hard to emulate. Still he cannot be said to be a benevolent man."

16. 曾子曰:"堂堂乎張也,難與並爲仁矣。"

译文:

曾子说:"子张学问高不可攀,使人无法和他一起成为仁人。"

英文:

Zeng Zi said, "In learning, Zi Zhang is too great to surpass. So it is impossible for people to cultivate benevolence together with him."

17. 曾子曰:"吾聞諸夫子:人未有自致者也,必也親喪乎!"

译文:

曾子说: "我听老师说过: 人不可能把自己的真实感情全部暴露出来, 除非是在父母死亡的时候。

英文:

Zeng Zi said, "I once heard my Master say that a man should not expose his feelings thoroughly unless in mourning for his parents."

18. 曾子曰: "吾聞諸夫子, 孟莊子之孝也, 其他可能也, 其不改父之臣與父之政, 是難能也。"

译文:

曾子说: "我听老师说过: 孟庄子的孝, 别的都容易做到, 而他不改换父亲的旧臣和父亲的政治措施, 这是别人很难做到的。"

注:

孟庄子: 名速, 鲁国大夫。他父亲是鲁国大夫孟献子, 有贤德。

英文:

Zeng Zi said, "My Master once said, others may be able to emulate Meng Zhuangzi in his filial piety toward his parents except in one thing: he did not remove those officials appointed by his father and abolish the political measures taken by his father. This is something difficult for others to follow."

19. 孟氏使陽膚爲士師，問於曾子，曾子曰："上失其道，民散久矣。如得其情，則哀矜而勿喜!"

译文:

孟孙氏任命阳肤当法官，阳肤向曾子**请教**，曾子说:"执政者无道，民心早已**离散**。你如果审理出犯罪者真情，应该怜悯他们，而不要居功自喜。

注:

阳肤: 传为曾子的学生。

英文:

Mengsun Shi appointed Yang Fu judge. Yang Fu asked Zeng Zi for advice. Zeng Zi said, "Those in authority have lost the way of good government and the common people have withdrawn their support. If you intend to gain the actual situation of those who have committed crimes, you should show sympathy for them, but not show off about it."

20. 子貢曰："紂之不善，不如是之甚也。是以君子惡居下流，天下之惡皆歸焉。"

　　子贡说:"纣王的无道,未必像现在传说的那样厉害。所以当权者最怕下台,只要一下台,天下各种坏名声都会加到他的身上。"

注:

　　纣: 商朝最后一位君主,为周武王所伐,自焚而死,被历代骂为暴君。

英文:

　　Zi Gong said, "Tyrant Zhou may not have been such a bad ruler as he has been said to be. Therefore, what a man in authority fears most is to be thrown out of power. Once out of power, all the bad names in the world will be imposed upon him."

　　Note: Zhou is the last king of the Yin Dynasty, who committed suicide by setting fire to himself after he was defeated by King Wu of Zhou. His name has gone down throughout history as a tyrant.

　　21. 子貢曰:"君子之過也,如日月之食焉;過也,人皆見之;更也,人皆仰之。"

译文:

　　子贡说:"君子的过错,好比日蚀月蚀:对他的过错,人人都看得见;改正之后,大家都敬仰他。"

Zi Gong said, "The gentleman's errors are like an eclipse of the sun and the moon: the whole world will see it when he errs, and he will be respected by all when he mends his ways."

22. 衛公孫朝問於子貢曰:"仲尼焉學?"子貢曰:"文武之道,未墜於地,在人。賢者識其大者,**不賢者識其小者**,莫不有文武之道焉。夫子焉不學? 而亦何常師之有?"

译文:

卫国的公孙朝问子贡:"你老师的学问是跟谁学的?"子贡回答说:"周文王、武王之道并未失传,都散在人间。贤人能抓住它的根本,庸人只能抓住它的末节。文王武王之道无处不存,我的老师也就无处不学习,何必一定要有固定的老师呢?

注:

公孙朝: 卫国大夫。

文武: 周文王、周武王,周朝两位君主,被孔子尊为圣人。

英文:

Gongsun Chao of Wei asked Zi Gong, "From whom does your Master acquire his learning?" Zi Gong answered, "The way of King Wen and King Wu of Zhou has not been lost yet. It is to be found in the multitude. The virtuous man grasps its essence while the mediocre grasps the details. The way of King Wen and King Wu is to be found everywhere. That is why my Master learns everywhere. What is the need to have a fixed teacher?"

Note: Gongsun Chao is a senior official of Wei.

King Wen, King Wu: two kings of the Zhou Dynasty whom Confucius considered to be sages.

23. 叔孫武叔語大夫於朝曰: "子貢賢於仲尼。"子服景伯以告子貢。子貢曰: "譬之宮墻，賜之墻也及肩，窺見室家之好。夫子之墻數仞，不得其門而入，不見宗廟之美，百官之富。得其門者或寡矣。夫子之云，不亦宜乎!"

译文:

叔孙武叔在朝廷中对官员们说: "子贡的学问比他的老师仲尼还要好。"子服景伯把这话告诉子贡，子贡说: "如果把学问比作宫墙，我的墙只有齐肩高，别人在外边就可以看见墙内结构美好的房屋。我老师的宫墙却有几丈高，如果找不到门进去，是看不见里面雄伟的宗庙建筑和各种结构的房舍的。能够找到门进去的人或许不多，所以叔孙武叔先生那样说也就不足为怪了。"

注:

叔孙武叔: 名州仇，鲁国大夫。

子服景伯: 名何，鲁国大夫。

英文:

In court, Shusun Wushu (a senior official of Lu) said to the officials, "Zi Gong's learning is greater than that of his Master's." Zifu Jingbo told this to Zi Gong. Zi Gong said, "Comparing learning to a wall, my wall is at shoulder height, so that the fine architecture of the buildings within can be seen from outside the wall. My Master's wall is thirty or forty feet high, so that one, if unable to find the entrance, cannot see the beauty of the solemn temples and the richness of the many palaces inside the wall. There may be only a few people who can find the entrance. So it is no surprise that Mr. Shusun Wushu made such a comment."

24. 叔孫武叔毀仲尼。子貢曰："無以爲也! 仲尼不可毀也。他人之賢者，丘陵也，猶可踰也; 仲尼，日月也，無得而踰焉。人雖欲自絕，其何傷於日月乎? 多見其不知量也。"

译文:

鲁国大夫叔孙武叔毁谤孔子。子贡说："这是徒劳的，仲尼是毁谤不了的。别的贤人好比是个小山丘，还可以超越过去；而孔子是太阳和月亮，是不可能超越的。有人要自绝于太阳和月亮，这对太阳和月亮有什么损伤呢？只能表示他自不量力罢了。"

英文:

Shusun Wushu, a senior official of Lu, slandered Confucius. Zi Gong said, "That is of no use. Confucius can never be slandered. Other virtuous men, like small hills, may be surmountable. But Confucius is the sun and the moon so that he is not surmountable at all. What harm does one do to the sun and the moon if he cuts himself from them? Is it not an overestimation of his own strength?"

25. 陳子禽謂子貢曰："子爲恭也，仲尼豈賢於子乎?"子貢曰："君子一言以爲知，一言以爲不知，言不可不慎也。夫子之不可及也，猶天之不可階而升也。夫子之得邦家者，所謂立之斯立，道之斯行，綏之斯來，動之斯和。其生也榮，其死也哀，如之何其可及也?"

译文:

陈子禽对子贡说："你是出于对老师的尊敬吧，仲尼真比你强吗?"子贡说："君子说一句话可以表现其是聪明还是愚笨，所以说话不可以不慎重。没有人能赶得上我的老师，就像不能搭阶梯爬上天一样。我的老师如果当上诸侯或卿大夫，老百姓就会懂礼，就会齐心协力跟他走，远方的百姓也会来归附。他生的光荣，死的可惜，我怎么能赶得上他呢？"

英文:

Chen Ziqin said to Zi Gong, "Do you really think that Confucius is greater than you? Is it out of respect for your Master?" Zi Gong answered, "One can tell whether a gentleman is wise or stupid in one word he utters. So he has to be careful in speech. Nobody is able to surpass my Master just as nobody can reach the sky with the help of a ladder. When my Master took office in court, the common people knew the rites, and followed my Master whole-heartedly. Moreover, people were attracted from afar. My Master will be honoured when alive and mourned when dead. How can I equal him?"

堯曰篇第二十

1. 堯曰："咨! 爾舜! 天之曆數在爾躬，允執其中。四海困窮，天祿永終。"舜亦以命禹。

曰："予小子履敢用玄牡，敢昭告于皇皇后帝：有罪不敢赦。帝臣不蔽，簡在帝心。朕躬有罪，無以萬方；萬方有罪，罪在朕躬。"

周有大賚，善人是富。"雖有周親，不如仁人。百姓有過，在予一人。"

謹權量，審法度，修廢官，四方之政行焉。興滅國，繼絕世，舉逸民，天下之民歸心焉。

所重：民，食，喪，祭。

寬則得衆，敏則有功，公則説。

译文:

尧让位给舜的时候说："舜呀! 按照上天的安排，帝位要传给你，你要坚持正确的治国之道，假如以后天下的百姓陷入困苦之中，上天会永远终止你的禄位。"舜在让位给禹的时候，也说了同样的话。

商汤在祈祷上天时说："小子履谨以黑色牡牛为祭品，忠实地向伟大的天帝禀告：我对有罪的人不敢赦免，对您的臣仆的善恶不敢隐瞒，这您是知道的。我个人若有罪，就不要牵连天下四方；天下四方若有罪，应该降罪我一人。"

周朝大封诸侯，使贤人得富贵。周武王说："我虽然有至亲，却不如有仁德之人。百姓如果有罪过，应该有我一人承担。"

统一度量衡，规范法律制度。恢复废弃的官职制度，政令便可通行天下。复兴被灭亡了的国家，接续已断绝的世族后代，选用被遗落的人才，天下百姓就会心悦诚服了。

执政者应该重视的是：人民，粮食，丧礼，祭祀。

宽厚待人就会得到人民的拥护，勤恳敏捷就会取得成功，公平合理就会使百姓高兴。

注：

尧：传说中的远古圣君。传说他让位于舜，舜又传位于禹。

履：商汤名履，商朝的建立者。

本章文字各段之间不连贯，可能中间有脱漏，或本非一章。

英文

When Yao let Shun succeed him, he said to him, "Oh, Shun! It is ordained by Heaven that you are to succeed me. You are to follow the right way of government. If the multitude fall in misery, Heaven will remove you from the reign forever!" When Shun let Yu take over the sovereignty, he spoke the same words as Yao did.

Praying to Heaven, King Tang of Shang said, "I, Lü, the little one, would dedicate sincerely a black bull and make this declaration to you, Great Lord. I dare not pardon those who have committed crimes; I dare not hide the good and evil deeds of your subjects since you know them already. If I commit a crime, do not extend the blame to the people; if the people commit crimes, it is I alone that is guilty."

In the Zhou Dynasty, a lot of virtuous men were granted dukes and fiefs so that they became rich. King Wu of Zhou said, "Although I have close relatives, I would rather enfeoff the benevolent men. When common people make mistakes, let me alone take the responsibility."

Government decrees will be carried out throughout the country when weights and measures are standardised, laws and regulations are well considered, and when the official posts that were abolished are reestablished. All the people under Heaven will be satisfied and won over if the states that were annexed are restored, and the lines of big families which were extinct are revived, and those talented who were forgotten are put into important positions.

Emphasis should be laid on affairs of the common people, on the food supply, on the funeral ceremonies, and on sacrifices.

Tolerance wins the support of the multitude; dili-

gence and quickness lead to success; fairness and justice
please the multitude.

Note: The incoherence of this chapter may be due to
some parts missing.

2. 子張問於孔子曰: "何如斯可以從政矣?"

子曰: "尊五美, 屏四惡, 斯可以從政矣。"

子張曰: "何謂五美?"

子曰: "君子惠而不費, 勞而不怨, 欲而不貪, 泰而
不驕, 威而不猛。"

子張曰: "何謂惠而不費?"

子曰: "因民之所利而利之, 斯不亦惠而不費乎? 擇
可勞而勞之, 又誰怨? 欲仁而得仁, 又焉貪? 君子無衆
寡, 無小大, 無敢慢, 斯不亦泰而不驕乎? 君子正其衣
冠, 尊其瞻視, 儼然人望而畏之, 斯不亦威而不猛乎?"

子張曰: "何謂四惡?"

子曰: "不教而殺謂之虐; 不戒視成謂之暴; 慢令致
期謂之賊; 猶之與人也, 出納之吝謂之有司。"

译文:

子张问: "怎样才能治理政事?"

孔子说: "尊重五种美德, 排除四种恶政, 就可以治
理政事了。"

子张问: "五种美德指什么?"

孔子说: "执政者使人民得到好处, 又不劳民伤财;

劳动百姓，而百姓却没有怨恨；追求仁德，而不贪图财利；性情安泰，不骄傲；态度威严而不凶猛。"

子张问："使人民得到好处，又不劳民伤财，这些应该如何去做呢？"

孔子说："让老百姓干对他们有利的事情，不就能使他们得到好处又不劳民伤财吗？让百姓干他们乐于干的事情，谁还会有怨恨呢？追求仁德而得到了仁德，还贪图什么呢？无论人多少，势力大小，执政者都不敢怠慢他们，还会骄傲吗？执政者衣冠整齐，目不邪视，态度庄重使人见了而生敬畏之心，不就做到了既威严而又不凶猛吗？"

子张又问："四种恶政又指什么？"

孔子说："不先进行教育就杀戮，叫做虐；不事先告诫而要求立即成功叫做暴；开始懈怠不问，而突然不令限期完成，叫做贼；应该给人财物而又舍不得，叫做吝啬。"

英文：

Zi Zhang asked, "How is one to take part in government?" "To respect the five virtues and spurn the four evils," answered Confucius," that is the right way for one to participate in government."

Zi Zhang asked, "What then are the 'five virtues'?" Confucius answered, "A gentleman should bring benefit to the people instead of toil; he should work the people while not incurring their complaints; he should pursue virtue but not be greedy for profit; he should have a calm disposition and not be arrogant; and he should inspire awe without being fierce."

Zi Zhang asked, "Can you explain for me 'bringing benefit to the people instead of toil' and so on?" Confucius said, "Doesn't it bring benefit to the people rather than toil that one allows them to do what is beneficial to them? Who will complain if made to do things they want to do? What more could one be greedy for if one desires benevolence and gets benevolence? Isn't one calm instead of arrogant if one does not dare to neglect anyone regardless of the number and the size of their clans? Isn't it awe—inspiring and not fierce if a gentleman dresses properly and looks dignified?"

Zi Zhang went on asking, "What then are the 'four evils'?" Confucius answered, "To impose the death penalty without first instructing the people is to be cruel; to demand immediate results without giving orders before—hand is to be brutal; to set a time limit all of a sudden without having paid any attention to the matter before is to cause injury; and to refuse to give something that should be given is to be miserly."

3. 孔子曰: "不知命，無以爲君子也；不知禮，無以立也；不知言，無以知人也。"

译文:

孔子说:"不知道命运，就做不了君子；不懂礼义，就难以立身处世；不会分辨别人的言论，就不能了解人。"

英文:

Confucius said, "One will never be a gentleman if he does not understand destiny. He will never get established if he does not follow the rites. He will never judge people if he does not understand their words."

Index

Table of the Different Names of Confucius' Disciples

According to Chinese tradition, people had a family name, a given name, a styled name, and sometimes a respectful name or another name. The family name could be followed by either the given name or the styled name. Both given name and styled name could be used independently. For example, Confucius himself was often called Kong Zi. "Kong" is his family name and "Zi" is a respectful title denoting master. His given name is Qiu, and his styled name is Zhongni.

This can be very confusing for readers. The table below lists the various names of Confucius' disciples in order to facilitate understanding.

1. Family Name	2. Given Name	3. Styled Name	4. Other Name
Bu	Shang	Zi Xia	
Chen	Kang	Zi Qin	
Dantai	Mieming	Zi Yu	
Duanmu	Ci	Zi Gong	
Fan	Xue	Zi Chi	Fan Chi
Fu	Boqi	Zi Jian	
Gao	Chai	Zi Gao	
Gongbo	Liao	Zi Zhou	
Gongxi	Chi	Zi Hua	Gongxi Hua
Gongye	Zhang	Zi Zhang	
Min		Zi Qian	
Nangong	Kuo	Zi Rong	Nan Rong
Qidiao	Kai	Zi Ruo	
Ran	Geng	Bo Niu	
Ran	Yong	Zhong Gong	Ran You
Ran	Qiu		
Shen	Cheng	Zhou	
Sima	Geng	Zi Niu	
Wuma	Shi	Zi Qi	Wuma Qi
Yan	Hui	Zi Yuan	Yan Yuan
Yan	Lu	Wu You	
You	Ruo		You Zi
Yuan	Xian	Zi Si	Yuan Si
Zai	Yu	Zi Wo	Zai Wo
Zeng	Dian	Zi Xi	Zeng Xi
Zeng	Shen	Zi Yu	Zeng Zi
Zhong	You	Zi Lu	Ji Lu
Zhuansun	Shi	Zi Zhang	

（京）新登字 134 号

责任编辑　蔡希勤

封面设计　张大羽

图书在版编目(CIP)数据

论语＝ANALECTS OF CONFUCIUS：文白、汉英对照/蔡希勤中文译
注；赖波、夏玉和英文翻译。—北京：华语教学出版社，1994.8
　ISBN 7－80052－407－8/H·460(外)

　I.论…II.①蔡…②赖…③夏…III.①论语－译文②论语－对照读物－
中、英③儒家－研究 IV.B222.22

　中国版本图书馆 CIP 数据核字(94)第 03047 号

论　语

*

ⓒ华语教学出版社

华语教学出版社出版

（中国北京百万庄路 24 号）

邮政编码 100037

北京外文印刷厂印刷

中国国际图书贸易总公司发行

（中国北京车公庄西路 35 号）

北京邮政信箱第 399 号　　邮政编码 100044

新华书店北京发行所国内发行

1994 年(大 32 开)第一版

1996 年第二次印刷

（汉英）

02900

9－CE－2895P